Judgment
on Nuremberg

Judgment on Nuremberg

AMERICAN ATTITUDES TOWARD
THE MAJOR GERMAN WAR-CRIME TRIALS

by William J. Bosch

The University of
North Carolina Press
Chapel Hill

Acknowledgments

On the long road to publication of *Judgment on Nuremberg* I have met many helpful friends and critics. Professor Robert M. Miller was the first to point me in the direction of this topic, and his continual encouragement and confidence were a major reason for the book's completion. He has been not only an inspiring mentor but also a valued friend. Credit and thanks are also due to Professors John E. Semonche, Charles Phipps, S.J., and John M. Anspacher for detailed critical readings of the entire manuscript. Professors Elisha P. Douglass and Frank M. Klingberg graciously reviewed the text at an early stage of its journey. Individual chapters have been improved through the kind advice of Professors Samuel F. Wells and Edward M. Conan.

Because of the vast amount of published material surveyed in this study, special acknowledgment is due to the dedicated members of the library staffs at the Library of Congress and at the newspaper division of the New York Public Library as well as to the librarians of Boston College, Catholic University, Duke University, LeMoyne College, Harvard University, and Syracuse University. The greatest debt, however, is owed to the librarians of the University of North Carolina who constantly amazed me by their generosity in time and energy.

All books are improved immeasurably by conscientious typists and editors. I appreciate greatly the labors of Mrs. Sue Killian and Mrs. Muriel Dyer, whose careful typing forestalled many technical errors. Mr. Leslie Phillabaum and the staff at the University of North Carolina Press receive my gratitude for their constant efforts and care during publication. Professor Cornelius Novelli of LeMoyne College supplied a helpful critical editing of the entire manuscript.

[v]

Mr. Bertrand Jarvis, Mrs. Eva Higgins, and Misses Jewel Williams, Betty Brandon, and Evelyn Shakir generously provided proofreading and constant interest and encouragement.

Research and publication were assisted by grants from the Smith Fund of the University of North Carolina, the LeMoyne Faculty Research Fund, a LeMoyne Community Grant, and the Jesuit Writers' Fund.

None of these considerate and helpful people share my responsibility for shortcomings in this book.

Contents

Judgment
on Nuremberg

1

The Road to Nuremberg

Bold headlines August 9, 1945 announced: "Soviet Declares War on Japan; Attacks Manchuria, Tokyo Says: Atom Bomb Loosed on Nagasaki." At the bottom of this first page was the headline: "4 Powers Call Aggression Crime In Accord Covering War Trials." [1]

Ironically, man's vast potential for destruction overshadowed the efforts which he was making at that moment to bridle the evils of aggression. The Allied nations' signing of the London Charter, which provided the law and procedures for the Nuremberg war-crime trials, hardly competed with the news of weapons that would be able to destroy the human race.

Although the search for safeguards for the rights of men and nations began centuries ago, never before has success in this seeking been so imperative. Modern communications and transportation have brought men closer in their destinies. Apart from the potency of new weapons, this closeness would be less disturbing if the future were not so imperiled by the emergence of modern totalitarianism with its tendency to violate the rights of its citizens and of neighboring states.

Opponents of totalitarianism have tried desperately to devise defenses against aggression and atrocities. Leaders have sought safeguards in several ways: politically, through collective security; militarily, through intimidating destructive might; and economically, through sanctions or elimination of frustrating poverty.

1. *New York Times*, August 9, 1945, p. 1. The word "trial" and "trials" can be used interchangeably. There were twenty-two trials and twenty-two verdicts in the Nuremberg proceedings. We will use the plural form. Again, "Nuremberg" can be spelled a number of ways. The form Nuremberg will be used, but variations occurring in citations will of course not be altered.

Another major effort to stop unjust wars and violations of human rights has been the development of an international legal code. Many hope that as individual states have curbed internal unrest and made men secure in their rights to life, liberty, and property, so the law of the nations might check international outlawry.[2] "Peace through law" has been a vision which has especially captivated America. Proud of the freedom and security provided by its legal tradition, the United States frequently has attempted through law to solve the nation's and the world's problems.

Perhaps the most striking illustration of this policy was the International Military Tribunal which tried Nazi Germany's leaders after the Second World War. The court which judged Hitler's warlords was significant not only because of the defendants' rank and the depravity and magnitude of their crimes, but also because the Allies sought to create a new international law through the Tribunal's decisions. Aggressive war was declared the "supreme crime"; national leaders who plotted unjust belligerency were held personally accountable; pleas of "head of state" and "order of superior" no longer bestowed legal immunity; and those who abetted aggressive war by their diplomatic, financial or industrial support were liable for the injustices perpetrated by their nation. In addition, an indictment for crimes against humanity was formulated.

The Nuremberg trials were not an impulsive decision by the Allied governments. They were the culmination of twenty-five years of legal development and psychological preparation. Twentieth-century men started on the road to Nuremberg immediately after World War I.

"Hang the Kaiser!"—a cry created out of wartime passion and the desire to mobilize national morale—expressed the Allies' determination to indict enemy leaders for war crimes at the end of World War I. Implementation of this policy began November 28, 1918 when the British Imperial War Cabinet decided to punish German leaders by legal tribunals rather than by executive action.

When the triumphant Allied and Associated powers assembled

2. Charles H. Tuttle, "The Lawyer and the Law," *New York State Bar Association Bulletin* 16 (February, 1944): 21.

in the Hall of Mirrors at Versailles to plan Europe's future, they assumed the former German government would be discredited by the trial of the kaiser. Mr. Robert Lansing, American secretary of state and president of the Committee on Breaches of Laws of War, informed them, however, that the committee had neither drawn up a list of criminals nor prepared for trials. The reason for the committee's inaction was that their judicial experts had decided "that the accused could not be brought before any legal tribunal, since they were only guilty of a moral responsibility." [3]

Because of this conclusion only the kaiser was indicted for starting the war. All other German leaders were charged with violations of the traditional rules and customs of war. These decisions were embodied in articles 227, 228, and 229 of the final draft of the Versailles treaty.

The first of these articles declared the victors' intention to bring the former German emperor to trial "for a supreme offence against international morality and the sanctity of treaties." A special tribunal was to be created, and the United States, Great Britain, France, Italy, and Japan would each supply one judge for the court.

Article 228 demanded German recognition of the victor's right to bring before its military tribunals enemy nationals accused of violations of the laws of war. Article 229 specified that the alleged criminal would be handed over to the aggrieved nation's military courts or, if he was charged with crimes by a number of nations, he would be brought before a military court composed of judges from the accusing nations. [4]

Article 227 had certain features which would reappear in the post-World War II Nuremberg trials: the indictment of government leaders, selection of the court's judges exclusively from the victorious powers; and high priority upon the demands of morality in international relations.

This last point, however, is also a source of fundamental

3. United States Department of State, *Papers Relating to the Foreign Relations of the United States: The Paris Peace Conference, 1919*, 13 vols. (Washington: Government Printing Office, 1943), 4:332 (hereafter cited as Department of State, *Paris Peace Conference, 1919*).
4. Ibid., 13:371, 376, 379.

difference between the plan proposed in Article 227 and the Nuremberg trials. The Versailles court was to try the kaiser exclusively on political and moral charges. At Nuremberg the indictment maintained that, over and above any ethical considerations, the acts committed by the Nazi chieftains were criminal in the strict judicial sense; that is, they were actions which broke the law and were punishable.[5]

In Article 229 the distinction between perpetrators of localized crime and those whose violations covered a large geographical area vaguely anticipated the twofold policy adopted at the Moscow Conference. Nazis who had committed atrocities within their territorial jurisdiction were turned over to the liberated countries by this World War II declaration. Major culprits, those whose crimes transcended the boundaries of any single nation, however, were to be punished by joint decision of the Allied powers.[6]

The well-laid plans of Articles 227, 228, and 229 of the Versailles treaty came to nought. On November 19, 1918 the kaiser fled to Holland, and when the victors requested his extradition the Netherlands refused to comply with what it considered a violation of neutrality.

With the major symbol of German war guilt beyond reach, Allied interest in postwar punishment slackened. On the other hand, incensed by the harsh treaty, Germany was eager to obtain jurisdiction over its own nationals.

Allied apathy and German zeal resulted in the Leipzig trials of 1920. All agree that these judicial proceedings were farcical. The Allies listed two thousand alleged war criminals and to German authorities they submitted as test cases the names of forty-five of the most notorious criminals. Twelve of the forty-five were brought to trial; six were acquitted, and the other six were given sentences averaging a few months.[7] Since time spent awaiting

5. Ibid., 13:371. The import of this distinction between illegal and criminal can be seen in regard to the Kellogg-Briand Pact. Many experts claimed that this treaty made aggression illegal because aggression violated its provisions. Aggression, on the other hand, was not criminal because the Pact established no definite sanction for contravening its declarations.

6. "Declaration of German Atrocities," *Department of State Bulletin* 9 (November 6, 1943): 311 (hereafter cited as "German Atrocities," *Department of State Bulletin*).

7. Department of State, *Paris Peace Conference, 1919,* 13: 379; Peter Calvocoressi, *Nuremberg: the Facts, the Law, and the Consequences* (New

trial was deducted from penalties, one defendant was found guilty and immediately released. All convicted submarine commanders "escaped" from prison.[8] Thus ended the first modern attempt at postwar legal punishment of war criminals.

In the years between the two World Wars, statesmen made little effort to create an international criminal law, but they did strive to control aggression in other ways. The major advance on the road to Nuremberg in the interwar years was the 1928 Paris Peace Pact. This treaty was the statesmen's political answer to aggression just as Nuremberg would be the legal response to unjust war.

The Kellogg-Briand Pact of 1928 stated that "the High Contracting Parties solemnly declare in the names of their respective peoples that they condemn recourse to war for the solution of international controversies, and renounce it as an instrument of national policy in their relation with one another." [9] This agreement was signed and adhered to by sixty-three nations including Germany.[10]

Two arguments were later urged against claims that the peace pact was a clear, binding law for Nuremberg's punishment of aggressors. First, the pact provided no penalty of any sort for violations. Second, the pact in no way assigned personal liability for any national leader who contravened the treaty.[11]

The argument frequently made in reply to these objections was that the pact represented a common international law which emerged between the World Wars. Analogous to common law development in Anglo-Saxon legal tradition, Nuremberg proponents urged that totality of government statements, legal writings, official resolutions, and pacts create an accepted international legal code which recognized aggression as the supreme

York: Macmillan, 1948), pp. 20–21 (hereafter cited as Calvocoressi, *Nuremberg*).

8. Robert K. Woetzel, *The Nuremberg Trials in International Law* (London: Stevens, 1960), p. 34 (hereafter cited as Woetzel, *Nuremberg Trials*).

9. Robert H. Ferrell, *Peace in Their Times: The Origins of the Kellogg-Briand Pact* (New Haven: Yale University Press, 1952), p. 268 (hereafter cited as Ferrell, *Peace in Their Times*).

10. Ibid., p. 258.

11. Oscar Svarlien, *An Introduction to the Law of Nations* (New York: McGraw-Hill, 1955), p. 406 (hereafter cited as Svarlien, *Introduction to the Law of Nations*).

crime and leaders of an unjust war as being personally accountable.[12]

Besides being witness to common law evolution, the Kellogg-Briand Pact was also significant because the United States was principle author of this treaty. Indeed this pact is often considered a classical expression of basic American attitudes in international affairs.[13] The Kellogg-Briand Pact, its critics asserted, reflected a national mentality determined on perpetuating the established world order so eminently favorable for the United States. America was a "have" nation, content with the status quo; it nursed no grudges from past defeats, was not avid for territorial acquisitions, and was not strangled by any vital shortages in economic resources. The treaty, moreover, was the American way in foreign affairs. It was that mixture of moralism and legalism which seeks to solve mankind's problems by statement of ethical principles and the creation of laws. The practical significance of the treaty, therefore, was not its half-hearted observance but the steadily increasing power of the moralistic-legalistic state whose fundamental attitudes it expressed. This nation would reach world military, industrial, and economic dominance in the period during the Nuremberg years immediately after the Second World War. What America wanted, America would get.

Similar was the importance of the Stimson Doctrine of 1932. This document announced that the United States would not recognize the results of aggression and that invasions were not ethically neutral acts but morally wrong ones. The doctrine illustrated America's determination to counter unjust war with legal means, even if its sword was the fragile blade of a legal fiction.[14]

12. Mitchell Franklin, "Sources of International Law Relating to Sanctions Against War Criminals," *Journal of Criminal Law and Criminology* 36 (September–October, 1945): 157 (hereafter cited as Franklin, "Sources of International Law").

13. Ferrel, *Peace In Their Times*, p. 264.

14. "Public opinion in America, eager to avoid a clash at all costs, warmly supported the cut-rate substitute for force known as the Hoover-Stimson Doctrine. Yet there was a bitter undercurrent of criticism from observers who argued the note was as useless as it was dangerous." Thomas A. Bailey, *A Diplomatic History of the American People*, 6th ed. (New York: Appleton-Century-Crofts, 1958), p. 697.

In the 1930's and 1940's aggression and atrocities marked the second great attempt of twentieth-century European states to settle conflicting national aspirations. During the war, Allied leaders articulated the view that it was no longer tolerable for national leaders to treat their citizens' lives and fortunes as expendable pawns in an international chess game. Repeatedly President Franklin Roosevelt, Prime Minister Winston Churchill, and Marshal Joseph Stalin threatened Nazis with the dire fate awaiting perpetrators of atrocities. Their intent to punish was formally proclaimed in the November 1, 1943 protocol of the Moscow Conference.[15]

The threatened sanctions could fall upon Nazi leaders in a variety of ways. There existed such alternatives as drumhead court-martial, summary execution by executive decree, and trial by enemy national courts, by neutral tribunals, or by an international criminal court.[16]

American leaders considered harsh military judgment or executive executions as probably unjust and revolting to the American conscience.[17] Among these leaders were Henry L. Stimson, secretary of war and Robert H. Jackson, an associate justice of the Supreme Court. Such violent solutions, while satisfying a desire for venegeance, would not reassert the rule of law in a world brutalized by the Third Reich's debasing legal order. Nor would such actions preserve the record of Nazi aggression and atrocities. Moreover, trial proponents argued, summary execution would create Nazi martyrs and an opportunity for revisionists and isolationists to claim once more that charges against the German enemy were fabrications.

The alternative of using German courts had little support. Men remembered Leipzig and wished no recurrence of the legal scandal perpetrated there.

The employment of neutral courts was exceedingly attractive

---

15. "German Atrocities," *Department of State Bulletin*, p. 311.
16. The genesis of the International Military Tribunal policy in the United States government is related in Chapter II.
17. Robert H. Jackson, *The Case against the Nazi War Criminals* (New York: Knopf, 1946), p. vi (hereafter cited as Jackson, *Case Against War Criminals*); Henry L. Stimson, "The Nuremberg Trial, Landmark in Law," *Foreign Affairs* 15 (January, 1947): 180 (hereafter cited as Stimson, "Nuremberg Trial").

and seemed to be a just and equitable method of punishment. Those urging international tribunals, however, held that this appeal was deceptive. They contended that after World War II no true neutral nation existed, for no state had refrained from hostilities because it was uninterested or impartial toward the outcome. Indeed a nation's desire for neutrality frequently had little relation to its actual status. Moreover, in states termed neutral the legal and political leaders had in fact chosen sides, or at least their self-interest was connected with one or the other of the belligerents.[18] Finally, it would be hard to find a man who was neutral to Dachau and Buchenwald, and, if such a man were found, would one wish him to sit in judgment?

By January of 1945 the United States government decided to conduct international trials. The three other major Allied powers accepted the American program at the San Francisco United Nations Conference.[19]

Meetings in London during the summer of 1945, attended by representatives of the United States, Great Britain, the Soviet Union, and the provisional government of France, marked the inception of the Allies' postwar punishment program. Associate Justice Robert Jackson, appointed by President Harry Truman as head of the United States delegation and future chief counsel for the American prosecution, was both guiding spirit and practical planner for the conference.[20]

Almost insurmountable problems faced Jackson. He had to

18. Calvocoressi, *Nuremberg*, pp. 19–22; Whitney R. Harris, *Tyranny on Trial, The Evidence of Nuremberg* (Dallas: Southern Methodist University Press, 1954), p. xxxii (hereafter cited as Harris, *Tyranny on Trial*); Winfield B. Hale, "Nuremberg War Crimes Tribunals," *Tennessee Law Review* 21 (December, 1949): 10.

19. Samuel L. Rosenman, *Working with Roosevelt* (New York: Harper, 1952), p. 545.

20. One of the many indications of the United States's guidance of the Nuremberg trials is that the American decision to indict the defendants for conspiracy to wage aggressive war was opposed by the British and Russians at the London Conference. Ernest O. Hauser, "The Backstage Battle at Nuremberg," *Saturday Evening Post* 218 (January 19, 1946): 18–19. The trials which the British conducted after the major Nuremberg sessions rejected the conspiracy charge and indicted the accused only for violations of the laws and customs of war. Morris Greenspan, *The Modern Law of Land Warfare* (Berkeley: University of California Press, 1959), p. 426 (hereafter cited as Greenspan, *Modern Law of Land Warfare*).

write the law for the court, reconcile four legal traditions, blend four courtroom procedures, and overcome the obstacle of five different languages.[21]

Solutions to these problems and many others were embodied in the London Agreement and Charter signed August 8, 1945. The agreement expressed the will of the Allies to create an International Military Tribunal to judge major Nazi criminals. The agreement further declared that the charter, which determined the court's constitution and jurisdiction, was the Tribunal's supreme law and that all of its provisions would be unchallengeable by prosecution or defense. The Big Four finally stated that other governments could adhere to the agreement, and nineteen members of the United Nations accepted this invitation.

The charter itself contained the law and procedure of Nuremberg. It determined the judicial character of the International Military Tribunal and the composition of the bench. The document stated that the defendants would be those whose crimes fell within three basic categories: crimes against peace, which consisted of conspiring, initiating, or waging a war of aggression; war crimes, which included all the traditional violations of the laws or customs of war; and crimes against humanity, which covered the atrocities of deportation, enslavement, and genocide.[22]

The charter further determined that the governmental position of defendants as heads of state could not confer immunity from punishment nor could such a defense be urged even to mitigate penalties. The defendant's plea that he was following the orders of superiors did not free him from responsibility, though it could be a factor in lessening punishment.[23]

Finally, the charter dealt with the problem of organizational

21. Jackson, *Case against War Criminals*, p. xiii; Harris, *Tyranny on Trial*, pp. 16–19; Svarlien, *Introduction to the Law of Nations*, pp. 401–2.

22. *Trial of the Major War Criminals Before the International Military Tribunal, Nurenberg, Germany: 14 November 1945–1 October, 1946*, 42 vols. (Nurenberg: International Military Tribunal, 1947–49), 1:11 (hereafter cited as *TMWC*). The prosecution in its indictment divided the charge of Crimes Against Peace into the two counts of conspiracy and of actually waging aggression. Ibid., 1:27–68.

23. Ibid., 1:12.

guilt. The document declared that the Tribunal might proscribe
a group or organization as being essentially criminal in its orien-
tation. If this were decided, prosecuting nations had the right to
bring any individual to trial for membership in such a body.

Once the Allies had created the law and the judicial forms
needed for trying the Nazis, a location for the trials had to be
determined. The Russian prosecutor opted for Berlin on the
ground that it was the former capital of the fallen foe. This
suggestion was rejected for the simple reason that Allied destruction of Berlin had been so complete that no building of the size
necessary for a large-scale trial remained intact.[24]

The pragmatic consideration of physical facilities led the Allies to choose Nuremberg for the International Military Tribunal.
Although bombs had destroyed large areas, the medieval Palace
of Justice and the large prison still stood amid the rubble. These
buildings provided accommodations for detention of prisoners
and conduction of trials.

If practical aspects determined the choice of Nuremberg, no
one was oblivious to the symbolism of the selection. During
former September days and nights Nuremberg was the Bavarian
city that had witnessed the spectacle of the Nazi party rallies. Its
streets and walls had echoed with four hundred thousand stri-
dent voices of Hitler's triumphant legions shouting "Sieg Heil!";
its stone stadium had reverberated with the drums and bugles
heralding a New Order which was to last a thousand years.
Moreover, the infamous decrees which deprived German-Jews of
their legal rights and left them defenseless against the atrocities
to come were entitled the Nuremberg laws.[25]

By common agreement twenty-four Nazis were selected for
trial before the International Military Tribunal.[26] Of these, Robert Ley, leader of the German Labor Front, committed suicide;
Gustav Krupp, head of the Krupp munitions works, was declared
too senile to stand trial; and Martin Bormann, head of the Party
Chancery, was tried "in absentia." Twenty-one defendants,
therefore, were arraigned at Nuremberg.[27]

24. Harris, Tyranny on Trial, p. 25.
25. Gustave Mark Gilbert, Nuremberg Diary (New York: Farrar, Straus,
1947), pp. 284, 404 (hereafter cited as Gilbert, Nuremberg Diary).
26. Jackson, Case against War Criminals, p. xi.
27. These men were: Hermann Wilhelm Goering, Commander-in-Chief
of the Air Force and successor designate to Hitler; Rudolf Hess, Deputy to

The trials started November 20, 1945 and ended August 31, 1946. The court conducted 403 open sessions. During the trials, 113 witnesses were called, 33 for the prosecution and 80 for the defense. One hundred thousand documents were accepted by the court. Five million words were recorded in evidence.

Final judgment was delivered September 30 and October 1, 1946. Ten of the defendants were sentenced to death by hanging. Goering, one of the condemned, cheated the hangman by suicide. Three defendants received life imprisonment; four were given prison sentences ranging from ten to twenty years; three were acquitted.

Five organizations were declared criminal: the leadership corps of the Nazi party; the SS (Schutzstaffel), an elite corps under Himmler; the SD (Sicherheitsdienst), a Security Service; the SA (Sturmabteilung), a paramilitary organization; and the Gestapo, the secret state police. The judges demanded, however, that personal responsibility for crimes be proved in any subsequent trial of members of these groups.[28] The court decided that the Reich Cabinet and the General Staff and High Command of the German Armed Forces lacked the cohesiveness required of an "organization" under the London Charter and therefore could not be condemned as criminal groups.

---

the Fuehrer and successor designate to Hitler after Goering; Joachim von Ribbentrop, Reich Minister for Foreign Affairs; Robert Ley, Leader of the German Labor Front; Wilhelm Keitel, Chief of the High Command of the Armed Forces; Ernst Kaltenbrunner, Chief of the Security Police; Alfred Rosenberg, Reich Minister for the Occupied Eastern Territory; Hans Frank, Governor General of Occupied Poland; Wilhelm Frick, Reich Minister of the Interior; Julius Streicher, Editor-in-chief of the antisemitic newspaper *Der Stuermer;* Walter Funk, President of the Reichsbank; Hjalmar Schacht, Reich Minister of Economics; Gustav Krupp von Bohlen und Halbach, head of the Krupp works; Karl Doenitz, Commander-in-Chief of the U-Boats and actual successor of Hitler; Erich Raeder, Commander-in-Chief of the Navy; Baldur von Schirach, leader of youth; Fritz Sauckel, Plenipotentiary for the employment of labor; Alfred Jodl, Chief of the Operations Staff of the high command of the armed forces; Martin Bormann, head of the Party Chancery; Franz von Papen, Vice Chancellor under Hitler; Arthur Seyss-Inquart, Reich Commissar for Occupied Netherlands; Albert Speer, Plenipotentiary for Armaments; Constantin von Neurath, Reich Protector for Occupied Czechoslovakia; and Hans Fritzsche, head of the radio division of the propaganda department of the party. Harris, *Tyranny on Trial,* pp. xxv–xxvi.

28. Harold Leventhal, et al., "The Nuremberg Verdict," *Harvard Law Review* 60 (July, 1947): 871; James Morris, "Major War Trials in Nurnberg," *North Dakota Bar Briefs* 25 (April, 1949): 100.

Thus ended the first great international criminal trial. But in many ways Nuremberg was just beginning. The length and the expense of the proceedings made other formal international tribunals unacceptable to the Allies, but courts of each of the four Allied powers and of the Germans themselves carried on the work of trying alleged Nazi offenders. When the denazification process was completed by 1950, these latter courts had tried over 3,500,000 Germans, using elements of Nuremberg's procedure and law.[29] Some of the Tribunal's principles were also embodied in such documents as the peace treaties with individual defeated nations, the army manuals of discipline for numerous countries, and other new national and international enactments. Nuremberg established for better or worse new developments in international law which had many future ramifications.

The Tribunal's most significant innovation was its legal definition of aggression as the "supreme crime." The novelty of this Nuremberg charge was that before the Tribunal's verdicts international law considered all wars ethically neutral and politically justifiable if a state deemed such belligerent action essential to its national interests. The court, going beyond even the dreams of those who wished to revive the concept that wars were either just or unjust, declared that aggression not only violated moral norms but also transgressed international law. Indeed, the judges asserted that aggression was the greatest of legal crimes for which death was the only fit penalty. Those who caused the murder of millions must pay with their lives.

A second principle enunciated was that government leaders were personally responsible for their policies. Previously, being a head of state created immunity from criminal liability. Decisions of political authorities were considered referrable to an abstract entity which was independent, sovereign, and supreme in its own affairs.[30]

Nuremberg declared all this changed. Government leaders no longer could hide behind the shield of "head of state" or "order of superior." The court and the charter maintained that international law can touch individuals within each nation in a fashion

29. Eugene Davidson, *The Death and Life of Germany* (New York: Knopf, 1959), p. 22 (hereafter cited as Davidson, *The Death and Life*).
30. Woetzel, *Nuremberg Trials*, pp. xiii–xiv.

analogous to the operation of United States federal law within the particular states. As the Nuremberg judges asserted: ". . . the very essence of the Charter is that individuals have international duties which transcend the national obligations of obedience imposed by the individual state." [31] Most of the other Nuremberg principles were corollaries of these two major innovations—the criminality of aggression and personal responsibility.[32]

Another decision important for the future was that all who aided criminal policies would stand trial as well as those who formulated the ultimate decisions for aggression and atrocities. Consequently, diplomats and financiers, industrialists and soldiers, all who make modern war possible could be called to account by international tribunals.

The judges, perceiving that the modern totalitarian state had the power to strangle its neighbors and to purge whole groups and organizations, nations, and races, enforced new laws condemning crimes against humanity. Previously, the rules and customs of war were adequate to sanction outrages because war crimes such as murder, looting, or rape were usually restricted to deeds of individual soldiers. At most, some commander might issue an order which resulted in a barbarity, but Nazism presented a different problem. Here was not an isolated outrage but a number of deliberate, extended policies officially adopted by a recognized government and executed by large organizations in a systematic fashion. The Nuremberg court decreed that not only the men who shot hostages and civilians, not only the men who turned on the gas in the chamber, but the political leaders who signed the orders and the propaganda chiefs who created the hysteria favorable to such genocide must pay for crimes against humanity.

Finally the Tribunal established a precedent demanding that any person charged with criminal action in international law has

---

31. *TMWC*, 1:223.
32. Alexander N. Sack, "War Criminals and the Defense of Act of State in International Law," *Lawyers Guild Review* 5 (September–October, 1945): 288–300; Alexander N. Sack, "War Criminals and the Defense of Superior Order in International Law," *Lawyers Guild Review* 5 (January–February, 1945): 11–17 (hereafter cited as Sack, "Superior Orders").

a right to a fair trial.[33] Anyone accused can demand that all the safeguards of due process be afforded him.[34]

The foregoing summary is a skeleton outline of the basic facts concerning the Nuremberg trials which judged the major German war criminals. Writers have studied many aspects of the Tribunal, and it is not our intention to repeat what these scholars have done so well. For this reason the reader will not find here a detailed examination of Nazi atrocities. The forty-two volumes of the Nuremberg trial record have carefully catalogued the systematic, diabolical cruelties of Hitler's regime which outraged all men with the slightest trace of moral or humane sensibility. Summaries of this proof of genocide and other atrocities have appeared in such books as Whitney R. Harris's *Tyranny on Trial: The Evidence of Nuremberg*. Moreover, the crimes have been graphically portrayed in documentary movies such as "Night and Fog" with an impact which no printed page could ever achieve. Hopefully such records will guarantee that America will long remember the barbarism of the gas ovens, the bulldozers covering the long ditches of dead, and the inhuman sufferings inflicted on over six million defenseless and innocent victims.

Nor is it our aim to relate a detailed history of the trials. The official record of the court's activities has been printed in full, and lawyers and historians have written at length concerning the facts of the Tribunal. Biographies of many of the defendants have been published. Nor do we propose to subject the court to legal examination in order to judge the legality, validity, or effectiveness of the trials. This path has been perhaps too well trod.

What, then, is the task we have chosen? It is to determine the judgment of Americans on the Nuremberg trials and to find out

33. Benjamin B. Ferencz, "Nurnberg Trial Procedure and the Rights of the Accused," *Journal of Criminal Law and Criminology* 39 (July–August, 1948): 144–45; Harris, *Tyranny on Trial*, pp. 558–59.

34. This enumeration of principles created by the Nuremberg court basically coincides with those listed by the United Nations International law commission's report to the General Assembly offered in fulfillment of that body's directive to "formulate the principles of international law recognized in the Charter of the Nürnberg Tribunal and in the judgment of the Tribunal," United Nations, "Report of the International Law Commission Covering Its Second Session, June 5–July 29, 1950," *American Journal of International Law*, Supplement of Documents 44 (October, 1950): 125.

the attitudes expressed by persons and groups in the United States toward the major war-crime trials. Our investigation is confined to those trials conducted from November 1945 to October 1946 by the International Military Tribunal which was created by the governments of France, Great Britain, Russia, and the United States in order to judge Hitler's major accomplices such as Hermann Goering, Rudolf Hess, Joachim von Ribbentrop, and Karl Doenitz. Reaction to the trials of relatively minor German officials, which were held by each of the Big Four following the Nuremberg Tribunal's action, and the trials of the Japanese leaders will be considered only by analogy or contrast. The secondary trials of German officials, doctors, lawyers, and industrialists did produce sensational evidence and did deepen our knowledge of Nazi depravity. However, these later trials did not have the importance of the major Nuremberg action either as legal innovation or as a conscious attempt by the victorious Allies to establish judicial precedents in international law.

To determine the American attitudes the opinions of many different individuals, professions, and organizations must be considered. The views of government officials and international lawyers, congress and the people, churchmen and "domestic" lawyers, historians and political scientists, military men and behavioral scientists—all will be examined so the full scope and diversity of American opinion may be revealed. We also will attempt to explain why various persons and groups held their particular judgments on the Tribunal, and we will try to situate their attitudes in the intellectual milieu of the post-World War II era.

We will view Nuremberg not as a legal drama performed in defeated Germany during 1945 and 1946. Here the Tribunal becomes a finely cut diamond whose facets reflected American intellectual commitments and emotional responses during those years, Americans' weariness and disgust with the ugliness of war, their dreams and plans for future peace, their loves and hates, their apathy and ambitions. Moreover, through analysis of the expressed or implied attitudes and assumptions, we seek insight into modern American sociological mythology—i.e., into those emotionally charged concepts, partly true, partly false, by which men live and die. We believe reaction to Nuremberg revealed in some ways the heart and mind of America, called upon for the first time to assume active world leadership and to make crucial decisions affecting war and peace.

Since these are the facts and insights that we seek, our method will be an objective presentation of American attitudes insofar as this is possible. The present study is an attempt not to judge but to record and analyze—to record what Americans actually said about the Tribunal, and to analyze what these statements expressed or implied in regard to patterns of American thought. We have found it difficult to refrain from judgment just as, we are sure, the reader will. Noteworthy positions seem so often to cry out for ridicule or commendation, qualification, or clarification. But it is not our own verdict on Nuremberg or on the opinions of others that we wish to present. We seek the judgment on Nuremberg of the American people.

To set the stage for the investigation of American attitudes, we will examine first the vital legal, political, psychological, and ethical issues which men saw embodied in the Nuremberg trials.

The novel aspects of Nuremberg caused men to debate four basic questions. The first, and the one of most consequence, dealt with the Tribunal's legality. Did any law exist by which these men could be judged, or were the trials an arbitrary exercise of power? Implicit in such a question is the accusation that although no one considered the actions of the German leaders criminal when they were doing them, the Tribunal would now, *ex post facto,* declare their acts to be crimes punishable by death and demand that the Nazis stand trial on this new interpretation.[35]

The second major issue concerned the composition of the court. Could nations guilty of similar offenses, or who even perhaps had an active part in the commission of the crimes under consideration, judge and condemn their fellow criminals and accomplices. Could the court declare Germany's belligerent action against Poland in the West to be a "supreme crime" and forbid mention in the courtroom of Russia's attack from the East? If Dachau and Buchenwald are declared open to investi-

35. The common phrase used by European lawyers to express the same idea is *Nulla crimen, sine lege,* that is, "no crime, without a [preexisting] law."

gation by an international court, are Hiroshima and Dresden also to be investigated?

Third, the verdicts of the Tribunal are called into question. Were the sentences too harsh? If the Allies had perpetrated similar brutalities, did they have a right to execute their German "brothers in crime"? Did the court have a right to deal out stern justice to military men who claimed merely to be obeying orders? Could the Tribunal condemn a man to death for talking? No crime of violence was proved against Julius Streicher, but he hanged for his propaganda. Hess seemed insane to many experts. Was life imprisonment an appropriate sentence for him?

Were the verdicts too lenient? Were the three acquittals really just? Were the judges right in excluding consideration of the millions of German-Jews and Christians slaughtered by the Nazis before 1939 just because these were not directly connected with aggressive war? Was the court's narrow interpretation of the charge of conspiracy for aggression realistic when its position resulted in only eight of the twenty-one major decision makers of Hitler's Germany being convicted on this indictment?

Finally, men wondered about the trials' effect on the future. Would Nuremberg be a deterrent to aggressive war? Or would the lesson be that a people must fight to the death knowing that to the victor went not only the spoils, but also the right to try the vanquished? Would the Tribunal be the inception of an international law recognizing the rights and duties of every individual in the world, or would it open the way for new barbarities committed in the name of law? Or, perhaps, was Nuremberg so novel an experiment that it would have no meaning as a precedent? [36]

Reaction to Nuremberg centered around these four issues—the legality of the trials, the composition of the court, the nature of the verdicts, and the consequence for the future. The intensity and diversity of attitudes on these four aspects of Nuremberg trials arose, as we shall see, because these four considerations are directly related to many of the most fundamental questions that men and society have posed throughout history.

The Tribunal, first of all, raises the timeless conflict of the

36. Victor C. Swearinger, "Nuernberg War Crime Trials," *Kentucky State Bar Journal* 12 (December, 1947): 20.

voluntarist and the rationalist in legal philosophy. Is law, as the former would claim, a creation of the sovereign's will? Or is it something discovered by man's reason as the rationalist asserts? Or might law be neither of these, but purely relative regulations which must pragmatically serve men's needs? Further, what is the relation between law and morality? Are they interchangeable or do their norms rule in essentially different spheres each with its own particular sanctions?

These legal and ethical considerations raised by Nuremberg are closely allied to the problem the Tribunal poses for the political scientist. What is the nature of the state? Is it an abstract Hegelian entity, absolutely sovereign, accountable to no higher authority? Or, on the other hand, are the state's actions open to inspection and judgment?

The Tribunal also raised basic questions in international relations. Should actions of a government be judged exclusively in terms of power and its own national interest or by norms of right and wrong? Was success or justice the standard for leaders? Could *individual* ethical norms be applied to nations?

The criminologist also saw Nuremberg in terms of other basic issues. What is the effect of punishment? Are legal sanctions effective deterrents to future lawlessness? How free is man in modern society? How accountable is he for his actions? Is the criminal evil or sick? Is crime a moral wrong or a social phenomenon?

Nuremberg also provoked questions about the role of the soldier in the modern world. Is the military leader merely a tool in the hands of the politician, blindly obedient? Or are the branches of a modern bureaucratic government so interrelated that the soldier must be implicated in ultimate policy decisions?

Our study of American attitudes toward the Nuremberg trials of the major Nazi war criminals will examine all of these questions and many other perplexing problems facing modern man in his political, legal, military, and ethical life. Obviously, no final solution which would satisfy all can be offered to any of these fundamental questions. Man has wrestled with these problems in some form from the beginning of his existence, and hopefully he will in the future.

2

American Policy Makers and the War-Crime Trials

For the men in the Executive Department of the United States government, the Nuremberg trials were essentially a matter of political policy, and they based their judgments on political norms rather than any other standard. To some extent they realized the importance of the legal, moral, psychological, and military factors that would be involved in any trial program, but they steadily viewed these aspects in relation to the question of whether trials would further or hinder the national interest of the United States.

The program of an international tribunal resulted from the interaction of a number of persons and ideas within the executive department of the United States government. President Franklin Delano Roosevelt indirectly determined the final United States policy of holding an international trial. It was Roosevelt who formally declared that Axis leaders would be punished and that this would involve some form of judicial procedure. As early as August 21, 1942 the president stated to all mankind that "the time will come when they shall have to stand in courts of law in the very countries which they are now oppressing and answer for their acts." [1] About two weeks later Roosevelt repeated this promise. "It is our intention," he said, "that just and sure punishment shall be meted out to the ringleaders responsible for the organized murder of thousands of innocent persons and the commission of atrocities which have

1. Franklin D. Roosevelt, *The Public Papers and Addresses of Franklin D. Roosevelt,* ed. Samuel I. Rosenman, 13 vols. (New York: Harper, 1950), 10:330.

violated every tenet of the Christian faith." [2] Note, however, that in these presidential proclamations aggressive war is in no way branded as the "supreme crime" nor is an international tribunal suggested.

When a decision became imperative on the exact manner in which the general program of postwar punishment would be implemented, Franklin Roosevelt followed a procedure characteristic of him. He gathered different plans, sought experts' advice, tentatively proposed various schemes, and gauged the reaction to each. The result of this experimentation was that the president apparently shifted his views, to a greater or lesser degree, three times.

The first official declaration of policy by the American government came in a joint statement by the United States, Russia, and Great Britain which was released by the Moscow Foreign Ministers' Conference on November 1, 1943. When these diplomats came to the Soviet capital, they had already received a common declaration, on war criminals, signed by the heads of the three nations.

The document issued a solemn warning to the Axis powers that violators of the rules of war and humanity would be punished in the place where they had perpetrated their atrocities. Major war criminals, however, because their outrages "have no particular geographical localization . . . will be punished by joint decision of the Governments of the Allies." [3]

We know that during these Moscow negotiations Secretary of State Cordell Hull attempted to determine exactly the method of dealing with alleged Nazi criminals. He proposed judgment by drumhead court-martials without any involved legal procedures.[4] It is probable that the secretary could not have urged this program without the knowledge and approval of the president. We note specifically that no formal state trials were promised in the conference's declaration and that the general tenor of Roos-

2. Ibid., p. 410.
3. "Declaration of German Atrocities," *Department of State Bulletin* 9 (November 6, 1943): 311.
4. Cordell Hull, *The Memoirs of Cordell Hull*, 2 vols. (New York: Macmillan, 1948), 1:128–29 (hereafter cited as Hull, *Memoirs*).

evelt's statements at this time also indicated his adoption of Hull's plan for swift military justice.

One month after the Moscow meeting of the foreign ministers, the first three-power conference in which Stalin personally participated was held at Teheran (November 28 to December 1, 1943). The president's words at this encounter apparently confirmed at least the spirit of Cordell Hull's proposal for summary executions.

At Teheran, Marshal Stalin raised his glass in a macabre toast. "I propose a salute to the swiftest possible justice for all Germany's war criminals—justice before a firing squad. I drink to our unity in dispatching them as fast as we capture them, all of them, and there must be at least fifty thousand of them." [5]

Elliott Roosevelt, a primary source for this story, reported that Churchill was instantly on his feet, enraged by the adoption of a policy in morbid humor which he considered unjust and illegal. "Any such attitude," he cried, "is wholly contrary to our British sense of justice! The British people will never stand for such mass murder. I take this opportunity to say that I feel most strongly that no one, Nazi or no, shall be summarily dealt with, before a firing squad, without proper legal trial, no matter what the known facts and proven evidence against him." [6]

Roosevelt, attempting to dissipate the tenseness of the situation, interposed the comment that the Russian marshal's number was perhaps too high. The president said he would be satisfied with 49,500.

The historian judging the seriousness of this dialogue may have to throw away all the usual scientific methods and resort to counting the number of toasts and estimating the alcoholic tolerance of the participants. Elliott Roosevelt related that his father told him in private that all was said in jest and that it was Churchill's misunderstanding to take it seriously. What is certain is that no evidence exists of any United States Army directive for the massacre of alleged German war criminals, nor in fact was any such program carried out.

5. Elliott Roosevelt, *As He Saw It* (New York: Duell, Sloan, and Pearce, 1946), p. 188.
6. Ibid., pp. 188–91.

The second method of postwar punishment which replaced the policy of drumhead court-martials was the Morgenthau plan. The president endorsed a shortened form of his program at the Second Quebec Conference held from September 11 to 16, 1944. Section XI of the full text opted for American adoption of a plan of "catch-identify-shoot" for Axis war criminals. The Allies must avoid trials of any type, according to Morgenthau, because such legal proceedings could only lead to confusion and to the guilty escaping just punishment.[7]

In fact, no definite decision for either shooting or trial was made by the Quebec conferees, but it was reported, perhaps erroneously, that the president had argued for a policy of executive executions which would have dispensed with legal procedures.[8]

Two months after the Quebec Conference, on November 21, 1944, Franklin Roosevelt revealed to the trial plan's chief advocate, Henry L. Stimson, the first signs that he was weakening in his endorsement of summary executions. The president on that day seemed intrigued by the secretary of war's idea that at postwar trials, men of all classes and professions who aided Hitler could be indicted on conspiracy charges.[9]

Realizing that there were a number of conflicting ideas and programs for war-crime punishment, the president finally turned the question over to a new committee headed by Judge Samuel Rosenman, his speech writer, "trouble-shooter," and confidant. The judge chose for his group Joseph P. Davis, Attorney General Biddle, and a number of minor officials in executive departments. This body, in its January 18, 1945 meeting, arrived at a consensus favoring legal rather than political action against the Axis leaders and a formal state trial for major criminals. Two days later, the secretary of war submitted for presidential consideration the program for trials prepared by the lawyers of his

7. Henry L. Stimson and McGeorge Bundy, *On Active Service in Peace and War* (New York: Harper, 1947), p. 584 (hereafter cited as Stimson and Bundy, *On Active Service*). Henry Morgenthau, Jr., *Germany Is Our Problem* (New York: Harper, 1945), p. 14; see also pages 3–4 and 12 (hereafter cited as Morgenthau, *Germany Is Our Problem*).
8. Stimson and Bundy, *On Active Service*, p. 585.
9. Ibid., p. 586.

department and endorsed by the State and War Departments.[10]

The hesitant but growing receptivity of President Roosevelt to Stimson's program for international trials has many explanations, most of them personal to Franklin Roosevelt. Secretary Stimson saw the Second World War as a spiritual crusade against the powers of wickedness. Consequently he desired the final act in the struggle to be an official seal that would stamp the enemy as evil and as the cause of all mankind's misfortunes. Arguing for postwar trials to achieve this aim, Stimson spoke to an American president who, for all his pragmatism and relativism in action, was still moralistic and religious in principle. Franklin Roosevelt, as did Stimson, considered the war an ideological conflict, and therefore a vast, symbolic trial had an appeal for the president.[11]

A second reason Roosevelt was predisposed to favor Stimson's idea of formal international trials was the president's awareness that revisionist historians and the isolationist had attempted to discredit America's entrance into the First World War and the Versailles settlement. These critics attacked the treaty's theory of exclusive German guilt for starting the war and had convinced a large segment of the Allied public that most reported enemy atrocities were merely Allied propaganda.[12]

The president was fearful of a recurrence of this skepticism. He feared that without irrefutable proof of their actions the Nazi leaders might someday be venerated as martyrs. "He was determined that the question of Hitler's guilt—and the guilt of his gangsters—must not be left open for future debate. The whole nauseating matter should be spread out on a permanent record under oath by witnesses and with all the written documents. . . . In short, there must never be any question anywhere by anyone about who was responsible for the war and for the uncivilized war crimes." [13] Guilt must be assessed, atrocities verified; for this, a formal tribunal was necessary.

Another reason international trials had a special appeal to Roosevelt was the very magnitude and drama of the undertak-

10. Ibid., pp. 586–87.
11. Ibid., p. 587; Hauser, "The Backstage Battle at Nuremberg," p. 18.
12. Rosenman, *Working with Roosevelt*, pp. 518–19.
13. Ibid., pp. 542–43.

ing. Certainly the journalist Ernest O. Hauser had a valuable insight into the psychological motives for the International Military Tribunal when he wrote that "the ambitious project of creating rather than merely applying international law, and of setting a new standard for good conduct in the family of nations, is essentially Rooseveltian. It can be traced directly to the late President, and it is fascinating to observe how the grandiose concepts as well as the vagueness characteristic of Franklin Roosevelt, are in evidence at Nuremberg." [14]

An indirect but probative indication that President Roosevelt had definitely committed himself to the program of international trials occurred when, upon Rosenman's presentation of his memorandum on war criminals to Roosevelt on January 22, 1945, the president gave him the assignment of convincing the London government of the advisability of an international tribunal. Rosenman's task was rendered particularly difficult by a consensus already existing among British officials to execute the top six or seven Nazis without trial, since English leaders feared that formal legal proceedings would provide a propaganda pulpit for the Third Reich's doctrines. [15]

Rosenman did not convince top British leaders, but he did succeed in delaying the decision on this matter until the general meeting of the Allies in San Francisco which had been called to establish the United Nations. When Rosenman attended the conference, he found that the English already had changed their opinion and were willing to support the American program. [16]

The British granted cooperation grudgingly. Although impressed by Rosenman's lengthy and eloquent pleadings in private conferences, Churchill at this time preferred executive exe-

14. Hauser, "Backstage Battle at Nuremberg," p. 18. A more critical statement of the "Rooseveltian" character of Nuremberg is provided by Alfred Vagts. "Perhaps this is New Deal justice—the overriding of precedent, the fight against the 'nine old men' who successfully stood out for precedent against administrative absolutism—transferred to the international scene, where no carefully administered law stood in its way. It is also New Deal jurisprudence without the tempering of justice with humanitarianism in which it usually prided itself." *Defence and Diplomacy, The Soldier and the Conduct of Foreign Relations* (New York: King's Crown Press, 1956), p. 327.

15. Rosenman, *Working with Roosevelt*, p. 542.

16. The reversal of British policy was influenced by a promise of a large postwar loan.

cutions for major criminals because such a nonjudicial program would be unassailable by charges that retroactive law had been employed. For this reason, one of the judge's moments of greatest personal triumph occurred in 1947 when at a dinner party Churchill remarked to him: "Rosenman, do you remember our talk at Chequers when I argued so strenuously against trying those Nazi war criminals? Now that the trials are all over, I think the President was right and I was wrong." [17]

No man can tell what plan Franklin Roosevelt finally would have adopted, for when the ultimate decision was made another man was president.

On April 12, 1945 Roosevelt died at Warm Springs, and Harry S Truman inherited not only the office but also the policies of the former president. In his first major speech on April 16, 1945, before a joint session of Congress, Truman stated that "we do not wish to see unnecessary or unjustified suffering. But the laws of God and men have been violated and the guilty must not go unpunished. Nothing shall shake our determination to punish the war criminals even though we must pursue them to the ends of the earth." [18]

When the Army General Advocate's departmental proposals for holding trials finally arrived at the president's desk, stamped with the approval of the War and State Departments, Truman gave the program his endorsement. The president appointed Robert Jackson, associate justice of the Supreme Court, as the chief American prosecutor and Francis Biddle, the attorney general, as the United States judge at Nuremberg. One motive the president had in appointing men of such rank and caliber was that he wished to influence the other Allied nations to send their best men and thus help ensure the success of the trials.

In his *Memoirs*, Truman has little to say concerning the Nuremberg proceedings, merely noting that it was the fulfillment of Roosevelt's and his own policy.[19] During the Tribunal's operation

17. Rosenman, *Working with Roosevelt*, p. 545.
18. Harry S Truman, *Public Papers of the Presidents of the United States, Harry S Truman*, April 12 to December 31, 1945 (Washington: Government Printing Office, 1961), 1:1 (hereafter cited as Truman, *Public Papers*).
19. Harry S Truman, *Memoirs of Harry S Truman*, 2 vols. (Garden City, N.Y.: Doubleday, 1955), 1:283–84 (hereafter cited as Truman, *Memoirs*).

the president maintained an attitude of noninvolvement. The final verdicts, however, elicited Truman's wholehearted praise because he held that the court had established an effective deterrent to future international banditry. "I think that's a fair trial, as far as I can see it," Truman told reporters, "and I think it's a good thing for the world—one of the greatest things to come out of this war." [20] The president also wrote at this time that "an undisputed gain coming out of Nürnberg is the formal recognition that there are crimes against humanity. . . . I am satisfied that the defendants received a fair trial. I hope we have established for all time the proposition that aggressive war is criminal and will be so treated." [21]

Other presidents and presidential aspirants had varying views, not always fully defined, about punishment for Nazi offenders and an international tribunal. The only former president still living at the time of the Nuremberg program, Herbert Hoover, advocated punishment of Axis leaders as one of the basic policies in his program for peace. The former president held that, although Americans should not think all Germans were villains, enemy leaders must be made to realize the vastness of their criminality. "There can be no moral distinction and there should be no legal distinction between such men and common criminals conspiring to murder. Too long has it been assumed that there is something sacred about the heads of state who project or provoke war and wholesale murder." [22]

The only uncertainty in understanding Hoover's policy is whether he would have wished these sanctions for Axis chieftains to be imposed by military courts or by an international tribunal. At the time of his writing in 1943 these alternatives had not been proposed.

Herbert Hoover's rival for the presidency in the 1928 election,

20. Truman, *Public Papers,* January 1 to December 31, 1946, 2:441.
21. Harry S. Truman, "Prosecution of Major Nazi War Criminals," *Department of State Bulletin* 15 (October 27, 1946): 954. See also Robert H. Jackson, "Final Report to the President from Supreme Court Justice Jackson," *Department of State Bulletin* 15 (October 27, 1946): 771–76 (hereafter cited as Jackson, "Final Report"), and Truman, *Public Papers,* January 1 to December 31, 1946, p. 459.
22. Herbert Hoover and Hugh Gibson, *The Problems of Lasting Peace* (Garden City, N.Y.: Doubleday, Doran, 1943), p. 252.

Alfred Emmanuel Smith, viewed the question of war criminals in much the same way as Hoover. When in May of 1944 the advancing Allied armies revealed Axis atrocities, Smith organized an appeal to the leaders of the United Nations requesting them to designate the United States as a temporary haven for persecuted minorities. This appeal was signed by eighteen governors, Coolidge's vice-president Charles G. Dawes, an associate justice of the Supreme Court, and many American intellectual, industrial, and political leaders. Smith's appeal called upon the United States to warn Nazi leaders that "no person who participates in crimes against the Jews and other minorities shall escape punishment" and that "the end of the war will bring swift retribution upon all those guilty of atrocities." [23] The exact manner in which Smith desired sanctions imposed cannot be ascertained. His death in October 1944 of course precluded any direct judgment by him on the International Military Tribunal.

The American press was intensely interested in the reaction to the Nuremberg verdicts of one individual who later became president, Dwight D. Eisenhower. Because at the time he was general of the armies, his views were considered as those of a soldier; therefore, we will study his statements when investigating military attitudes toward Nuremberg.

Eisenhower's successor, John Fitzgerald Kennedy, evaluated Nuremberg tangentially when writing of Senator Robert A. Taft in *Profiles in Courage*. Although President Kennedy never explicitly delivered his judgment on the Tribunal, it is perhaps implied by his answering the rhetorical question "but what kind of trial was this?" with a quotation from Supreme Court Justice William O. Douglas roundly condemning the Tribunal. Kennedy added that "these conclusions are shared, I believe, by a substantial number of American citizens today." [24]

23. *New York Times*, May 26, 1944, p. 19.
24. John Fitzgerald Kennedy, *Profiles in Courage* (New York: Harper, [Inaugural edition] 1961), pp. 216–17 (hereafter cited as Kennedy, *Profiles in Courage*). Professor Allan Nevins, who wrote the foreword to President Kennedy's book, disagrees with this interpretation of an anti-Nuremberg stand. "The late President Kennedy never talked with me about the Nuremberg Trials, beyond saying that he greatly admired the courage of Senator Taft in condemning the American position. I was left with the impression that he himself had never clearly formulated a position on the equity of the trials." Letter to the author, August 25, 1965.

At this point we consider a presidential nominee who, although not a serious contender, was a constant and thoughtful voice on national issues. Norman Thomas, the Socialist candidate, held that Axis criminals should be punished, but he had serious misgivings about the inclusion of the indictment for aggression. "Our socialist proposals never precluded the trial and punishment of those guilty of atrocities against civilians and prisoners of war," Thomas wrote. "For that there was sufficient law already recognized. They did preclude trials of the sort that are dragging along in Nuremberg and Tokyo as this is being written. Aggressive war is a moral crime but this will not be established in the conscience of mankind by proceedings such as those at Nuremberg, where Russians sit on the bench and exclude evidence of Hitler's deal with Stalin. What was the latter's war against Finland, Poland and the Baltic states but aggression? Indeed, what major power had not in comparatively recent years been guilty of acts of aggression? Mr. Justice Jackson makes much of the analogy of the growth of common law to justify the Nuremberg proceedings. The very composition of the court by victors who are at once judges and prosecutors refutes his analogy." [25]

It is interesting to reflect that Norman Thomas's condemnation appeared some time before the dissent of any other nationally known figure. It occurred months before the statement of Senator Robert Taft. Observe, moreover, that Thomas and Taft, seldom in agreement on other issues, both attacked Nuremberg for the same reasons—it applied retroactive law, and the victor nations could not be impartial in judgment.

Henry Agar Wallace, secretary of commerce in the Nuremberg years, was another presidential aspirant of the postwar period. Wallace ran as the candidate of the Progressive party in 1948. In his book *The Century of the Common Man*, Wallace held that the first problem of the postwar period would be to decide what to do with the defeated: ". . . revenge for the sake of revenge would be a sign of barbarism. But this time we must make

25. Norman Thomas, *Appeal to the Nations* (New York: Holt, 1947), pp. 68–69.

absolutely sure that the guilty leaders are punished, that the defeated nation realizes its defeat and is not permitted to rearm." [26]

Although Henry Wallace was in favor of punishment for Axis chiefs, he did not publicly approve of Nuremberg during the proceedings of the trials, nor did he respond to Senator Taft's criticism of the court. As he wrote at a later date, "I gave no opinion at the time. This far after the event I hate to give an opinion. I have never been blood thirsty. On the other hand, it is disturbing to see certain Nazi criminals operating in Egypt today." [27]

Thus spoke the American presidents and those who sought the presidency.

If ultimate decisions on American foreign policy are reserved for the president, selection of the practical means of implementation is the province of the secretary of state. While a postwar occupation program for Germany became the immediate responsibility of the War Department, the State Department had an active role in the war-crime trials.

One strange fact that the evidence reveals is that most men in the secretariat, during the period of the trials' proposal, action, and accomplishment, had strong reservations about, if not aversion to, an international tribunal.

Cordell Hull, secretary of state until November 21, 1944, strenuously urged that swift, sure execution be the fate of Axis criminals. As he expressed his opinion at the Moscow Foreign Ministers' Conference: "If I had my way, I would take Hitler and Mussolini and Tojo and their arch-accomplices and bring them before a drumhead court-martial. And at sunrise on the following day there would occur an historic incident." [28] The secretary of state promoted this manner of postwar punishment because he felt that the vicious aggressions and atrocities of the Nazis had to be eliminated in a dramatic fashion.[29]

26. Henry A. Wallace, *The Century of the Common Man* (New York: Reynal and Hitchcock, 1943), p. 45.
27. Henry A. Wallace, letter to the author, September 20, 1965.
28. Hull, *Memoirs*, 1:1289.
29. Ibid., 1:1289–90.

Although Hull earlier argued vehemently for military execution, after the international trial was decided upon he diplomatically acquiesced in the Nuremberg program. "I do not want, however, to be understood as being opposed to the Nuremberg trial," he explained. "I heartily supported that course when it was later decided upon. My thought has only to do with the difference in the form of trial." [30]

Edward R. Stettinius, Jr., who succeeded Cordell Hull on November 21, 1944, delegated State Department activity on war-crime punishment to his subordinates, but his personal support for the administration policy was never in doubt. [31] Dean Acheson was appointed to act as liaison officer between the executive branch and the legislative branch concerning measures for punishment, and Joseph C. Grew, voice of the State Department, introduced the public to the problem. [32]

One of Grew's first duties was the official announcement of discontinuing the services of Mr. Herbert C. Pell as United States representative at the United Nations War-Crimes Committee in London. Grew's press conference of January 26, 1945 assured the American people that they would continue to be represented by Pell's deputy commissioner and that there would be "no diminution in the interest or activity of this Government in the general subject of the punishment of war criminals." [33]

It was also early in 1945 that Grew, as acting secretary of state, informed the American people that the final decision on the method of dealing with Axis criminals was being worked out with the other Allies through the forum of the United Nations War-Crimes Commission, and he also pointed out that certain general guidelines were already established by the statements of President Roosevelt and the Moscow Declaration. [34]

Finally, Joseph Grew, as one of his last official acts, issued Departmental Order No. 1326 on June 22, 1945 announcing the

30. Ibid., 1:1291.
31. *Cong. Rec.*, 79 Cong., 1 Sess., 91:3692.
32. Ibid., 4283–84.
33. Joseph C. Grew, "Discontinuance of Services of Herbert C. Pell," *Department of State Bulletin* 12 (January 28, 1945): 123.
34. Joseph C. Grew, "Punishment of War Criminals," *Department of State Bulletin* 12 (February 4, 1945): 154–55.

State Department's policy of full cooperation with the United States chief of counsel for the Tribunal.[35]

James Byrnes, succeeded Edward Stettinius as secretary of state July 1, 1945 and held that office during the entire proceedings at the Nuremberg trials. The new cabinet official's attitude may be characterized as pragmatic and cautious. During policy discussions in Roosevelt's cabinet prior to his appointment, Byrnes considered that the executive execution program advocated by the State Department under the influence of the Treasury was too punitive. He thought that if fair trials were held some Germans might be acquitted or receive sentences lighter than death.[36]

At the Potsdam Conference (July 17 to August 2, 1945) the secretary of state brought about a modification of the Russian proposal demanding that Allied nations immediately submit lists of war criminals. Byrnes urged care and sound planning with such effectiveness that the conference agreed to a statement of a general principle favoring punishment of Axis criminals but postponed naming the accused until more detailed investigation of the individuals and the alleged charges could be made.[37]

During the trials the State Department continually published material favorable to the Tribunal. Lectures and radio broadcasts were employed to explain Nuremberg to the American people and to solicit their support for it. The Department of State *Bulletin* printed many documented defenses of Nuremberg. No comment adverse to the trials ever appeared in its pages.

The public policy of the State Department toward international trials did not change either during or after the prosecution of the Nazis, but its unpublicized attitude did shift during the proceedings. The new policy emerged as early as June 1946, three months before the Tribunal's verdicts. James Byrnes realized that the International Military Tribunal had been an expen-

35. Joseph C. Grew, "Cooperation with the United States Chief of Counsel for the Prosecution of Axis Criminality," *Department of State Bulletin* 12 (July 1, 1945): 40.

36. James F. Byrnes, *Speaking Frankly* (New York: Harper, 1947), p. 183.

37. "Tripartite Conference at Berlin," *Department of State Bulletin* 13 (August 5, 1945): 158.

sive, time-consuming spectacular whose point had been made, if it ever would be made. Nuremberg, moreover, was re-evaluated because of new hostilities between Russia and the United States. The secretary feared that subsequent international trials might achieve little more than the alienation from the West of new German leaders.[38]

On June 17, 1946 Brigadier General Telford Taylor, who was in charge of the trials after the major Nuremberg tribunal, conferred with Mr. Benjamin Cohen, State Department representative in Paris, on the continuation of international trials. After Taylor presented documents written by Justice Jackson and himself, Cohen sought the secretary of state's decision. On June 21 the Paris agent relayed to Taylor, Byrnes's statement that "the United States cannot afford to appear to be in the position of obstructing another trial. . . . If the plans for a second trial break down because of disagreement among the other three governments, or because one or more of the three will not agree to conditions or requirements which are really necessary from an American standpoint, well and good. But if the three countries definitely want a second trial and are prepared to meet our requirements, we had better play along with them." [39]

When Secretary Byrnes's policy decision was published in 1949 it received some notoriety because Malcolm Hobbs, in his article "Nürnberg's Indecent Burial," cited Byrnes's communication as evidence of the State Department's disenchantment with the war-crime trials.[40] This communique, however, probably did not have for either Telford Taylor or Secretary Byrnes the momentous import that Hobbs assigned to it.[41] Still the document seems to indicate some shift in the State Department's policy toward the international tribunal.

38. Telford Taylor, *Final Report to the Secretary of the Army on the Nuernberg War Crime Trials Under Control Council Law No. 10* (Washington: Government Printing Office, 1949), p. 92.

39. Ibid., p. 282.

40. Malcolm Hobbs, "Nürnberg's Indecent Burial," *Nation* 169 (December 3, 1949): 534–35 (hereafter cited as Hobbs, "Indecent Burial").

41. Letter of Telford Taylor to the author, May 14, 1965. "I do not recall ever writing General Maxwell (sic) Taylor, or for that matter, anyone else, a secret letter about the Nuremberg Trials"; Letter of James F. Byrnes to the author, May 14, 1965.

In this way the attitudes of the secretaries of state had shifted from Cordell Hull's desire for swift, sharp justice by drumhead court-martial, to official approval of an international trial under Stettinius and Grew, and finally to Byrnes's trying to eliminate a program that had not proved an unqualified blessing to American foreign policy.

If the State Department's attitude toward Nuremberg underwent alteration, the other branch of the government intimately connected with the proceedings was a model of consistency. The reason for this was simple. Henry L. Stimson, secretary of war, was the chief governmental proponent of judgment on Axis warlords by an international tribunal.

Stimson early realized that a conflict existed over the future policy for Germany and the punishment of enemy leaders. One faction, led by Secretary of the Treasury Henry Morgenthau, Jr., championed a program of immediate execution upon apprehension of alleged war criminals. Morgenthau opposed any trials because they would "reap a crop of martyrs" for Germany and "the trials would be a sounding board for Nazi dogma." [42]

Stimson led the other faction. He never lost hope even when he found that his advocacy of an international tribunal made him a minority of one in the cabinet.[43] Indeed it was when success seemed most remote that the secretary of war set his departmental lawyers to the task of working out the procedures for a trial. The legal group created by Stimson, and headed by Colonel Murray C. Bernays of the Judge Advocate General's staff, arrived at the same conclusions as their dynamic leader.

One important addition was made to the postwar trial program at this time. Colonel Bernays urged the inclusion of the charge of conspiracy to wage aggressive war. Stimson, overcoming a former hesitation regarding this charge, now gave his hearty approval to the idea, motivated perhaps by his own success as United States attorney with an analogous conspiracy charge against American business monopolies.[44]

42. Morgenthau, *Germany Is Our Problem*, p. 14.
43. Stimson and Bundy, *On Active Service*, p. 584. Lucius D. Clay had heard this view of Stimson in the summer of 1945. *Decision in Germany* (Cambridge, Mass.: Harvard University Press, 1946), pp. 53–56.
44. Stimson and Bundy, *On Active Service*, pp. 586, 587.

After this preparation Stimson repeatedly pleaded his views with Franklin Roosevelt, and on November 21, 1944 the president first indicated that he might be interested in an international trial. Soon after this date other government leaders rallied to support Stimson's proposal, and by January of 1945 the secretary of war could claim that ultimate victory was inevitable for the formal trial program.

Officially, Stimson had little subsequent involvement with Nuremberg. Unofficially, however, even after his resignation as secretary of war September 21, 1945, Henry L. Stimson did not cease his advocacy for the international tribunal. As voices of opposition were heard in the land, the former secretary presented in the periodical *Foreign Affairs* an eloquent defense of the Tribunal. Stimson's essay was of the greatest importance. His arguments were constantly reproduced by the trials' defenders, and he was frequently cited as an authority.[45] The secretary eloquently verbalized the attitude of most Americans and rallied traditional assumptions and principles of United States foreign policy to the support of the Nuremberg Tribunal.

In his essay the former secretary of war developed his interpretation of Nuremberg almost exclusively through consideration of the one indictment of conspiracy to commit aggression.[46] Other lawyers' difficulties with this charge were nonexistent for Stimson because the "proposition sustained by the Tribunal is simple: if a man plans aggression when aggression has been formally renounced by his nation, he is a criminal." [47]

This article is important because it reveals the mind and spirit of Stimson, whom many consider a typical American statesman. The former secretary of war clearly epitomized what George Kennan, the well-known diplomat and historian, characterized as the "moralistic-legalistic" mind in American foreign policy.

45. *New York Times*, December 19, 1946, p. 28; *Cong. Rec.*, 79 Cong., 1 Sess., 91:A 2923; Telford Taylor, "Nuremberg Trials, War Crimes and International Law," *International Conciliation no. 450* (April, 1949), p. 345 (hereafter cited as Taylor, "Nuremberg Trials"); Francis Biddle, "The Nurnberg Trial," *Virginia Law Review* 33 (November, 1947): 686 (hereafter cited as Biddle, "Nurnberg"); Robert H. Jackson, "The Significance of the Nuremberg Trials to the Armed Forces," *Military Affairs* 10 (Winter, 1946): 3–4.
46. Stimson, "Nuremberg Trial," p. 180.
47. Ibid., p. 184.

International law for Stimson was equated with "the moral judgment of the civilized world," and alternatives to the International Military Tribunal were rejected because "the whole moral position of the victorious Powers must collapse if their judgments could be enforced only by Nazi methods." Nuremberg, moreover, was for Stimson "the enforcement of a moral judgment. . . . we must bring our law in balance with the universal moral judgment of mankind." [48]

If the secretary hammered away at the equation of law and morality, he also stressed Nuremberg as a legal device to achieve peace. Its juridical outlawing of aggression established the principle "upon which we must henceforth rely for our legal protection against the horrors of war." [49]

According to his critics Stimson also displayed the typical American view of international relations in his apparent lack of comprehension of the complexities of modern political right and wrong, good and evil. The secretary always assumed that the Axis powers alone had any responsibility for the start of the war and its resultant evils. This simplistic view, while perhaps patriotic, led the secretary to adopt a double standard. Actions which were criminal for Axis leaders and followers were noble and virtuous, or at least necessary, when performed by the victorious powers. This alleged myopia was attacked by one of Stimson's biographers, Richard Current, when he suggested that "if, unfortunately, the Japanese had won the war, they might have tried Stimson himself as a war criminal according to his own concepts of international law." [50] Current based his opinion on his conclusion that Stimson continually urged a preventive war to stop Japanese expansion.[51]

The other cabinet position officially connected with the Nuremberg proceedings was that of the attorney general. Francis

48. Citations in order, ibid., pp. 180, 179, 185.
49. Ibid., p. 189.
50. Richard N. Current, *Secretary Stimson, A Study in Statecraft* (New Brunswick, N.J.: Rutgers University Press, 1954), p. 220.
51. Ibid., pp. 154, 163 and *passim*. Stimson's support of Nuremberg was continued by the War Department under his successor, Robert P. Patterson, and by the Navy Department under James Forestal. "Navy Department Participation in the Prosecution of War Crimes," *Journal of Criminal Law and Criminology* 36 (May–June, 1945): 39–40.

Beverly Biddle, who held the post during much of Franklin
Roosevelt's administration, resigned in order to become the
United States judge on the International Military Tribunal. His
appointment by President Truman was a logical one. Biddle was
a respected jurist who added dignity and competence to the
court. Moreover, he had pleaded the government's case against
the Nazi saboteurs who were put ashore on the eastern coast of
the United States, and consequently Biddle was conversant with
many of the legal questions certain to arise at Nuremberg such
as "superior orders" and "act of state." [52]

After the trials, the former attorney general wrote a number of
articles in defense of Nuremberg in which he revealed the same
attitudes and arguments as those found in Henry L. Stimson's
writings. Besides these essays Biddle furthered the trials' effects
by requesting President Truman to petition the United Nations
to adopt the Nuremberg principles and to establish a permanent
international criminal court. [53]

When Biddle went to Nuremberg, Tom Clark succeeded him
in the attorney general's office. At the Tribunal's commencement,
Clark, apprehensive lest the proceedings be drawn out and end
in a farce, publicly hoped that the Nuremberg court would "deal
out what we in Texas call 'Law west of the Pecos'—fast justice,
particularly fast." [54]

At the end of the trials, one of the longest and most involved
courtroom battles in history, Tom Clark had totally forgotten his
"let's-get-it-over-with" views. He gave the Attorney General's
Department ecstatic endorsement on the accomplishment in Germany. "Mankind has known great moments in the history of the
law," Clark explained in a speech for the Voice of America
broadcasts. "The Ten Commandments, Magna Carta and the
Constitution of the United States have been giant forward steps

52. Willard B. Cowles, "Trial of War Criminals by Military Tribunals,"
American Bar Association Journal 30 (June, 1944): 331 (hereafter cited
as Cowles, "Trial of War Criminals"). The judge and the prosecutor,
Biddle and Jackson, were exactly reversed in the Saboteurs and Nuremberg
trials.
53. Francis Biddle, "Prosecution of Major War Criminals, Report from
Francis Biddle to President Truman," *Department of State Bulletin* 15
(November 24, 1946): 956–57.
54. "West of the Pecos," *Time* 46 (November 25, 1945): 28.

on the slow and dreadful path to human justice. This age has just given us the judgment of Nuremberg. . . ." [55]

From our study of the executive branch, we begin to realize that the trials were a result of the attitudes and activities of many men in the administration. At the White House were the presidents who endorsed the necessary measures and also Judge Samuel Rosenman who supplied skilled diplomacy. At the State Department, Secretaries Stettinius, Grew, and Byrnes, as well as many minor officials, aided efforts for a tribunal. At the War Department were those master architects of the assize, Secretary Stimson, his assistant John McCloy and Judge Advocate General Murray C. Bernays. At the Department of Justice were Attorney General Biddle, later Nuremberg judge and staunch defender of the trials, his successor Tom Clark, and Biddle's assistant Herbert Wechsler, a strong force in planning, publicizing, and defending the Tribunal. [56] To this list certainly would have to be added many less prominent government officials who, by their loyal service and personal initiative, aided in the countless operations needed to create the complexity of the Nuremberg trials. These American leaders were searching for a solution to the problem of how to provide the proper punishment for alleged enemy criminals. Their answers stemmed essentially from a political pragmatism or a moralistic-legalistic attitude, both of which sought the program most advantageous for the United States in the confused and fast-moving postwar world of 1945. Over strenuous objections American decision makers concluded that the best policy for the nation would be the Nuremberg Trials. Their decision created the events in the Bavarian courthouse which would later fall under the judgment of their fellow Americans.

55. *New York Times,* October 21, 1946, p. 15; "The Nürnberg Novelty," *Fortune* 34 (December, 1946): 259.

56. Herbert Wechsler, "The Issues of the Nuremberg Trial," *Political Science Quarterly* 62 (March, 1947): 11–26 (hereafter cited as Wechsler, "Issues of Nuremberg").

3

Positivism, Pragmatism, Natural Law, and Nuremberg: The Judgment of International Lawyers

Of all the groups who commented on Nuremberg, the international lawyers most fully revealed the profundity and complexity of the Tribunal. These specialists posed the fundamental legal questions concerning Nuremberg and its ramifications. The trials were the special province of the international lawyer. No matter how frequently commentators evaluated the trials by the law code of the United States, Nuremberg was neither established nor conducted according to American or Anglo-Saxon legal standards. Nor was the Tribunal an informal expression of a popular demand for justice. The proceedings were an intricate application of international law principles to the adjudication of crimes against peace and humanity. Because of the technical nature of this assize, lawyers specializing in the law of the nations were most aware of the deeper implications of the proceedings and were most competent to evaluate the event. How did these experts judge Nuremberg?[1]

Professors of international law, because of their greater technical knowledge and concern with abstract theory, presented generally consistent and integrated positions. They often evaluated

1. In the twenty years after the major Nuremberg trials, at least thirty books by international lawyers have considered the Tribunal, the London Charter or the Nuremberg principles. Of these thirty writers, twenty-one were favorable to the court, six condemnatory, and three attempted an objective recital of the facts. In articles appearing in the semiofficial publication *The American Journal of International Law*, seventeen different authors evaluated the Tribunal. Twelve writers approved (some with qualifications), and three disapproved of the legal proceedings, while two refused to pass judgment.

Nuremberg according to the norms of a specific legal philosophy. Quincy Wright, professor of international law at the University of Chicago and an editor of the *American Journal of International Law*, incisively recognized this crucial insight when he wrote that "the favorable or unfavorable character of comments upon events related to international law often depends less upon the nature of the events than upon the theory of international law assumed by the commentator." [2] Investigation bears this out. What happened or did not happen at Nuremberg was only tangential to the different evaluations of the Tribunal; philosophical presuppositions were the real determinants.[3] Logically, then, we must analyze the international lawyers' judgment by an examination of their legal principles as well as of their final positions.

Numerous systems and theories in the areas of law, diplomacy, and metaphysics were in conflict about Nuremberg. In the field of international law conflicting ideas tended to polarize into two groups. We might loosely label these basic categories legal positivism and the pragmatic-natural-law coalition. Actually these terms are oversimplifications, for all the theories to be considered departed somewhat from the model of either system. Yet for purposes of identification we can deal with the variety of viewpoints within the framework of these two categories.

It is imperative to remember that we are not saying that the various legal philosophies in either camp were merely diverse enunciations of a common view. For example, a community of interests and principles did exist between the theory of realism and the theory of legal positivism, but they did not necessarily or perfectly coincide.[4] Similarly, as we will explain in detail later,

2. Quincy Wright, "Legal Positivism and the Nuremberg Judgment," *American Journal of International Law* 42 (April, 1948): 405 (hereafter cited as Wright, "Legal Positivism").

3. Ibid., see also Whitney Harris, Review of *Nuremberg Trials* by August von Knieriem. *American Journal of International Law* 54 (April, 1960): 444 (hereafter cited as Harris, Review of Knieriem). Maximilian St. George and Lawrence Dennis, *A Trial on Trial, The Great Sedition Trial of 1944* (New York: National Civil Rights Committee, 1946), p. 132 (hereafter cited as St. George and Dennis, *Trial on Trial*).

4. Percy E. Corbett, *Morals, Law and Power in International Relations* (Los Angeles: John Haynes and Dora Haynes Foundation, 1956), pp. 2–3 (hereafter cited as Corbett, *Morals, Law and Power*).

the frame of mind termed sociological jurisprudence or legal pragmatism in American domestic law was closely allied by some common goals and criteria to the natural law or Grotian philosophy in international law. On the other hand, these last two legal philosophies also diverged widely and radically on fundamental principles and methods.

Legal positivism, which enjoyed almost complete acceptance by both statesmen and scholars from the Treaty of Vienna, 1815, until the First World War, had been given its classical systematization by John Austin (1790–1859) in his *The Province of Jurisprudence Defined*. This jurist built his theory upon a definition of law as a regulation established by a political superior, noncompliance with which called for a definite punishment. Regulations not imposed by the political superior or which had no definite sanction, such as rules of honor, customs, and much international "law," were for this nineteenth-century jurist part of positive morality, but not positive law. Finally, unenforceable international legal codes were for Austin merely expressions of tender persuasions, pious hopes, and traditional mythologies.

Although there has been in modern times an evolution in the mainstream of legal positivism as well as the appearance of various subdivisions, the system today still retains many tenets of Austin's classical presentation.[5] All these variations and varieties within the legal-positivist philosophy concur on a hard core of basic assumptions concerning law, sovereignty, morality, power, and their interrelationships. "Positivism tends to assume that the sovereign state is the only subject of international law; that it is under no obligation except those which it has accepted by valid agreement or clear acquiescence in a general custom; that such obligations are to be narrowly construed under the assumption that consent to qualifications of sovereignty cannot be assumed; and that consequently concrete obligations cannot be implied even from formal consent to general principles."[6]

When we turn our consideration from the general principles of

---

5. Arthur A. Nussbaum, *A Concise History of the Law of Nations* (New York: Macmillan, 1954), p. 311 (hereafter cited as Nussbaum, *History of the Law of Nations*); Wright, "Legal Positivism," p. 504; Svarlien, *Introduction to the Law of Nations*, p. 420.
6. Wright, "Legal Positivism," p. 405.

positivism to its view on Nuremberg, we can formulate this system's first thesis in this way: the pragmatic and natural-law legal systems were wrong because they were merely mental constructs without relevance to the real order.

The typical Austinian proponent applied this thesis to the Nuremberg process first by attacking the frequently proposed legal basis for the trials, the Kellogg-Briand Pact.[7] The positivist contended that only one nation that signed this Treaty thought the document would eliminate belligerency from the world. All the other states still considered war to be an accepted instrument for resolving problems unamenable to diplomacy—a "dreadful necessity," but a necessity none the less. The proof that starry-eyed Americans were the only ones who thought the "international kiss"[8] was a pledge of undying love was that all of the European states entered the armament race soon after signing the pact.

Second, the Allies, who condemned German leaders at Nuremberg for violations of the peace pact and other international treaties, during the 1930's had repeatedly and officially recognized as not criminal the Nazi government's use of aggression as an instrument of national policy. The Rhineland and Austria were occupied "with a whimper and not with a bang." Then the nations went to Munich to acquiesce officially in another take-over and violate their solemn pacts and treaties pledging defense of the victim nation. "If the aggression against Czechoslovakia was an international criminal act, then all the participants in the Munich Agreement were equally guilty."[9]

The next test of the Kellogg-Briand Pact was Poland. Russia, proud occupant of a seat of judgment at Nuremberg, gave Germany a free hand to invade Poland by the Molotov-Ribbentrop Treaty and attacked from the East as the Wehrmacht rolled in from the West.[10] If Nuremberg and the pragmatic-natural-law

7. Corbett, *Morals, Law and Power*, p. 23.
8. This metaphor was applied to the Pact by Senator Reed of Missouri, *Cong. Rec.*, 70 Cong., 2 Sess. 70:1186.
9. George A. Finch, "The Nuremberg Trial and International Law," *American Journal of International Law* 41 (January, 1947): 27 (hereafter cited as Finch, "Nuremberg Trial and International Law").
10. Herman Finer, *America's Destiny* (New York: Macmillan, 1947), p. 257 (hereafter cited as Finer, *America's Destiny*).

coalition held the "rape of Poland" to be an international crime "then there follows an irrefutable implication that Soviet Russia and its officials were *participes criminis*." [11]

The legal positivist further pointed out that the United States itself miserably failed the natural-law advocates and their just-war doctrine at the invasion of Poland. The American government acknowledged the realities of power and sent official notification to Poland and Nazi Germany that it "is on terms of friendship and amity" not only with the inhabitants of both countries but also their governments.[12] The Austinian claimed that if Nuremberg's belated judgment were valid and the invasion of Poland was a "supreme crime" by a despicable outlaw, then Americans in September 1939 had at least compounded an international crime.

Another reason for the positivist's contention that Nuremberg's condemnation of aggression was unrealistic and unjust was that careful study of wartime warnings of punishment for Axis leaders highlighted a very curious fact. Not once during the war did an Allied chieftain raise the specific charge of aggression as a legal offense. The president, the marshal and the prime minister always limited their threats of sanctions to war crimes and atrocities. The United Nations' War-Crime Committee, moreover, never urged the criminality of aggressive war.[13]

But why, the Austinian continued, limit the argument to citing Allied condoning of what later they labelled Germany's crimes, when one could adduce numerous examples of Allied aggression and violations of treaties including the Kellogg-Briand Pact. In the real world, as opposed to the dream land of the pragmatic-natural-law coalition, what can one say in defense of the Russian occupation of Latvia, Estonia, Lithuania, Finland, Rumania, and Hungary? What answer did America have to the indictment that it grossly violated international law by bombing Rumania while technically at peace with that nation, by invading Vichy-France without legal right, and by insisting that the Soviet Union violate the Russo-Japanese nonaggression pact although Japan had given no provocation?

How could the American prosecution working on natural law

11. Finch, "Nuremberg Trial and International Law," p. 28.
12. Ibid.; Finer, *America's Destiny*, pp. 36, 37.
13. Finch, "Nuremberg Trial and International Law," p. 28.

principles demand death for conspiracy to wage aggressive war, the positivist asked, when Hitler frustrated Great Britain's invasion of Norway by anticipating their move by only a few weeks? What could the prosecution say about the American secretary of war's plans which advocated aggressive action against Japan if American interests were threatened in the Far East? The Austinian concluded that the pragmatist-natural-law doctrines of international law were applying an unrealistic double standard of law and morality and forcing facts to fit their theories.

If the positivist held that his opponent's systems did not reflect reality in regard to the Kellogg-Briand Pact, what did he say of Nuremberg? Both friend and foe agreed that the Tribunal was a concrete expression of the pragmatic and natural law philosophies. The Austinian consistently affirmed that the trials were a chimera, a natural-law myth which cloaked a reality far different from what the Tribunal purported to be.

Most critics ultimately decided that beneath the idealistic jargon Nuremberg was a show of crude, irresponsible force by the conquerors, "victors' vengeance." The only alternative which could explain the trials, according to the positivist, was that the London Charter expressed the legal code of a superstate, a world government.[14] The positivist maintained that the Grotian and legal progressives were applying a nonexistent world law, because such a new international criminal code was not valid or feasible. One foundation for this objection was that such a law demanded, as a necessary prerequisite, a political unity and a supranational authority. If such an accepted power with competence over all nations did not exist, then there was no arbitrator, no one with the right and duty to bring alleged outlaw states before the bar of world justice.[15]

14. "The latest evidence of the change from international to a superstate municipal law, is found in the proceedings of the Nuremberg trials. . . . Attention must be called to the fact that it was not an old or new international law which was applied, but a new municipal law, a criminal law which was not theretofore known"; Edwin Borchard, "International Law and International Organization," *American Journal of International Law* 41 (January, 1947): 107 (hereafter cited as Borchard, "International Law"). See also Philip Marshall Brown, "World Law," *American Journal of International Law* 40 (January, 1946): 159–60 (hereafter cited as Brown, "World Law").

15. Corbett, *Morals, Law and Power*, p. 24; Borchard, "International Law," p. 107.

The Austinian attempted to prove by many arguments the actual absence of the supranational authority essential for the justification of Nuremberg. First, the legislative body necessary to enact world law did not exist at the time of the trials. The United Nations Organization, a mere symbol of the reality the natural-law doctrine required for its legitimacy and feasibility, was hardly constituted when Nuremberg came to pass, and that organization had nothing to do with drawing up the London Charter which established the jurisdiction and law of the Tribunal.

Even if one were to grant all sorts of hypothetical powers to the United Nations, this organization gave Nuremberg only limited and qualified approbation.[16] The world society refused to define aggression, adopted only some of the trials' efforts to protect human rights, and did not demand compulsory jurisdiction in international criminal cases.[17]

Not only had the United Nations not endorsed all the principles of Nuremberg, it had enacted a law which many considered a censure of the Tribunal. The General Assembly on December 9, 1948 "had adopted the Declaration of Human Rights of which Article 11 (2) provides that: 'No one shall be held guilty of any penal offense on account of any act or omission which did not constitute a penal offense, under national or international law, at the time when it was committed.' "[18] Since a major indictment against the International Military Tribunal's code was that it was *ex post facto* law, a few legal positivists gave special significance to this United Nations' condemnation of such law.

Some positivists doubted if any world organization in the future would ever legalize trials such as Nuremberg. An international criminal court such as the Tribunal was not a minor invasion of sovereignty which nations might tolerate, but an institution which pierced to the very heart of national power and

16. Manuel R. Garcia-Mora, *International Responsibility for Hostile Act of Private Persons against Foreign States* (Hague: Martinus Nijhoff, 1962), pp. 38–40 (hereafter cited as Garcia-Mora, *International Responsibility*).
17. Louis Henkin, *Arms Control and Inspection in American Law* (New York: Columbia University Press, 1958), p. 123 (hereafter cited as Henkin, *Arms Control and Inspection*).
18. Julius Stone, *Aggression and World Order, A Critique of United Nations Theories on Aggression* (Berkeley: University of California Press, 1958), pp. 138–39 (hereafter cited as Stone, *Aggression*).

independence.[19] "[Nuremberg's] principles if generally accepted may reduce the unity of the state, increase the difficulties of maintaining domestic order, and deter statesmen from pursuing vigorous foreign policies when necessary in the national interests."[20]

The Austinian drew two conculsions from his first major thesis which asserted the lack of conformity between his opponent's principles and international reality. First, he held the correctness of his own theory's insistence that power was the final arbitor. The strong imposed their will on the weak if their self-interest counseled such a policy.[21] Indeed, the war-crime trials themselves proved the validity of this principle, for only when one had adequate military power could one force an aggressor nation to trial and judgment. Conversely, no state victorious in war would ever allow its leaders to be arraigned as war criminals.[22]

The positivist's other conclusion was that the trials were essentially a political not a legal action. This point will be developed at length when we now consider the second major positivist thesis, that the opposing system produced multiple errors concerning the particular subjects of aggression and individual accountability.

Aggressive war, for the Austinian, was too complex to submit to legal action. The final burst of belligerency only culminated the interaction of a multitude of social, economic, and political forces which often defied analysis or which were understood only after detailed investigation.[23] Critics called attention to the

19. Henkin, *Arms Control and Inspection*, p. 123. Note the United States' decision in the Connelly Resolution. *Cong. Rec.*, 79 Cong., 2 Sess., 92:10694–95.

20. Quincy Wright, "The Law of the Nuremberg Trial," *American Journal of International Law* 41 (January, 1947): 45 (hereafter cited as Wright, "Law of Nuremberg").

21. Edwin D. Dickinson, *Law and Peace* (Philadelphia: University of Pennsylvania Press, 1955), p. 121 (hereafter cited as Dickinson, *Law and Peace*).

22. Hans Kelsen, *Peace Through Law* (Chapel Hill: University of North Carolina Press, 1944), p. 114 (hereafter cited as Kelsen, *Peace Through Law*); Percy E. Corbett, *Law and Society in the Relations of States* (New York: Harcourt, Brace, 1951), p. 236 (hereafter cited as Corbett, *Law and Society*).

23. Charles G. Fenwick, *International Law*, 3rd ed. (New York: Appleton-Century-Crofts, 1948), p. 672 (hereafter cited as Fenwick, *International Law*).

perhaps astonishing fact that the International Military Tribunal and later the United Nations were unable to define exactly what constituted the international crime of aggression or the exact criminal mentality required for its commission.[24] According to the positivist this problem of definition arose from the fact that military coercion was essentially a political and not a legal act. War was the method which states adopted when they were convinced that self-interest compelled them to achieve a goal unobtainable through diplomacy.[25] The Austinian concluded that to allow other states to question the nation's protestation that it fought a just war and had not committed an aggressive act would open a pandora's box of ruthless vengeance, for the question would never be settled on objective grounds but solely on the judging nation's self-interest and demands on its national policy.[26]

Because the positivist maintained that belligerent actions were political, he logically concluded that any adequate deterrents to war must also be primarily political and not legal. This was true for the Austinian, not only because of the nature of aggressive war itself but also because of the simple fact that legal deterrents did not work. The effectiveness of judicial punishment to deter crime even in the highly organized system of municipal law was questionable, but the weakness of legal sanctions to inhibit crime was particularly true in the case of national leaders. Retribution was a remote possibility; the vast majority of countrymen approved the successful chieftain's conduct.[27] The Nazis certainly would not have been checked by the precedent of legal sanctions if such a trial as Nuremberg had occurred before their advent to power. German leaders knew that failure most likely would mean death, but they accepted this possibility.[28]

24. Stone, *Aggression*, pp. 135, 136, 141.
25. F. B. Schick, "The Nuremberg Trial and the International Law of the Future," *American Journal of International Law* 41 (October, 1947): 774, 776 (hereafter cited as Schick, "International Law of the Future").
26. Corbett, *Law and Society*, p. 58; St. George and Dennis, *Trial on Trial*, p. 110; Wright, "Legal Positivism," p. 413; Fenwick, *International Law*, p. 673; Corbett, *Law and Society*, p. 58.
27. Schick, "International Law of the Future," p. 771.
28. Percy E. Corbett, *The Study of International Law* (Garden City, N.Y.: Doubleday, 1955), p. 34–36 (hereafter cited as Corbett, *Study of International Law*).

In the past, the positivist pointed out, the leaders of the world realized the political nature of aggressive war and insisted that deterrents also had to be political. In their wisdom these statesmen sought peace and order through the effective means of balance of power, collective security, economic sanctions, coalitions, and alliances. Another example of their prudent practicality was that these leaders realized that only by holding international law to a bare minimum of firmly established and universally accepted rules could this code be maintained and enforced.

The diplomats' past reluctance to codify law resulted in Nuremberg's applying retroactive law. A few authors writing on international law emphasized the *ex post facto* charge, but most legal positivists conceded that this principle was not binding in the code of the nations as it was in domestic law, or they granted that it constituted a principle of justice and not a restriction upon legal action.[29] Holding this view Nuremberg opponents among international lawyers differed from critics, writing in newspapers, magazines, and American law reviews, who most frequently objected that the Tribunal had applied *ex post facto* law.

If the legal positivist rejected strict legal difficulties arising from the prohibition of retroactive law, he stressed that the Tribunal, by its unprecedented expansion of the international legal code, was totally out of step with the common sense that had formerly prevailed among nations. To the mind of the Austinian the Tribunal's impatience with the traditions of the past, with the organic development of the law, and with technical legal safeguards resulted in the court's openly flouting the accepted tradition which held war to be a legally neutral act.[30] The result of Nuremberg's reversal of standard doctrine would be an upheaval in the relations between states and widespread

29. St. George and Dennis, *Trial on Trial*, pp. 110–11. Hans Kelsen, a positivist, denied the validity of this principle of *ex post facto* in international law and granted that the war crimes trials were one occasion when morality could be equated with a legal foundation; *Peace Through Law*, pp. 87–88.

30. Quincy Wright, "The Munich Settlement and International Law," *American Journal of International Law* 33 (January, 1939): 28–29; Corbett, *Law and Society*, p. 236.

confusion about and opposition to international law. We have already cited the neutral nature of war that the Austinian proved by facts: the many Allied acts similar to the crimes of Germany; the statements of the conquerors, before their entrance into the war, denying the criminal nature of the enemy's acts; and the fact that during the hostilities no Allied leader affirmed the criminality of aggressive war. Nuremberg, the positivist claimed, was a little late to change the rules of the game.

If the Tribunal's sentences cast past actions of nations under a cloud of uncertainty, the positivist argued that its role for the future would certainly not be one of pure enlightenment. The blanket condemnation of aggression as criminal caused many practical difficulties. Any action of the Security Council of the United Nations aimed at warding off war might easily fall under the vague criterion of unjust belligerency as determined by the Nuremberg court.[31] Some positivists were also "concerned lest the free decision of their government to make a 'preventive war' be impaired." [32] Thus Nuremburg, designed as an instrument for peace, would frustrate sound practical political means for maintaining order and security in the world.

Nor were these the only evils incorporated into Nuremberg's declaration against aggression. The critics asserted that the vague manner in which the London Charter designated this crime meant that a whole nation or a large segment of a nation could be indicted as guilty of this crime and punished accordingly. Faced with this legal threat a nation now would be forced to fight to the bitter end rather than face extinction by the conqueror's vengeance in some legal drama.[33]

If the positivist held that Nuremberg was an evil omen for the losers, he also believed that it was a destructive delusion for the victors. Outlawing aggression created a false sense of security, for men somehow thought that the new law would end all unjust conflicts. The truth was just the opposite. Any future application of the Nuremberg principles against unjust war would demand as a prerequisite that a conflict had taken place. The world needed political and military preventives that would stop war,

31. Stone, *Aggression*, pp. 137–38.
32. Wright, "Law of Nuremberg," p. 47.
33. Schick, "International Law of the Future," p. 787.

not legal shows to mop up the mess remaining after the evil had been done.[34]

For the positivist another evil derived from Nuremberg's condemnation of aggression was that the moralism contained in the Tribunal's verdicts would be viewed in days to come as self-righteous hypocrisy and an attempt to shift a common guilt to a convenient German scapegoat. As sure as the *Diktat* of Versailles echoed in the streets and stadium of Munich, so the name Nuremberg would reverberate down the corridors of future European history as a cry for vengeance.[35] For all these reasons, positivists saw Nuremberg's pronouncements on aggression as the "supreme crime" as a dangerous precedent that would come back to haunt its creators.

Another major aspect of the Tribunal that raised the wrath of many Austinians was the novel principle which held heads of state individually accountable for their deeds in international law. Just as all nations had assumed war to be an "indifferent" act, all had supposed that the principle of personal responsibility was foreign to the code of the nations.[36] National leaders would have to submit perhaps to a day of reckoning for their policies, but this settling of accounts was to be done in an extralegal manner with their own states.

On the theoretical level the principle of individual responsibility clashed with the positivist's tenet, accepted by all nations before Nuremberg, that the state and only the state was the object and subject of international law. Even the Paris Peace Pact established no penalties whatsoever for individuals and considered only nations as the contracting parties to its declaration against war. Any attempt in 1929 to write in the novelty of personal responsibility would certainly have meant that the pact would not have been ratified by the nations of the world.[37]

34. George A. Finch, "The Progressive Development of International Law," *American Journal of International Law* 41 (July, 1947): 614; Finch, "Nuremberg Trial and International Law," p. 35.

35. Corbett, *Law and Society*, p. 236; Finch, "Nuremberg Trial and International Law," p. 24.

36. Corbett, *Law and Society*, p. 231; Quincy Wright, "War Criminals," *American Journal of International Law* 49 (April, 1945): 280–82 (hereafter cited as Wright, "War Criminals").

37. Hans Kelsen, *Principles of International Law* (New York: Rinehart, 1959), p. 138; Corbett, *Law and Society*, pp. 231–32.

Indeed it was problematical if even the signers of the London Charter, in their very act of creating individual responsibility, thought that this principle was of universal validity rather than an *ad hoc* way of "getting" the Nazi leaders. If a sudden reversal of fortune had put them in the hands of the Germans, did they really think that they should personally have to answer for signing the charter? Most likely the framers of this theory thought of it as a one-way street that would lead the Nazis to the gallows, but it could not bring retribution to them.[38]

Against this principle of individual responsibility, the positivists avowed that the defenses of "act of state" and "order of superior" must be recognized as creating legal immunity. The first plea, "act of state" had always been acknowledged in the past, and any other course would be invalid and unjust because it subjected the leader of an independent state to the jurisdiction of another.

Lawyers who condemned the Tribunal thought the rejection of the second plea for immunity, "superior orders," would cause havoc in the relation of the soldier or the government official to his country. "Anarchy might result if the individual placed his duty to the world community ahead of obedience to his government and set himself up as the judge of his obligations superior to the judgment of his government." [39] The only exceptions which the Austinian allowed to this rule were acts obviously illegal. Some Nazis had indeed committed atrocities, but these crimes could be punished under the existing rules of warfare and needed no novel enactments. Because of a few infamous cases the Nuremberg Court should not have created new and unsound laws which would beget more evils than they were supposed to solve.

This then was the positivist stand as propounded by international lawyers. It is a strong position buttressed by legal logic, traditional practice, and practical considerations. If it is not the system that would spontaneously appeal to the man on the street, it is the creed of the diplomat and many a legal scholar.

38. Wilbourn E. Benton and Georg Grimm, *Nuremberg: German Views of War Trials* (Dallas: Southern Methodist University Press, 1955), pp. 22–23.

39. Wright, "War Criminals," p. 263; Kelsen, *Peace Through Law*, p. 104.

What possible answer could the natural-law proponents and the pragmatists have to all of the legal positivist's arguments and accusations? From the general principles of these two antipositivist theories developed an inner logic which led to their conclusions on the Tribunal.

The pragmatic or sociological school of jurisprudence is more a method than a philosophy, more a way of looking at the law than theorizing about it. For the pragmatist law is an instrument which adapts principles and tenets to human conditions; therefore the test of any legislation's validity is how well it improves man's lot or organizes society so that the system better fulfills the needs of men.[40] The human factor is given primacy by these legal scholars, and logic, reasoning, and consistency are relegated to the position of instruments for social engineering rather than ends in themselves. People, not any theoretical system, are the important thing. "Sociological jurisprudence was, however, more than a method. It had substance and an affirmative program. It held that the truth of law, like truth in general, was something to be found through experience, that it was relative, and that it could be created. It asserted that good law was what worked best for society, that law was functional and to be understood in terms of ends rather than origins, and that the actual workings of the law were more important than its abstract legal content."[41]

From this brief summary the basic differences which separate legal pragmatism from the natural-law philosophy become patent. The former epistemologically is derived from a relativism and empiricism that stands diametrically opposed to the absolutism in thought and being of the natural-law system. The pragmatic philosophy rejects a law of natures and affirms that law is not absolute but mutable, not static but dynamic, not rigid but progressive. A legal code, for the pragmatist, is not discovered through the analysis of metaphysical essences; it is created by human reason learning from experience. Only in the crucible of

40. Roscoe Pound, *Interpretations of Legal History* (New York: Macmillan, 1923), pp. 163–64.
41. Henry Steele Commager, *The American Mind: An Interpretation of American Thought and Character Since the 1880's* (New Haven: Yale University Press, 1950), p. 379.

trial and error can the legal rules for human progress be forged.[42]

Radical as these differences between legal pragmatism and the natural-law philosophy are, a certain common mind existed on international law and Nuremberg because of a concurrence on some objectives and norms. Both theories ascribe a certain primacy to reason whether as an instrument for solving problems or as a faculty for discovering basic principles.

At times both theories have played major and effective roles in defending the individual person against the state and vested interests. Both stand strong against absolute power and insensitive exercise of authority, even if they aim at this goal in different ways. The Grotian seeks this limitation of force by the concept of absolute natures with inviolable rights; the pragmatist, by placing man in the center of a relativistic, individualistic universe and making his experience the criterion of truth and goodness.

Both systems hold a "higher law" doctrine which breaks through the technicalities and statutory limitations imposed by the legal positivists. These theories place something above the law book, something above the written pact and treaty. For the natural-law philosopher this higher consideration is the nature of a human being; for the pragmatist it is the value of the person. Both standards are an anathema to classical positivists who declare the sovereign state and its sanctionable enactments to be of supreme value in international affairs.

Both theories, moreover, assert that international law can not

42. Certainly one cause of conflict between the two systems is the degenerate form of natural law philosophy which the pragmatists encountered in the period 1870–1900. "They [pragmatists] were repelled also from what they thought was natural law by two brands of pseudo-natural law. First, that represented by the excessively theoretical and abstract creations of the French revolutionary mind with its succession of paper constitutions echoed by the closet-spun codes of Bentham. Second, the Spencerian identification of natural law with the brute struggle for existence and individualistic, atomistic laissez-faire. Indeed it was the humanitarian revulsion at abuses of the capitalistic system run riot and proletariat protest that brought into being the progressive movement of the first part of this century. Pragmatism was a powerful weapon against the *status quo* and it is not without significance that so many leaders of the movement were pragmatists"; Ben W. Palmer, "The Natural Law and Pragmatism," *Notre Dame Lawyer* 13 (March, 1948): 339.

exist if there is an unlimited right to make war. The reason for this conclusion again divides these schools. The Grotian affirms this fact because he evaluates war by the medieval concept that the motive of any resort to arms is to promote justice; the pragmatist reaches this conclusion from his determining the justice of a war by evaluating its tendency to preserve international peace and security.[43]

Even if the pragmatist from his twentieth-century American experience had deep misgivings concerning the natural-law doctrine, he still realized that the real enemy in the international field was legal positivism. It was in the latter theory that he found the real absolutism and rigidity, the insensitive defense of the traditional order, and the arbitrary dictates of crass power which are utterly abhorrent to his system.

Because of the likenesses and differences between the pragmatic and natural-law philosophies, we will study their views on Nuremberg by noting common positions and distinguishing principles.

The pragmatist's first thesis relevant to Nuremberg, which the natural-law philosopher fully endorsed, was that their common adversary's theory was outmoded, unrealistic, and dangerous. As we have seen, these accusations were identical with those which the Austinian hurled against supporters of the Tribunal. The pro-Nuremberg forces declared that the positivist's concept of the sovereign Hegelian-Hobbesian state, which was an abstract artificial political entity, perhaps aided understanding of the world situation in an earlier age but was bankrupt in regard to the contemporary scene. Historical events were voiding the theory of any conformity to realities. The modern totalitarian state differed essentially from the national state of the nineteenth century, and the growing interdependence of nations made effective supranational controls ever more imperative.[44] Nuremberg stood as symbol and signpost of this change by announcing that states were accountable to the world community and that

43. Josef Kunz, "Bellum Justum et Bellum Legale," *American Journal of International Law* 45 (July, 1951): 528.
44. Wright, "Law of Nuremberg," p. 72; Dickinson, *Law and Peace*, p. 75; Wright, "War Criminals," p. 264.

international tribunals had jurisdiction over individuals who were now personally responsible for their violations of international law.[45]

The pragmatist and the natural-law advocate both maintained that the positivist was talking to past ages not only because of the changing forms of political power but also because of changes in modern warfare. A theory which held war to be a legitimate or "indifferent" policy might be tolerable in an era of limited conflicts, but mankind had blundered into an age of total war. In this type of holocaust, the positivist's position seemed to be the product of a neanderthal mind. "For if it is not a crime, punishable at the bar of international justice, to engage in aggression by force in today's thermonuclear age, or to commit genocide or other crimes of enormous magnitude against humanity itself—mankind is, indeed, on the verge of extinction." [46] Because of the escalation in destructive power, the state's almost automatic declaration that it was fighting in self-defense must be open to judgment by an authority superior to the state itself.[47]

If both pragmatist and natural-law philosopher agreed on the first negative thesis—that the Austinian doctrine was antiquated —the first positive thesis of these philosophies also can be stated in terms common to both. The primary goal of law must be to protect man and assure him of his rights.

We can see that Nuremberg enacted concrete applications of the pragmatist's desire that law serve mankind.

First, the court maintained that aggression must be outlawed because man could not survive if such international conduct was allowed in the future. Second, experience showed that sanctions falling upon the artificial moral entity of a Hegelian state proved an ineffective instrument for preventing war, so retribution must fall upon guilty individuals.[48] Third, the Tribunal's judgment

45. Percy Elwood Corbett, *The Individual and World Society* (Princeton: Princeton University Press, 1953), pp. 9–10 (hereafter cited as Corbett, *Individual and World Society*). Greenspan, *Modern Law of Land Warfare*, p. 448; Wright, "Law of Nuremberg," pp. 71–72.

46. Harris, Review of Knieriem, p. 444.

47. S. McDougal Myres and Associates, *Studies in World Public Order* (New Haven: Yale University Press, 1960), pp. 189–90.

48. Herbert W. Briggs, *The Law of Nations* (New York: Appleton-Century-Crofts, 1952), p. 97 (hereafter cited as Briggs, *Law of Nations*). Even

upon Julius Streicher also vividly illustrated the pragmatist's desire to defend human rights under modern conditions. Streicher was put "to death for crimes against humanity, although he took no administrative or military part in such crimes." [49] In the modern world of mass communications the demagogue who swayed a nation to hatred and blood-lust was at least as dangerous as the man who finally committed the racial atrocity. The international lawyer demanded cognizance of the new realities bred by the modern totalitarian state with its frighteningly efficient organization, its ability to mold public opinion, and its terrifying new police powers.

An implicit assumption of the legal pragmatist on these questions was that, by its very nature, law was dynamic. The International Military Tribunal in its final judgment gave a classic expression of this progressive quality of law. "In interpreting the words of the [Kellogg-Briand] Pact, it must be remembered that international law is not the product of an international legislature, and that such international agreements as the Pact of Paris have to deal with general principles of law, and not with administrative matters of procedure. The law of war is to be found not only in treaties, but in the customs and practices of states which gradually obtained universal recognition, and from the general principles of justice applied by jurists and practised by military courts. This law is not static, but by continual adaptation follows the needs of a changing world." [50]

As this declaration of the Nuremberg court indicated, the dynamic theory presupposed that law is derived from a number of sources and is not limited, as the classical positivist asserted,

---

Professor Corbett agreed with this pragmatic argument, although he saw it primarily under the guise of the positivist concepts of power and law as the sanctionable. "Apart from monetary penalties or acts of formal apology and restitution—rarely adequate to the occasion—what retribution could be visited upon this abstract entity?" Corbett, *Study of International Law*, pp. 34–35. Quincy Wright, "International Law and Guilt by Association," *American Journal of International Law* 42 (October, 1949): 752–53 (hereafter cited as Wright, "Guilt").

49. Quincy Wright, "The Crime of 'War Mongering,'" *American Journal of International Law* 42 (January, 1948): 133 (hereafter cited as Wright, "War Mongering").

50. International Military Tribunal (Nuremberg), "Judgment and Sentences," *American Journal of International Law* 41 (January, 1947): 219.

to statutory enactments.[51] Three sources were most significant for the international lawyer who stressed pragmatic principles: analogy with common law, customary law, and the consensus of mankind.[52] The first of these, the comparison with the gradual evolution of English common law from court opinions and judges, decisions, will be seen again when we consider the views of American "domestic" lawyers who tended to be imbued with the same pragmatic principles that guided the progressives in international law.

Although a number of legal pragmatists asserted that customary law was the basis of expansion of the legal code, this opinion did not have the popularity among them that it enjoyed among popular writers and American lawyers. Perhaps scholars in international law realized the difficulties involved in establishing a valid custom from the vague and often unratified pacts, treaties, and resolutions entered into between the World Wars, but a more important reason for this lack of emphasis arose from the fact that these writers often blended customary law with the third major source of law, the consensus of mankind.[53]

The pragmatist's argument stemming from consensus was that the almost universal demand on the part of peoples and nations, for the principles finally enacted at Nuremberg, reflected human reason's search for practical and efficient solutions to answer the problems that confronted it. This new desire for effective legal safeguards for personal rights and for the judicial condemnation of aggression and aggressors might be called an instinctive longing, a sense of justice, or the demands of a "conscience of humanity," but it was a key element in an evolutionary, dynamic

51. Wright, "Law of Nuremberg," p. 58. See also Dickinson, *Law and Peace*, p. 67; Philip C. Jessup, *Transnational Law* (New Haven: Yale University Press, 1956), p. 106; Carl J. Friedrick, *The Philosophy of Law in Historical Perspective* (Chicago: University of Chicago Press, 1958), pp. 207–8.

52. Wright, "Law of Nuremberg," p. 59; Svarlein, *Introduction to the Law of Nations*, pp. 399–400, 402–5; Joseph B. Keenan and Brendan F. Brown, *Crimes Against International Law* (Washington: Public Affairs Press, 1950), pp. 43, 70 (hereafter cited as Keenan and Brown, *Crimes Against International Law*).

53. Quincy Wright, "Due Process and International Law," *American Journal of International Law* 40 (April, 1946): 402; Greenspan, *Modern Law of Land Warfare*, p. 428.

adaptation of the instrument of law for the betterment of human society.[54]

A corollary to this tenet concerning the progressive nature of international law was the pragmatist's demand that obsolete obstacles to development be eliminated. Regarding Nuremberg he considered these primarily the defenses of "act of state" and "superior orders" which for the pragmatist were legal anachronisms that protected vested interests against the demands of reason and the orderly development of human society.[55]

In accord with this principle, the progressive viewed Nuremberg as an emphatic affirmation of his theory that law was not for the past but for the future. Consequently, the assertion that Nuremberg's law was retroactive aroused little terror in him because he asserted that it was much more imperative to establish accepted principles of international law for future guidance than to apply an antiquated dictum such as *ex post facto*.[56] His proof that Nuremberg did point out the direction in which international law would develop was that subsequent war-crime trials and enactments of national and international assemblies followed and confirmed the court's principles.[57]

When the progressives marshalled on the legal battlefield of Nuremberg looked to their flanks, they certainly must have marveled at their strange compatriots in the coalition to defend the trials. In domestic-law conflicts the pragmatist's great adversary had always been the natural-law school, yet now as the warriors of social jurisprudence stood in the dawn of what they hoped

54. Joseph Walter Bingham, "Current Notes: The Continental Shelf and the Marginal Belt," *American Journal of International Law* 40 (January, 1946): 178; see also page 174.

55. Corbett, *Individual and World Society*, pp. 9–10; William W. Bishop, Jr., *International Law, Cases and Materials* (Boston: Little, Brown, 1962), p. 644.

56. Wright, "War Criminals," p. 285; William W. Bishop, Jr., "Robert H. Jackson—Obituary," *American Journal of International Law* 39 (January, 1955): 47; Briggs, *Law of Nations*, p. 1020.

57. H. B. Jacobini, *International Law* (Homewood, Ill.: Dorsey Press, 1962), p. 228; H. B. Jacobini, *Study of the Philosophy of International Law as Seen in the Works of Latin American Writers* (Hague: Martinus Nijhoff, 1954), p. 36; Greenspan, *Modern Law of Land Warfare*, p. 444; Norman D. Palmer and Howard C. Perkins, *International Relations, The World Community in Transition* (Boston: Houghton-Mifflin, 1953), p. 317 (hereafter cited as Palmer and Perkins, *International Relations*).

would be a new day in international law, they welcomed their old foes as allies.

The natural-law philosophy's application to international relations as enunciated by Hugo Grotius in his classic *De Jure Belli Ac Pacis* can be reduced to four major principles. "First, Grotius would hold states to the same rules which regulate the lives of individuals and make the violation of them a crime subject to punishment. Second, . . . he formulated the 'law of peace' which became the foundation of his whole system. Third, he argued that states may properly punish other states which violate the law. Fourth, he accepted natural law—or right reason—as the primary basis for determining rules for the right conduct of states." [58]

Grotius defined natural law as "the dictate of right reason which points out that a given act, because of its opposition to or conformity with man's rational nature, is either morally wrong or morally necessary, and accordingly forbidden or commanded by God, the author of nature." [59]

An examination of Nuremberg on these four basic principles will reveal how the war-crime trials are based upon Grotius' natural-law philosophy and will exemplify its tenets. That our analysis is not forcing facts to fit a theory is supported by the assertions of international lawyers who, whether they approved of the Tribunal or not, agreed that the Nuremberg court was based on a natural-law philosophy.[60] Moreover, the language of the judges and the prosecution, the concepts and principles of

58. Cornelius von Vollenhoven, "Hugo Grotius," *Encyclopedia of Social Sciences*, 15 vols. (New York: Macmillan, 1937), 7:177, as paraphrased in Palmer and Perkins, *International Relations*, p. 311.

59. Hugo Grotius, *De Jure Belli Ac Pacis Libri Tres, The Classics of International Law*, trans. Francis W. Kelsey, ed. James Brown Scott. 2 vols. (Oxford: Clarendon Press, 1925), 2:38.

60. As the publisher summarized in his foreword to Keenan and Brown, *Crimes Against International Law:* "It is the authors' contention that the Tokyo and Nuernberg war crimes trials were a manifestation of an intellectual and moral revolution which will have a profound and far reaching influence upon the future of world society. . . . They maintain that the international moral order must be regarded as the cause, not the effect, of positive law; that such law does not derive its essence from physical power, and that any attempt to isolate such law from morals is a symptom of juridical schizophrenia caused by the separation of the brain of the lawyer from that of the human being," p. v–vi. See also Corbett, *Study of International Law*, p. 16; Nussbaum, *History of the Law of Nations*, p. 114; Harris, Review of Knieriem, pp. 443–44.

the court, all revealed the pervasiveness of this legal system at the trials.[61]

Nuremberg's application of Grotius' first fundamental principle, which bound nations by the same regulation as individuals and which made violations of these rules punishable crimes, had a number of ramifications. First, many statutory and customary foundations were suggested for the Tribunal's law, but apparently the judges and prosecution assumed that moral laws condemned the wrong actions of the accused even when human lawmaking had been deficient. This principle also meant that law ruled individuals, not artificial political entities. Even in momentous decisions involving the very existence of the nation, such as the initiation of war, natural-law philosophy judged the event on the moral quality of the personal motives of the sovereign or ruler.[62]

Nuremberg's application of this principle of individual responsibility was not only consonant with Grotian ideas, it was perhaps an ideal for which the doctrine's early champions could have only timidly hoped. In the past the only way to enforce the ethical judgment that an individual had violated the natural law was by the sanctions of war or rebellion. After World War II the Tribunal had finally established legal punishment for violators of law; in this way the court hoped to answer a basic theoretical objection of the positivists who held that the natural law was not real "law" for it had no juridical sanction and had to appeal to war as a final arbitrator.

A corollary of Nuremberg's application of individual responsibility in international law was that it foreshadowed world federation.[63] "Regularly enforced world criminal law applicable to

61. On the other hand, we should note that the prosecution did not adopt these principles in a doctrinaire manner, but in a typically American practical adaptation of assumptions to the situation. "I have no training in jurisprudence, and therefore hardly feel that I am qualified to comment on your inference that I assume 'the legal principles of the Grotian or naturalist legal philosophy of international law.' My conceptions about the war crime trials were formulated *ad hoc* as I went along. . . ." Letter of Telford Taylor to the author, May 14, 1965.

62. Corbett, *Law and Society*, p. 58; Wright, "War Criminals," pp. 263–64; Wright, "Law of Nuremberg," pp. 55–56; Garcia-Mora, *International Responsibility*, p. 38.

63. Quincy Wright, *Problems of Stability and Progress in International Relations* (Berkeley: University of California Press, 1954), pp. 78, 261; Wright, "Legal Positivism," p. 409.

individuals necessarily makes inroads upon national sovereignty
and tends to change the foundations of the international community from a balance of power among sovereign states to a universal federation directly controlling individuals in all countries on
matters covered by international law." [64] Adherents to natural
law welcomed Nuremberg's assumption of international jurisdiction over any individual who had committed crimes anywhere
against the law of the nations.

Intimately connected with the principle of individual responsibility was the principle of criminality of aggression. Authorities
agreed that unless national leaders acted beyond their competence, as determined by international law, they were immune
from punishment. That the German warlords had broken
through the limits of their legitimate sphere of activity was
decided on the basis of Grotius' second principle, the theory of
"just" and "unjust" war, i.e., that belligerent action was justified
only when its cause was in conformity with right reason, the
natural law. Nuremberg (with an assist from the modern American idea that aggressive war was always wrong) declared that
Nazi aggression was morally evil and consequently criminal. [65]

This natural-law verdict on aggressive war agreed with the
pragmatist's judgment that unjust war was an evil which was no
longer tolerable. The Grotian, however, did not condemn aggression because man's experience proved that it was a socially
undesirable act but because such hostilities violated ultimate,
eternal, and objective norms. Therefore they were acts intrinsi-
cally evil, *malum in se*.[66] Aggressive wars were declared "unnatu-
ral acts" devoid of right order or finality.

Nuremberg obviously applied Grotius' third principle, that
other nations can punish violators of the natural laws regulating
international behavior. The third principle was particularly an
anathema to the positivists because jurisdiction over the leaders
of a sovereign nation by other countries violated their cherished
principle of state sovereignty.[67] The two principles of universal

64. Wright, "Law of Nuremberg," p. 47. See also Wright, "Legal Positivism," p. 409.
65. Corbett, *Law and Society*, p. 58; Wright, "Legal Positivism," p. 409;
Dexter Perkins, *The American Approach to Foreign Policy*, rev. ed. (Cambridge: Harvard University Press, 1962), pp. 94–95.
66. Wright, "Law of Nuremberg," p. 63.
67. Dickinson, *Law and Peace*, p. 81.

jurisdiction and the criminality of aggression meant that a su-pranational power had been created which could interfere in domestic affairs, stand in judgment on all state acts, and even demand that the plea of self-defense be questioned.[68] The advo-cate of natural law conceded that this was exactly the signifi-cance of these tenets, because he held that even the most unscru-pulous nations cried "self-defense" to cloak aggrandizement.

Writers suggested that Nuremberg's implementation of the second and third principle stood witness to a new mentality in world relations, a reversal in the popularity of the two basic international legal philosophies. For these writers the trials held after World War II were the high point for the just war concept since the Middle Ages.[69] "Indeed, in our esteem for international conduct based on moral principles and in our growing convic-tion that peace-loving states must accept the obligation to punish lawless states, we are closer to the spirit and mind of Grotius than were the men of the nineteenth century with their glorifica-tion of sovereignty." [70]

Finally, we note that the achievement of objectivity was a fundamental aspiration of the natural-law proponent. He real-ized that if judgment lacked this quality then the positivist was right, and punishment would be merely an act of revenge. What the natural-law doctrine needed was not only the principle of universality of jurisdiction, as enunciated in Grotius' third dic-tum, but also a norm for sanctions which could be applied without bias or prejudice. This lacuna was filled by the fourth principle.

Grotius' final tenet stated that natural law was right reason which determined rules for the proper conduct of states. Because of the universal and absolute nature of this norm, the proponent of natural law claimed that international criminal law could be impartially administered. The act of the accused nation was measured by the eternally objective principles of the law of nature, and the verdict finally arrived at expressed absolute justice. The objective validity of the verdict was the ultimate

68. Robert W. Tucker, *The Just War, A Study in Contemporary American Doctrine* (Baltimore: Johns Hopkins Press, 1960), pp. 131–32.

69. Nussbaum, *History of the Law of Nations*, p. 277; Svarlien, *Law of Nations*, p. 340; Keenan and Brown, *Crimes Against International Law*, pp. 70–73.

70. Palmer and Perkins, *International Relations*, p. 311.

refutation of the positivist's charge that Nuremberg was "victors' vengeance." [71]

Although the Grotians held that law once discovered was objective, eternal, and unequivocal, they also maintained that there were many sources from which man learned exactly what the natural law was. They agreed with the pragmatist in his acceptance of numerous fonts of law and also in his enumeration of the same three specific sources: analogy with common law, customary rules, and the consent of mankind. Often these sources and laws are united, blended, fused by the naturalistic writer to create a "general code which God, nature, reason, human usage, and consensus imposed upon the rulers of men as a limitation on their use of the authority and material power entrusted to them." [72] As lawyers explained: "In substance, the international criminal law incorporated in the Nuernberg Charter was not statutory. It was customary law and law based on the recognition of international morality by treaties, by a long and distinguished line of juridical experts, by the School of Natural Law Jurisprudence, and by a great part of world public opinion." [73]

The primary use of these three sources—analogy, custom, and consensus—by the natural-law advocate was not to hold that these equaled statutory law but that they were concrete manifestations of attempts by human reason to imbue temporal law with eternal justice. Nuremberg was reason's verdict upon Nazi evil.

This schematic, simplified treatment of the positions of international lawyers demands some notes of caution and qualification. Few legal writers consistently followed a strictly doctrinaire approach; few presented a systematic philosophical exposition. Indeed the opposing systems even engaged in an eclectic borrowing from each other. For example, a number of lawyers who favored Nuremberg attempted to justify the proceedings by appealing to the realistic and positivistic doctrine of power. They argued that what one victorious nation had the

71. Wright, "War Criminals," pp. 282–83.
72. Corbett, Morals, Law and Power, pp. 19–20.
73. Keenan and Brown, Crimes Against International Law, p. 43. See also Greenspan, Modern Law of Land Warfare, p. 432; Joachim von Elbe, "The Evolution of the Concept of the Just War in International Law," American Journal of International Law 33 (October, 1939): 685.

right to do, all the conquerors acting in concert could do. Germany's unconditional surrender constituted the Allied powers as the absolute sovereign and therefore as the legitimate lawmaking body for that country.[74]

The Austinians, on the other hand, borrowed pragmatic and natural-law principles to prove that Nuremberg was unjust and a mistake. Often they presented their condemnation of Nuremberg in the typically Grotian terms of moral denunciation for violation of ethical standards.[75] The Tribunal's injustice arose from its contravening law and equity which made the proceedings an immoral act. Another example of this eclecticism was that Josef Kunz, a positivist, agreed with the pragmatist's demand for a dynamic law for the nations, but, on the other hand, held that this development would be achieved not by judicial process but by international legislation.[76] Hans Kelsen, although opposed to many natural-law principles, accepted the Grotian "just war" doctrine but maintained that this was a political rather than a moral decision.[77]

We further note that many characteristics, opinions, or attitudes were common to the opposing sides. Some positivists as well as natural-law advocates gave a high priority to morality.[78] The philosophies diverged regarding whether the application of moral standards was a practical possibility at the time or whether it was an ideal for achievement in the future. The positivist usually had reservations that such principles must be

74. Greenspan, *Modern Law of Land Warfare*, pp. 429–30; Svarlien, *Introduction*, p. 369; Wright, "Law of Nuremberg," pp. 50–51; Wright, "Legal Positivism," pp. 411, 412.

75. Wright, "Law of Nuremberg," p. 45; Harold R. McKinnon, "Natural Law and Positive Law," *Notre Dame Lawyer* 23 (January, 1948): 125–39.

76. Wright, "Legal Positivism," p. 409.

77. Kelsen, *Peace Through Law*, pp. 87–88.

78. F. S. C. Northrop, *Philosophical Anthropology and Practical Politics* (New York: Macmillan, 1960), pp. 176, 186–87; Corbett, *Morals, Law and Power*, p. 16. "Even if such justification is of moral rather than strictly legal significance it is of great importance; for, in the last analysis, international morality is the soil which fosters the growth of international law. It is international morality which determines the general direction of the development of international law. Whatever is considered 'just' in the sense of international morality has at least a tendency of becoming international 'law' "; Hans Kelsen, *Law and Peace in International Relations* (Cambridge, Mass.: Harvard University Press, 1942), pp. 37–38.

codified in statutory law before legal punishment could support the healthy instincts of mankind.

These ethical considerations of anti-Nuremberg international lawyers were atypical of any pattern perceived in other literary media. In newspapers, magazines, and law reviews, the affirmation of the pertinence of morality to international conduct almost inevitably was united to approbation of Nuremberg. This connection was not necessarily true among experts in the law of nations.

Another topic on which some natural-law philosophers and positivists often reached agreement was their approval of international organizations and even of ultimate federation. Austinians perceived that the world's political evolution was going in this direction, and many of them heartily approved steps toward a more united world, even toward a transnational government in some qualified form.[79] Nuremberg's condemnation by these authors stemmed from the fact that they believed that world organizations had to come before world law, political developments before legal ones.[80]

Finally we observe that as writers in the various literary media become more knowledgeable, the topics of interest and discussion became fewer. It became clear what was important and what was not. Extraneous and superficial considerations were cast aside. The international lawyer brought to the Nuremberg discussion his reputation as a scholar, his zest for solving difficult problems in his specialty, and also a philosophical allegiance. These legal experts studied Nuremberg with care, candor, and conviction.

79. Corbett, *Morals, Law and Power,* p. 48.
80. Kelsen, *Peace Through Law,* pp. 111–12; Corbett, *Study of International Law,* pp. 35–36.

4

Congress Gives Its Judgment

The men Americans send to Washington as their representatives reflect, in general, the attitudes and assumptions of the popular mind. Two circumstances, however, may occasion exceptions to the rule. Some congressmen, because of investigation or personal motives, reject the judgment of popular opinion and champion an alternative which seems preferable to them. Some other legislators adopt minority views because they are the agents of particular sections of the nation which have distinctive views and interests not shared by the average American. The representatives' judgment on Nuremberg reflected both conformity with popular attitudes and divergence from them.

During the war Congress confined its action on war-crime trials to expressing the desire for certain punishment of evildoers, because most members willingly acknowledged that the ultimate disposition of Axis leaders was in executive rather than legislative competence.[1] Congressmen knew, however, that a judicial farce had allowed World War I criminals to escape punishment; they knew that the current enemy had committed outrageous barbarities; and they knew that the American people, who had made extreme sacrifices, did not want justice to abort once more. The members of Congress, therefore, informed the president that they expected a stern punitive policy.

As early as 1943 Senator Alben W. Barkley introduced a resolution for the "Condemnation of and Punishment for Outrages Inflicted upon Civilians in Nazi-Occupied Countries." As one would expect, this measure passed unanimously because the vote was taken during wartime, atrocities against the Jews were

1. *Cong. Rec.*, 79 Cong., 1 Sess., 91:4286.

front page news, other legislative bodies had expressed their indignation, and the resolution was essentially no more than a statement that murderers of millions "shall be held accountable and punished in a manner commensurate with the offenses for which they are responsible." [2]

Further congressional demand for punishing Axis leaders grew in intensity as victory became certain. In February 1945 Herbert Claiborne Pell was recalled by the State Department from his post as American representative on the United Nations War Crimes Commission. The department's announced reason for Pell's removal was that it did not have the money for his salary.[3] Pell, on the other hand, charged he was fired because he had urged punishment of Axis leaders for atrocities committed within their own territory and against their own citizens.[4] The reaction, particularly of the Jewish community, to the State Department's explanation and Pell's accusation can well be imagined.[5]

Congressmen such as Thomas J. Lane of Massachusetts, Samuel Dickstein of New York, and Chet Holifield of California repeatedly raised the question of Pell's recall and demanded stern prosecution of Axis criminals even if these had been "heads of state" or if their crimes had been committed within the borders of their own state.[6]

2. *Cong. Rec.,* 78 Cong., 1 Sess., 89:1723.

3. Ibid., 79 Cong., 1 Sess., 91:906. As the debate in the Foreign Affairs Committee revealed, the State Department's claim of lack of money was not an absurd declaration that the Department did not have $25,000. It was rather a statement that the Department was technically strangled by red tape. The UNWCC agent was a presidential appointment under certain wartime powers which terminated at the end of the calendar year. A special grant would be needed after January 1. This excuse was a rather obvious pretext.

Proceedings of the Foreign Affairs Committee also revealed confusion about the dismissal. For example, Pell did not know whether he was permanently removed from his position until the chairman of the Committee informed him that this was the case. *Punishment of War Criminals: Hearings Before the Committee on Foreign Affairs, House of Representatives, Seventy-Ninth Congress, First Session on H. J. Res. 93* (Washington: Government Printing Office, 1945), pp. 28–30 (hereafter cited as *Punishment of War Criminals*).

4. *Cong. Rec.,* 79 Cong., 1 Sess., 91:906.

5. Ibid., A76, A763.

6. Ibid., 906, A735, A763. Intensified interest in postwar sanctions engendered by the Pell incident prompted New York Congressman Vito Marcantonio to insert in the *Record* the American Labor Party's proposals for

There were two cruxes of congressional concern for war-crime trials, the Pell affair and the King resolution. The man who linked the two was Congressman Emmanuel Celler.[7] On March 22 and March 26, 1945 the New York congressman appeared before the House Committee on Foreign Affairs to plead for his joint resolution which would direct "the President to appoint a Commission to cooperate with the United Nations War Crimes Commission, or any other agency or agencies of the United Nations in the preparation of definite plans for the punishment of war criminals of the Axis countries."[8]

Celler testified before the committee that his bill signified "the first time that any official recognition, as far as Congress is concerned, had been taken of the paramount subject of war crimes and punishment."[9] The congressman contended that his measure was needed because, although the War, Navy, State, and Justice Departments had all started programs for trials, apparently there was no coordination between the branches.

The chief witness Celler called in support of his resolution was Herbert C. Pell. The former United States representative to the UNWCC maintained that confusion reigned concerning postwar sanctions. Many of those involved in deciding on a program, Pell contended, did not even realize that a new type of violation had to be treated. Formerly, "war crimes" were limited to such individual acts as murder, rape, or looting, but now German leaders had initiated criminal programs as official government policy. Outmoded procedures could not deal with these outrages; new concepts had to be created to punish these crimes on a common-law analogy.[10]

Hearings on Celler's resolution were continued March 26, but

---

punishment. This program, published three months before the London Charter's provisions were released, was a noteworthy example of the tradition of third party anticipation of future measures of major parties. The resolution embodied all the essential charges which would be contained in the actual indictment. Ibid., A932.

7. During the months of March and April of 1945, postwar punishment absorbed the interest and efforts of Emmanuel Celler. *New York Times*, March 23, 1945, p. 3; April 14, 1945, p. 3; April 25, 1945, p. 3; April 27, 1945, p. 6.

8. *Punishment of War Criminals*, p. i.

9. Ibid., p. 1.

10. Ibid., pp. 29–30.

on that day a sudden change in legislative programming occurred. The second meeting opened with Congressman Cecil R.
King of California introducing a new measure as a substitute for
Celler's bill. This was House Concurrent Resolution 30, a measure declaring the "sense of Congress" urging postwar trials of
war criminals, the exclusion in such tribunals of immunity on the
pleas of "head of state" and "superior orders," and the barring of
neutral asylum to Axis criminals.[11]

The key to the technical difference between Celler's and
King's measures was that a joint resolution, such as that of the
New York congressman, was legislation which bound the executive to implement the program demanded by Congress. The
Californian's concurrent resolution merely recommended to the
executive a general policy which the legislators deemed advisa-
ble.

The House Committee on Foreign Affairs decided to send
Congressman King's resolution, rather than Celler's bill, to the
floor. Apparently the State Department influenced the committee's choice because Congressman King submitted his measure to
Secretary Stettinius on April 2, 1945 and eleven days later received official approbation.[12] Celler, on the other hand, was
informed that the department considered his proposed coordi-
nating and investigating committee to be "superfluous." [13]

The climax of congressional activity regarding war criminals
occurred on May 7, 1945, one month before the drafting of the
London Charter which would provide the law for the Nuremberg Tribunal. At that time the House Foreign Affairs Committee formally presented Congressman King's concurrent resolution.

A dozen representatives spoke in favor of the measure, and no
one directly opposed it.[14] The only desire of the legislators was to
make the document stronger by appointing "watchdog" and

11. Ibid., p. 41.
12. Ibid., p. 126.
13. *Cong. Rec.*, 79 Cong., 1 Sess., 91:A2022.
14. Luther A. Johnson (Dem., Texas), Rogers (Rep., Mass.), Neeley
(Dem., W. Vir.), Celler (Dem., N.Y.), Grossett (Dem., Tex.), Voorhis
(Dem., Calif.), McCormack (Dem., Mass.), Patrick (Dem., Ala.), Murdock
(Dem., Ari.), Brooks (Dem., Lo.), Kee (Dem., W. Vir.), Mundt (Rep.,
S.D.).

investigating committees, by suggesting hanging as a fit penalty, and by requesting that a permanent record be made of Nazi atrocities.[15] Congressman McCormack of Massachusetts claimed for himself the role of "gadfly," again and again demanding clear declaration, by members of the committee, that the bill did express the effective and stern determination of Congress to punish enemy criminals.[16]

The only discordant note was sounded by Emmanuel Celler, who, although not against the King bill, demanded action rather than pious platitudes. "One could no more be against a declaration of this sort than one could be in favor of sin," the New York congressman declared. "It is probably just as right as the dictionary, but of no avail unless it is used and followed up by action." [17] He still wanted a commission.

After a short debate King's resolution was passed unanimously. Suggested strengthening amendments were not voted on because they were technically inadmissible since the bill had been introduced under a suspension of the rules. In this way the official policy of the House of Representatives was declared.

At the time of the Nuremberg verdicts in October of 1946, congressional comments reflected the attitude of most Americans. President pro tempore of the Senate, Kenneth McKellar, and Senator Thomas Steward, his fellow Democrat from Tennessee, thought the judicial sentences would be an effective deterrent to future aggressors and expressed the hope that the occupation authorities would not delay the executions. New York Congressman Sol Bloom said that "you cannot make the penalty too severe." [18]

It was a long time after the conclusion of the trial that words of approbation for Nuremberg once more echoed through the congressional chambers. In January of 1959 Senator Morse pleaded with the Cuban government of Fidel Castro to desist from its legalized murder. The Oregon Democrat thought that this crime was being committed by the Revolutionary govern-

15. These proposals were urged by Celler, Grosett, and Brooks respectively.
16. *Cong. Rec.*, 79 Cong., 1 Sess., 91:4283.
17. Ibid., 4285.
18. *PM*, October 2, 1946, p. 10.

ment's execution of members of the Batista regime after trials lasting minutes. Morse enunciated the principle: "We recognized that if we are to keep faith with moral and spiritual values in the relations between nations we must repudiate any doctrine for handling prisoners of war which is based on the jungle law of vengeance." [19]

Senator Morse raised the possible Cuban retort that the United States had followed a similar "jungle policy" with the German war criminals at Nuremberg. The Senator, who claimed to be a buff on the Tribunal, replied: "As an American, with pride I point to that record, because it is a glorious record in support of fair trial procedure for the protection of both the innocent and the guilty. Sincere men and women may disagree as to whether the German war criminals should have been prosecuted. It was determined as a matter of public policy, on the part of the governments concerned, that the trials should be held. They were held in accordance with established principles of international law." [20] Morse pleaded with Castro for like procedural fairness when the Cuban leader tried his enemies.

In the contrast between approval of the trials by some legislators and disapproval by others, the most obvious pattern is the temporal one. During the first half of 1945, when congressmen were eagerly voting in favor of trial and punishment of Axis leaders, no legislator declared his opposition. The reason for this acquiescence is obvious. Few Americans completely rejected punishment for war criminals, especially in the vague terms in which it was being discussed during this period. Even a program of trials, rather than summary execution, was acceptable to almost all congressmen. Conflict arose when the generic wish for judicial sanctions was transformed into the specifics of the London Charter and into the gray walls of the Palace of Justice at Nuremberg.

The first real storm clouds of direct congressional disapproval of Nuremberg appeared November 27, 1945, a few days after the convening of the court in Bavaria. The Tribunal was discussed tangentially in a senatorial debate on the advisability of the United Nations Security Council legally defining aggression.

19. *Cong. Rec.*, 86 Cong., 1 Sess., 105:925.
20. Ibid.

Senator Shipstead, Republican from Minnesota, argued for an authoritative definition and charged that private individuals at the war-crime trials were attempting to codify international law on their own initiative. Their efforts, the Senator added, were establishing principles which would intimidate men from following military careers.[21] According to the new doctrine, he said, if there had been a "Nuremberg" after the Civil War, General Lee would have been tried and shot. Senator Burton K. Wheeler, Montana Democrat, seconded Shipstead's ideas and stressed that the soldiers' trepidations were a hard fact to be reckoned with no matter what the legal validity of the prosecution's theory.[22]

Senator Shipstead's remarks were not accepted with a polite silence. Senator William Fulbright of Arkansas interrupted his colleague to declare that his comparison of Robert E. Lee to the Nazis was invalid because an essential difference existed between the two situations. In 1860 war was considered a legitimate means of national policy; now attitudes had changed, and a war of aggression was illegal and criminal.[23]

When the verdicts for the Nazi leaders were announced, Robert Alphonso Taft, Republican senator from Ohio, became an outspoken critic, probably the best known, of the proceedings. Taft's negative judgment was not a foregone conclusion. In fact, his previous speeches on war crimes and international law reveal both agreements and contradictions with his later Nuremberg stand.

What were Taft's ideas before the verdicts? First, although Nazi war crimes and atrocities were not Taft's major interest, he frequently stated his abhorrence for the deeds of the German leaders. These declarations were usually prompted by his efforts to save the Jews of Europe or to establish Palestine as a free, independent Jewish commonwealth.[24] Senator Robert Wagner, Democrat from New York, and Senator Taft proposed a resolution requesting the United States government to use its "good offices and to take the appropriate measures" to create a Jewish homeland (S.R. 247). Taft constantly urged this measure in and

21. *Cong. Rec.*, 79 Cong., 1 Sess., 91:11019.
22. Ibid.
23. Ibid.
24. *Cong. Rec.*, 78 Cong., 1 Sess., 89:9305.

out of the Senate during the pre-Nuremberg period.[25] He stated
his motive thus: "I have supported the resolution because
we owe the best retribution we can give to the Jewish people
who first bore the brunt of the Hitler attack, who have suffered the most intolerable tortures and the most frightful
decimation. . . ."[26]

Second, Taft considered aggression to be Germany's major
crime. The senator's one basic speech, which he repeated with
minor variations for three years (1943–45), always gave special
prominence to the idea that aggression had to be punished
ruthlessly.[27] The sanction would consist mainly of the terrible
devastation of modern war which was necessary for Allied victory. The destruction would prove a deterrent to any future
aggressor, but postwar policy must reinforce this example.
"Many steps," Taft said, "may be taken in the transition period
which are unthinkable as permanent policy. During the transition period the world will be dominated by the United Nations.
The Axis nations will be completely disarmed and subjected to
every penalty which seems wise and effective." [28]

Third, Taft stressed that peace and freedom should come by
elimination of the world's economic problems, by an international society modeled on the League of Nations, and by an
international court.[29] This tribunal, in the Senator's mind, should
have compulsory jurisdiction over international disputes. This
last opinion led Taft to make a statement one might not have
expected of him. Exactly two months before his speech on the
Nuremberg judgment, the senator spoke against restrictions by
the United States on the jurisdiction of the United Nations'
court. He said: "I do not think we shall have peace in the world
until the nations submit their disputes to impartial tribunals for
decisions by them. I do not care whether there is existing law or
not, for I am willing to let the court decide the issues on the
basis of justice. I would be willing to let the court consider such
matters without having any treaty as a basis for its decision; and

25. *Cong. Rec.*, 78 Cong., 2 Sess., 90:963, 7261; 79 Cong., 1 Sess., 91:
12139, 9217; 79 Cong., Sess., 92:6376–77.
26. *Cong. Rec.*, 79 Cong., 1 Sess., 91:12141, 12168, A 1411.
27. *Cong. Rec.*, 78 Cong., 1 Sess., 89:5092–94, A 1510, A 3783.
28. Ibid., 5093.
29. Ibid., 5093–94.

until we do that, I say we cannot have peace, even though we set up all the force we want and all the tribunals we want. . . . To say that if there is no written law, just as there was no written law for many years in respect to the common law of England, the Court shall not take jurisdiction, will mean, I think, that there will be no hope for peace in the world." [30]

Finally, although Taft favored a world court with compulsory jurisdiction, he rejected a fundamental Nuremberg principle of individual responsibility. "The theory of an international state bearing the same relation to the nations and their citizens as our federal Government bears to the States and its citizens appears to me to be fantastic, dangerous, and impractical." [31]

These points summarize Taft's position before the judgments at Nuremberg.

The quiet college town of Kenyon, Ohio, in October of 1946, presented a great contrast to the majestic display of judicial formality at Nuremberg and the frenzied congressional press interviews held at Washington. Senator Robert A. Taft had agreed to contribute to a symposium on America's Anglo-Saxon heritage a survey of that tradition's contribution to the legal system of the United States. Events induced the senator on that occasion to state his belief that the Anglo-Saxon tradition of justice had been perverted at Nuremberg. "The hanging of the eleven men convicted," Taft declared, "will be a blot on the American record which we shall long regret." [32]

In his speech, "Equal Justice Under Law," Taft asserted that Nuremberg's deterrent value would be nil. No potential aggressor expects to lose, and consequently the threat of a trial subsequent to defeat can hold little terror for him. Moreover, he objected, the court employed retroactive law; the victorious powers were unable to judge impartially; and Nuremberg embodied the Russian concept of a legal system because it served governmental policy and not justice.

No authority claimed that Taft did not know what he was doing. No experienced politician could be insensitive to the

30. *Cong. Rec.*, 79 Cong., 2 Sess., 92:10700.
31. *Cong. Rec.*, 78 Cong., 1 Sess., 89:A 3784.
32. Robert A. Taft, "Equal Justice Under Law," *Vital Speeches* 13 (November, 1946): 48.

American people's approval of Nuremberg's punishment of Nazi criminals.[33] Arthur Krock, *New York Times* news analyst, was informed by Taft's friends and advisers that "Mr. Republican" fully understood how hostile would be the reception to his stand. "Their estimate is that he made it nevertheless because, as a lawyer and son of a Chief Justice of the United States, he holds this opinion passionately and seriously believes that the effect of the Nuremberg trials and sentences on courts and laws in democratic nations will be degrading. Such being his state of mind, say these persons, no consideration of possible harm to his political ambitions or to those of other Republicans could keep him silent." [34]

Taft's biographer, William Smith White, presented a slightly different explanation of the Kenyon address in *The Taft Story*. This writer thought the Senator's "enormously tactless position" showed him to be a "genuine, honest-to-God strict Constitutionalist of rare vintage (if perhaps a slightly frozen one)." [35]

White incisively noted another basic consideration which would turn Taft against Nuremberg. The court was something new and spectacular. "The approach, moreover, had for him the great defect of novelty; he did not as a rule care for novelty in any field, quite apart from the high field of the Constitution. Nor did he relish dramatic solutions to anything." [36] Indeed the theatrical side, the "show to be remembered" aspect, of an international tribunal was as abhorrent to Robert Taft as it was appealing to Franklin Roosevelt.

No matter whether Senator Taft foresaw the force of the protest which would greet his Kenyon speech, the reaction did come.[37] Sharp as it was, the intensity and extent of the opposition has frequently been exaggerated in later accounts. We find only a few inches of objective coverage of Taft's speech in most

33. *New York Mirror*, October 17, 1946.
34. *New York Times*, October 9, 1946, p. 17.
35. William Smith White, *The Taft Story* (New York: Harper, 1954), p. 47 (hereafter cited as White, *Taft Story*).
36. Ibid., p. 48. Taft in his clarification of the Kenyon speech declared he was not opposed to the verdicts because Nazi leaders would hang, but rather because of the "whole *novel* and hypocritical procedure of the victors trying the vanquished for the crime of making war, under the form of judicial procedure" (italics mine). *Charlotte Observer*, October 9, 1946.
37. *New York Times*, October 8, 1946, p. 15.

national magazines.[38] One generally must seek diligently to find the news item; only columnists and politicians were greatly concerned with his statement.

The protest which did arise against Taft's views was centered mainly in New York State. Two interconnected reasons explain this localization. First, New York at the time of Taft's speech was in the middle of an election campaign, and Democrats hoped for a general political advantage by publicizing the Kenyon stand. Second, politicians thought that the large Jewish vote in New York City and the large Polish vote in Buffalo would be particularly sensitive to the Nuremberg issue.

Herbert Lehman, Democratic nominee for the United States Senate from New York, led the attack upon the Ohio senator. Lehman informed reporters that he was "deeply shocked" by Taft's stand and that he thought all right-thinking Americans would repudiate the Senator's opinion. "For a year the civilized world has followed these trials," Lehman said, "and has been impressed by the meticulous fairness with which they were conducted. Mass murder and violations of the laws of war were recognized crimes at the time they were committed by the convicted individuals. In respect to these charges no question of *ex post facto* can fairly be raised." [39] Other New York Democratic and American Labor Party politicians reiterated Lehman's view in less temperate fashion.

New York Republicans were prompt in their reaction. Governor Thomas E. Dewey and Irving N. Ives, Lehman's rival for the Senate seat, issued a formal statement attacking Taft's stand and affirming their belief in the justice of the Tribunal's verdict.[40] Jacob K. Javits, Republican congressional candidate from the twenty-first Manhattan district, in a telegram to Senator Taft, asserted that the Kenyon address was a "disservice to all we fought for and to the cause of future peace." [41]

No leading Republican in New York State came out in support of Senator Taft's Nuremberg judgment. This certainly was not a

38. "Nuremberg Blot," *Newsweek* 28 (October 14, 1946): 59; "The Nürnberg Debate," *Time* 48 (October 14, 1946): 29.
39. *New York Times*, October 8, 1946, p. 15.
40. Ibid.
41. Ibid.

case of cowardice or expediency for all, if for any. Governor Dewey, for instance, had stated in June of the previous year his support for a world court to achieve international justice. In a speech to the American-Irish Historical Society the governor endorsed a basic natural-law philosophy as well as expressing his belief in the dynamic, progressive nature of international law.[42] These legal tenets pitted him in direct conflict with Senator Taft on a much more basic level than that of political expediency.

Although intense political reaction to Taft's statement was centered in the greater New York City area, national Democratic spokesmen also commented on the Kenyon address. President Truman was asked in a press conference if he had any comment on Senator Taft's views. The president gleefully responded: "Well now, I think that's a matter that he and Dewey can settle, don't you?" The reporters responded with laughter.[43]

Senator Alben Barkley, Democrat from Kentucky, who sponsored the first resolution demanding sure punishment for war criminals, issued a thunderous rejoinder to the senator from Ohio. Barkley said that Taft "never experienced a crescendo of heart about the soup kitchens of 1932, but his heart bled anguishedly for the criminals at Nuremberg."[44] Senator Scott Lucas, Democrat from Illinois, told reporters that "Senator Taft, whether he believed it or not, was defending those culprits who were responsible for the murder of ten million people."[45]

Politicians could not match, however, the savage, bitter attacks and defenses of Senator Taft which were found among newspaper columnists. These writers jumped for the jugular. No charge was too crude, no item too far-fetched if it could be used to damn the Ohioan or, on the other hand, to manhandle his assailants.

Walter Winchell had never been favorable to Taft, but the senator's statement on Nuremberg sent Winchell to his venom well. His column began with the general observation: "Give Senator Taft's record the once-over and you'll come across shoddy facts that you wouldn't want to touch. His astounding

42. Thomas Dewey, "International Justice Requires the World Court," *American Bar Association Journal* 31 (June, 1945): 296.
43. Truman, *Public Papers, January 1 to December 31, 1946*, p. 448.
44. *New York Times*, October, 25, 1946, p. 15.
45. Ibid., October 19, 1946, p. 10.

comment about the hanging of the Nazi unspeakables is only the last act in the tragedy of his career." [46] The column continued: "Ohio's spurious gift to the Senate recoils in horror about the Nuremberg verdict and the prosecution of alleged seditionists. He tags the judgment of the Allied Tribunal as 'an outrage of justice.' But he is mum about the truly outrageous crimes of the convicted Nazis and turns his back on the subversive acts of their home-front chums. Taft concentrates on aiming his indignation at the force of law and order UPHOLDING JUSTICE. . . . International ghouls and domestic goons bring out the Yankee Doodle in Taft." [47] Winchell concluded by agreeing with the conservative *Herald-Tribune*'s judgment that Taft would only help to manufacture a future legend of martyrdom for which there would be no justification.

Winchell's asperity against Taft was matched by Westbrook Pegler's hostility to the senator's critics. Pegler's article eulogized Senator Taft and noted that a "quick, nasty response" to his Kenyon address came from Republicans as well as Democrats. The columnist judged such vilification to be the "punishment that honest men must be brave enough to face when they express unpopular opinions on sensitive subjects." [48]

In Pegler's view Dewey and Ives were cowards, just as Taft was courageous. The challenge of the Democratic chairman demanding that Taft come to New York to plead for convicted Nazis was "dirty politics" because the chairman hoped that Taft would be mobbed if he presented a "reasoned argument against a group execution which he regarded as a lynching." Democratic candidate Herbert Lehman, Pegler admitted, might be right in asserting that Americans generally favored Nuremberg and that they opposed Taft. It might also be true, the columnist added, that Americans were giving up their right to trial by an impartial court, and they were also exposing themselves to retroactive law. [49]

We conclude from our evidence that adverse reaction to Taft's judgment on Nuremberg was sharp and bitter, but also short and

46. *Charlotte Observer*, October 17, 1946.
47. Ibid.
48. Ibid., October 14, 1946.
49. Ibid.

limited.[50] Criticism was confined almost exclusively to the month after the Kenyon speech, and discussion of the issue was minimal once the 1946 campaign was over. During the time of interest, scattered voices of censure sounded throughout the land, but New York State was the center of disapproval. Leaders of the Democratic party seized upon the senator's speech with the idea of making it a major emotional consideration in the 1946 elections. These politicians believed that although few Americans could comprehend Nuremberg's involved legal questions, they would respond favorably—with the war and all its sacrifices fresh in their memories—on the issue of swift, severe punishment for the Nazi leaders who were guilty of aggression and atrocities.

Democratic expectations proved sterile. More immediate and personal issues—jobs, rationing, inflation, housing—led to an overwhelming victory for the Republicans, and as a result they dominated both houses of the federal government. Even in the New York elections Republicans were successful, and Taft's Nuremberg statement had little if any influence upon the Jewish voters or upon any other ethnic "bloc vote" in the city or the state.

By 1948 Taft's stand was considered not a burden but a political asset by Republican leaders. Felix Morley, in a *Life* article urging Taft's presidential nomination, devoted a major portion of his article to the story of the senator's speech at Kenyon College. Morley believed that more and more lawyers with high professional standards were doubting the justice of Nuremberg, but "it was the achievement of Senator Taft to express that doubt at a time when it was politically dangerous and could do him no possible good." [51]

50. How quickly the Nuremberg statement evaporated as a political question is indicated by the fact that when Professor Allan Nevins wrote his biography of Herbert Lehman, the senator "did not mention to me Senator Taft's criticism, probably because it simply escaped his memory." Letter of Professor Allan Nevins to the author, August 25, 1965.

Apparently Lehman made no speech on Taft's stand except that cited. Mrs. Herbert Lehman writes: "There is no record of any speech concerning the Nuremberg Trials during the senatorial campaign of that year. As a matter of fact, I strongly doubt if the subject would be an issue in the campaign." Letter of Mrs. Herbert H. Lehman to the author, September 24, 1965.

51. Felix Morley, "The Case for Taft," *Life* 24 (February 9, 1948): 56.

If Morley believed that by 1948 Nuremberg was a political asset for Taft, other writers at least considered it no handicap. Even by February 1947, four months after the Kenyon speech, *Time* magazine held that the major obstacle to Taft's selection by the Republicans as their presidential candidate was "lack of political sex appeal." [52] Nuremberg was not cited as a deterrent. At a later date Eric Goldman listed the liabilities which he thought defeated Taft's bid for the nomination, but he did not mention the Nuremberg issue.[53]

If Nuremberg and Senator Taft's opposition are known by the man on the street today, it is most likely because of John F. Kennedy's *Profiles in Courage*, familiar to millions of young Americans either in book form or as a television serialization. President Kennedy's interpretation has much in common with previous studies of Taft's Nuremberg statement. The theme of courage came naturally to the minds of all but the senator's most violent critics. The senator's firm, inflexible integrity also is an accepted factor in any explanation.

Kennedy agreed with White and Krock that Taft's rigid constitutionalism was the basis for his condemnation of the trials. "The Constitution of the United States was the gospel which guided the policy decisions of the Senator from Ohio. It was his source, his weapon and his salvation. And when the Constitution commanded no *ex post facto* laws, Bob Taft accepted this precept as permanently wise and universally applicable." [54]

This judgment of the liberal John F. Kennedy was echoed at a later date by the conservative Russell Kirk. In *The Political Principles of Robert A. Taft*, a work highly laudatory of the senator, Kirk and coauthor James McClellan maintained that "Taft refused to remain silent concerning the Nuremberg Trials because he could not in conscience ignore this fatal exercise of arbitrary power, this affront to the rule of law." [55]

Congressional opposition to Nuremberg grew after the Tribunal concluded its operations. This resulted from the renewal

52. "Taking Stock," *Time* 49 (February 24, 1947): 27.
53. Eric Goldman, *Crucial Decade, America, 1945–1955* (New York: Knopf, 1959), pp. 81, 89–90.
54. Kennedy, *Profiles in Courage*, p. 217.
55. Russell Kirk and James McClellan, *The Political Principles of Robert A. Taft* (New York: Fleet Press, 1967), p. 102.

of bitter partisan politics, the advent of the Cold War, and growing discontent with the policy of American occupation. The mismanagement of the trials following Nuremberg tended to discredit the whole tribunal policy and added arguments to the critics' arsenals. Stories of lack of talent among the American prosecutors and judges as well as of the use of torture to obtain evidence were entered into the *Congressional Record*.[56]

Although a number of congressmen and women objected to the trials, a triumvirate of opponents was preeminent—John E. Rankin, George A. Dondero, and William Langer. Other legislative critics of the Tribunal confined their objections to inserting in the *Appendix* their own adverse views or their constituents' condemnatory writings. Only these three voiced opposition on the floor. Curiously, although they are in basic agreement on Nuremberg's baneful nature, each had his own reason for condemnation, and all reflected the hopes, fears, and values commonly identified with their respective constituents. Because their views were extreme they received only passing notice in national deliberations.

Congressman John E. Rankin of Mississippi took the House floor to express his delight with President Truman's directive of July 15, 1947, repudiating the "Morgenthau Plan" with its harsh measures for turning Germany into an agricultural state. The Congressman hope that this declaration of policy would "put a stop to the racial persecution of the people of Germany who are now helpless at our feet. . . . If we people of the Southern States had been treated in the same manner after the War between the States as those people have been treated under the pressure of a certain racial minority, you would not have heard the last of it until doomsday. . . . treat the people of Germany . . . with

56. *Cong. Rec.*, 80 Cong., 1 Sess., 93:8563, 11468; 81 Cong., 1 Sess., 45: A 3741. Lawrence H. Smith, Representative from Wisconsin, in a speech entered into the *Congressional Record*, stated: "Julius Streicher, for example, was obliged by Americans to kiss the feet of Negro soldiers, to swallow spittle, and was offered urine when he asked for water; . . ." Ibid., A 3742.
A listing of the congressmen, with their party affiliations, who in any way opposed Nuremberg supports a supposition of political partisanship: Schwabe (Rep., Mo.), Shipstead (Rep., Minn.), Wheeler (Dem., Mon.), Luce (Rep., Conn.), Willis (Rep., Ind.), Dondero (Rep., Mich.), Rankin (Dem., Miss.), Langer (Rep., N.D.), Smith (Rep., Wis.), St. George (Rep., N.Y.), Sheehan (Rep., Ill.), Taft (Rep., Ohio).

humanity and decency and [do] not permit racial minorities to vent their sadistic vengeance upon them and charge it up to the United States." [57]

Rankin later repeated this view that the Tribunal was in effect an instrument of (Jewish) vengeance. "Mr. Speaker," he said in the House on November 28, 1947, "as a representative of the American people I desire to say that what is taking place in Nuremberg, Germany, is a disgrace to the United States. Every other country now has washed its hands and withdrawn from this saturnalia of persecution. But a racial minority, 2½ years after the war closed, are in Nuremberg not only hanging German soldiers but trying German businessmen, in the name of the United States." [58]

Congressman George A. Dondero, Republican of Michigan in 1948, developed the idea that the Tribunal's prime evil was that its principles demoralized Allied military men and broke down necessary army discipline. These sanctions created the precedent that patriotic service to the nation, the soldiers' obeying of orders, was possibly criminal.[59] The court's verdicts, consequently, exposed future defenders of the United States to ruthless vengeance if international Communism ever were victorious.

Although Congressman Dondero's major worry was about the trials' effects upon the military, he also was anxious over the Tribunal's indictment of industrialists and financiers. The congressman considered this a covert attack upon American manufacturers, a group of men Dondero thought deserved better treatment because they had put forth such noble efforts to protect the United States against Hitler. These entrepreneurs, moreover, were vital to America's defense against Russia.

Considering the Nuremberg court's indictment of representatives of private enterprise, Dondero became convinced that Communists had infiltrated the war-crime trials in Germany. He

57. *Cong. Rec.*, 80 Cong., 1 Sess., 93:9054.
58. Ibid., 10938.
59. Ibid., 80 Cong., 2 Sess., 94:A 2369. Congressman Dondero states that he had no special connection with the military at the time of these statements in Congress and of his inclusion in the appendix of items on Nuremberg. "I had no special contact or association with the Army any more than any other Member of Congress during that period." Letter of George A. Dondero to the author, May 11, 1965.

gave as examples Max Lowenthal, a top legal adviser to occupation military authorities, whose "record of Communist affiliation
is on file with the FBI." He also charged that "the conduct of the
Nuremberg trials in Germany is under the guidance of well-
known left wingers and ideologists like Josiah Dubois and so
forth." [60]

This last theory, that Nuremberg's trials were Communist
influenced, was the major argument of Republican Senator William Langer of North Dakota. He attempted to distinguish
clearly between the first trials of the major Nazis and the subsequent proceedings, but he still viewed even the major assize as a
Russian attempt to hang the industrialists.

Langer asserted that the trial procedures were adopted at
Moscow and conformed to Communist principles. In Russia,
Marshal Stalin employed like trials to liquidate his internal
enemies. "At Nuremberg the Communists used the war-crimes
trials to liquidate their external enemies." [61] The North Dakota
senator explained: "It is the Communist's avowed purpose to
destroy the Western World which is based on property rights.
The war trials were aimed directly at property rights. It was
intended to try the accused as aggressors, convict them as having
started the war, and then confiscate their property as a
penalty." [62]

The Communists, according to Langer, failed in their effort to
destroy German industrialists and financiers at the first major
assize, and so they worked through stooges during the trials
which followed. "Senator will find that those war-crime trials
have been most ardently supported by Communist-front organizations." Moreover, Langer continued, "if the payrolls of the
Nuremberg prosecution staff are supoenaed by the Judiciary
Committee, headed by the distinguished Senator from Nevada, it
will be seen that practically the entire prosecution staff was
composed of leftists and men who since have been exposed as
Communists and members of Communist-front organizations." [63]

The factors which probably motivated Senator Langer fell into

60. *Cong. Rec.*, 80 Cong., 1 Sess., 93:8563.
61. Ibid., 81 Cong., 2 Sess., 96:16708.
62. Ibid.
63. Ibid., 16709.

an interesting pattern. An ethnic consideration might have been operative because a good percentage of the legislator's constituents were of German descent and might not have been enthusiastic supporters of a harsh policy of occupation. Then the senator's zealous and doctrinaire isolationism may well have gagged on the idea of an international tribunal and American involvement in what might be considered a European problem. Finally, the anti-Communist theme in Senator Langer's attack on Nuremberg may be explained by the fact that it was spoken in 1950 during the McCarthy Era. Langer's background resembled that of the senator from Wisconsin in that both had constituents who were violently interested in the topic of Communism and who desired to prove their first-class citizenship by opposition to it. Moreover, both men had in their right-wing Catholicism an ideological basis for this political aversion.[64]

Nuremberg's implications for American legislators and politicians continued for some time after the judgments. Robert Taft's opposition to the trials was, in the eyes of his fellow Republicans, a sign of courage and integrity. At the same time active support of Nuremberg turned into political advantage for some. Participation in the Tribunal stamped one as a crusader against tyranny. As late as the 1962 election, William Donovan mentioned his Nuremberg activities to Jewish groups in spite of his having worked only on the preparations of the prosecution rather than on the trials themselves.[65]

Even more recently, on October 2, 1964, *Time* magazine noted that an "unkind cut" had been dealt to William Miller, the Republican vice-presidential candidate by the *New York Herald-Tribune*. That paper questioned a claim made in the party's official literature that candidate Miller had "played a major role in the prosecution of Nazi war criminals during the famous trials at Nuremberg." The New York newspaper's research found that Miller's activities had consisted of examining captured war documents during four months with the War Crimes Office. "Miller's

64. Ibid., 16705–6. Langer kept up his attack on the punishment dealt out at Nuremberg and the policy of a hard peace for Germany. The senator called attention to the role of Harry Dexter White in the genesis of the Morgenthau Plan; Ibid., 84 Cong., 2 Sess., 102:6466.

65. *New York Times*, November 5, 1962, p. 27.

'lame response' was 'I never claimed I was one of the trial lawyers.' " [66]

So Nuremberg lives on to aid or to haunt the American politician and statesman. It was an issue that allowed him to display his best or his worst: his catering to a spirit of revenge, or nurturing man's zeal for justice; his courageous stand for principle, or his passion for turning everything against a political opponent. It illuminates the chauvinistic or isolationist mind that judges everything by exclusively American or Anglo-Saxon standards, or it reveals a fuzzy-minded, right-hearted desire to make law at any cost serve justice.

Often only the politician or statesman himself could tell why he made his particular judgment on Nuremberg, and perhaps nearly as often as not even he was unable to answer because of the complexity of attitudes and the variety of circumstances that determined his stand.

66. "On the Receiving End," *Time* 84 (October 2, 1964): 43.

5

The Views of the American Public

"What was the American judgment on Nurem-
berg?" The inquirer usually wishes to find out by this question
how the majority of citizens evaluated the major war-crime
trials. He seeks to know the view of the typical man on the street
and not the opinion of experts or of a particular profession.

There is validity in this approach because the ordinary American's judgment on Nuremberg is of vital importance. Not that
the average citizen could understand fully the intricate factors
involved in the United States's trial program, nor could he
control the details of the administration's actions. Still, the
wishes, goals, emotions, and ideals of the American people do
influence foreign policy decisions. "To an extent that it is true in
no other country," historian Dexter Perkins tells us, "the motivating force in government has come up from the people, rather
than down from a political or diplomatic elite. The average man
in America, be he well-informed or ill-informed, is likely to think
that he has a right to express an opinion in politics, and to have
that opinion considered. . . . The great questions of foreign
policy have often been submitted to public debate, often discussed with great frankness from more than one point of view,
and often decided by the test of public opinion. No one can
understand American diplomacy who does not grasp the importance of the democratic motif in its historic evolution." [1]

In light of these facts, it is interesting to see how the program

1. Perkins, *American Approach*, pp. 74–75. For a less sanguine view concerning the knowledge and ability of Americans in foreign affairs, see Gabriel A. Almond, *The American People and Foreign Policy* (New York:
Praeger, 1960), pp. xxii-xxiii, 4, 5 (hereafter cited as Almond, *American
People and Foreign Policy*).

of the Nuremberg trials was received by the people and to discover whether it fits into the suggested pattern of governmental responsiveness to the people's basic desires.

The popular view of Nuremberg is also worthy of investigation because it illustrates a frame of reference in which Americans view international affairs. Public opinion on this event in 1946 revealed some of the fundamental concepts, presuppositions, and values which influence modern Americans as they survey the world scene.

To comprehend in some depth the popular judgment on Nuremberg, three questions may be asked. First, what was the people's verdict on the trials? To answer this, we will briefly indicate the evolution, during and after World War II, of views on the punishment of the enemy, the punitive measures which people wished to see employed, and their specific evaluation of the trials in Bavaria.

Our second question: what were the immediate sources of information and opinion that the American people used in forming their judgments? The average American gains his knowledge about the facts and personalities of the war-crime trials from the opinion media readily accessible to him—the daily newspaper, the columnists' feature articles, and popular magazines. These publications not only provided him with the basic information upon which he formed his judgment, they also presented him with definite evaluations of the trials with which he could agree or disagree. Especially in a matter so technical and complicated as the Nuremberg proceedings, the man on the street almost had to rely upon his favorite oracle in the popular press in order to select a view as his own.

Finally, we will investigate and offer some hypotheses concerning a third question: what were the basic attitudes operative in deciding the popular judgment on Nuremberg? As we will see, the Tribunal did fit into a definite pattern and showed specific characteristics which experts in foreign affairs have asserted to be the "American way" in international relations.

The attitude of the people toward the trial and punishment of the leaders of Nazi Germany crystallized during the years of the Second World War. Pearl Harbor enraged the ordinary citizen, and the long years of blood, sweat, toil, and tears confirmed him in his determination that those he believed had caused the holocaust must pay. This idea of sanctions for individuals was but one element in the "hard" peace which Americans were determined would follow the end of hostilities. During the war years an overwhelming majority of Americans insisted that the enemy should be treated with much more rigor than that imposed by the Versailles treaty, because they believed that the leniency shown after the First World War was a cause of the recurrence of German aggression.[2] One way that Americans expressed this determination was by strongly approving the president's demand for "unconditional surrender."[3] This battle cry, as Franklin Roosevelt explained, did not mean the total destruction of the German nation or the annihilation of its citizens, but it did entail the elimination of the enemy's capacity to wage war and the stern punishment of all war criminals.[4]

As the war came to an end, the American people placed their hope for containment of the enemy and his reformation primarily in a proposed United Nations Council which would rule Germany for at least ten years and eventually make that nation adopt a democratic government. The second plank in the ordinary citizen's blueprint for peace was the trial and execution of the chief Nazi officials who had led the German nation on its path of aggression and atrocities.[5]

Later, when the Allied governments implemented their plan of occupation, a growing number of Americans expressed satisfaction with the administration's handling of the problem. A large segment of the population, however, still worried about the enemy's being coddled by the conquering powers. Almost no

2. *Public Opinion Quaterly* 8 (Summer, 1944): 297; 8 (Fall, 1944): 448; 10 (Fall, 1946): 425.

3. The National Opinion Research Survey of May 7, 1944, found that 81% approved of the unconditional surrender policy; 10% disapproved. A Gallup poll about a year later found that three-fourths of those surveyed still approved of this program. *Public Opinion Quarterly* 8 (Summer, 1944): 296; 9 (Spring, 1945): 95.

4. Rosenman, *Working with Roosevelt*, p. 528.

5. *Public Opinion: 1935–1946*, ed. Hadley Cantril, prepared by Mildred Strunk (Princeton: Princeton University Press, 1951), p. 1114 (hereafter cited as Cantril, *Public Opinion*).

American in the postwar period thought that the program of denazification and punishment was too harsh.[6]

A perhaps surprising aspect of the popular attitude during this wartime period was that the vast majority of Americans, rejecting any hysterical propaganda about the total depravity of the enemy, clearly distinguished between Hitler's government and the German people. Popular opinion held that the leaders and not the German citizens were the enemy to be battled, subdued, and punished.[7] When Americans were asked how many of the enemy deserved death, they rejected suggested estimates of four hundred thousand and fifty thousand and expressed the view that those to be executed did not exceed five hundred.[8]

If the American public thought that few of the enemy should be punished severely as war criminals, they were united in what they thought the penalty for these few should be. Their overwhelming response was: "Kill them!" No judicial frills were desired—no legal process or possibility of escape or commutation. Exiling the German warlords as was done with Napoleon or Kaiser Wilhelm was a policy to be avoided rather than repeated. The idea of imprisonment received limited and very erratic endorsement. Leniency or forgiveness for the men who had plunged the world into the blood bath of World War II was not popular among Americans in the 1940's.[9]

6. *Public Opinion Quarterly* 9 (Winter, 1945–46): 534.
7. The surveys asked the question: "In the war with Germany do you feel that our chief enemy is the German people as a whole or the German government?" This information is found in *Public Opinion Quarterly* 7 (Spring, 1943): 173; 7 (Fall, 1944): 448; 9 (Spring, 1945): 95.
8. Minnesota Survey, No. 22. 5/45, Roper Public Opinion Research Center. This number was in startling contrast with official calculations. The American prosecutor at Nuremberg, Justice Robert Jackson, thought that about two million Germans could be tried as war criminals. In fact, the court's acceptance of the accusers' demand that mere membership in certain Nazi organizations be declared criminal would have placed an estimated 980,000 Germans in danger of death. Eugene Davidson, "The Nuremberg Trials and One World," in *Issues and Conflicts, Studies in Twentieth Century American Diplomacy*, ed. George L. Anderson (Laurence, Kan.: University of Kansas Press, 1959), p. 242; *Time* 49 (January 6, 1947): 29; Dina Ghandy McIntyre, "The Nuernberg Trials," *University of Pittsburgh Law Review* 24 (October, 1962): 103 (hereafter cited as McIntyre, "Nuernberg Trials").
9. Cf. the chart on pages 92–93.

In light of the future adoption of trials for war criminals, it is interesting to note that this program had little appeal for the public during the war. Only a fraction of Americans polled favored dealing with the enemy by judicial process.[10] When a trial was suggested specifically for Hermann Goering, the number two Nazi, only a handful favored a day in court for the very man who, as it happened, would be the main defendant before the International Military Tribunal a few months later.[11]

No matter what the American people and their Allies desired, however, their governments decided on the International Military Tribunal to try the major Nazi war criminals. When the public learned of this determination, no protests were heard even though adoption of the trial program meant rejection of the prompt extermination policy which they had overwhelmingly favored. Popular opinion greeted with satisfaction the legal methods chosen.[12] All newspaper editors, commentators, and politicians who were sensitive to the mood of the nation, whether they personally approved or disapproved of the trials, assumed that the man on the street favored the Tribunal.[13] As John F. Kennedy stated: "The Nuremberg Trials, in which eleven notorious Nazis had been found guilty under an impressively documented indictment for 'waging an aggressive war,' had been popular throughout the world and particularly in the United States. Equally popular was the sentence already announced by the high tribunal: death."[14]

The Nuremberg trials, indeed, did not present any problem for the vast majority of Americans, for without hesitation or doubt they agreed that the accused Nazis were guilty, that the enemy leaders deserved death rather than life imprisonment and that

10. *Washington Post*, April, 1945.
11. Cantril, *Public Opinion*, p. 117.
12. NORC, Survey No. 54–243, Q. 13, Roper Opinion Research Center.
13. *Baltimore Sun*, October 1, 1946; *Miami Herald*, October 2, 1946; *Brooklyn Eagle*, October 2, 1946; *Philadelphia Inquirer*, October 9, 1946; William L. Shirer, *The End of a Berlin Diary* (New York: Alfred A. Knopf, 1946), pp. 365–66 (hereafter cited as Shirer, *End of Berlin Diary*). Among those disapproving of Nuremberg see Westbrook Pegler, *Charlotte Observer*, October 4, 1946; "Nurnberg Confusion," *Fortune* 34 (December, 1946): 120.
14. Kennedy, *Profiles in Courage*, p. 216.

TIME	POLL	QUESTION	None of our Affair	Take Power	Be Lenient	Hard Labor	Trials	Isolate-Exile	Reeducate	Imprison	Torture	Kill Them	As they treated others	Forgive	Control	Punish	Other Answers	No Opinion	No Answer
March 26, 1942	OPOR	If we win the war, how should we treat Nazi leaders?		3				8		17	3	40	6	3	3	7	4	5	1
June 9, 1942	AIPO	After the war is over, how should we treat the Nazi leaders?	2		2		2			31	2	35	5				5	12	4
July 15, 1942	OPOR	When the war is over in Germany, how do you think we should treat the Nazi leaders?		6	2		4	7		11	5	44	10				2	8	2
February, 1945	AIPO	After the war is over, how should we treat the Nazi leaders?	1		3		10	2		13	7	41				18		5	
April 27, 1945	AIPO	After the war, what do you think should be done with members of the Nazi Party who defend themselves by claiming that they committed crimes under orders of higher-ups in the party?	2				19		3	42		19						15	

TIME	POLL	QUESTION	None of our Affair	Take Power	Be Lenient	Hard Labor	Trials	Isolate-Exile	Reeducate	Imprison	Torture	Kill Them	As they treated others	Forgive	Control	Punish	Other Answers	No Opinion	No Answer
May 15, 1945	AIPO	What punishment, if any, do you think we should give Goering?	1				4			6		67					5	17	10
June 9, 1943	AIPO	After the war is over, how do you think we should treat Hitler?	2				1	6		23		39	5			10		3	11
April 4, 1945	AIPO	When Germany is defeated, do you think Hitler should be punished?						12		19		51				14			4
May 15, 1945	AIPO	What do you think should be done with the members of the German Gestapo and the Nazi Storm Troopers?			1	3	15	5		6		39	5			8	2	6	10

justice was done at Nuremberg.[15] If the court had been deficient in any way, it was in being too lenient.[16] The average American also optimistically believed that the trials had been a beneficial and prudent policy of the United States government, and they hoped that the verdicts would prove a deterrent to potential aggressors.[17]

Public opinion and the press interact. The views and values of the people directly or indirectly influence popular publications, for these survive only if they are read and most people read what generally agrees with their own views. On the other hand, the average citizen has insufficient time, energy, and interest to research each issue current in domestic or international affairs and, therefore, must rely for many of his views upon the ideas presented to him by the popular press. We will perceive this interaction when we briefly study the judgment on Nuremberg as found in such printed matter as daily papers, syndicated columns, and popular magazines.

By military aircraft and war-ravaged rail system, the world's reporters flocked to the gray-walled castle of Baron Faber-Castell which would be their home at Nuremberg. Mankind had long awaited this trial, this "day of reckoning," and looked to its news agencies to convey the facts, human interest, and significance of this aftermath of six bloody years of the European war. Because of worldwide interest, Nuremberg in November 1945 held the largest group of journalists ever gathered in one place to cover one event—over a hundred sixty writers. Most of these were from the world's largest newspapers.[18]

Eleven months, four hundred three sessions, nearly two hundred witnesses, one hundred thousand documents, five million words of evidence later, one writer, Rebecca West, re-

15. "If you were on the jury would you find the defendants guilty or not guilty?" By a majority of nearly five to one, Americans thought that the accused Nazis were guilty. Minnesota Survey, No. 37, Q: 2, 9/46. When asked for their choice of punishment, the people voted two to one for death rather than life imprisonment. Ibid., Q. 3. "Had justice been done at Nuremberg?" Americans resoundingly answered fifteen to one in the affirmative. Ibid.
    16. *Public Opinion Quarterly* 10 (Winter, 1946–47): 645; Minnesota Survey No. 38, Q. 13, 10/46.
    17. Minnesota Survey No. 38, Q. 14 and Q. 15, 10/46.
    18. Genêt, "Letter from Nuremberg," *New Yorker* 21 (March 16, 1946): 84.

marked: "For however much a man loved the law, he could not love so much of it as lies about at Nuremberg." [19] Those who had been assigned to constant attendance at the court grimly joked that they were the last victims of Nazi persecution.[20] The news story that was supposed to be finished in a few days, a month at most, had trudged along for nearly a year. The reporter's work had become dull, routine and of minor interest to their editors and readers.[21]

In spite of all of these factors, almost every newspaper in the United States did devote its front page spread and its major editorial to Nuremberg on three occasions: the start of the trials (November 21, 1945), the announcement of the verdicts (October 1, 1946), and the executions (October 16, 1946). By editorials and reporting, newspapers formed and reflected the popular judgment on Nuremberg.[22]

We discover in the newspapers basically the same evaluation held by the average American citizen, in the sense that a large majority of editors approved the trials. On the other hand, we are able to discern for the first time on the popular level the reasons proposed for the favorable or unfavorable judgment and the discussion of specific aspects of the trials rather than the mere declaration of a general evaluation.

Newspapers which echoed the public's approbation of Nuremberg claimed that the court had rendered justice almost divine.

19. The figures may be found in *Newsweek* 28 (September 9, 1946): 52, and *Life* 21 (September 16, 1946): 40. The comment appeared in Rebecca West, "Reporter at Large," *New Yorker* 22 (September 7, 1946): 40.

20. *Charlotte Observer*, October 6, 1946.

21. The editorial in the *Atlanta Constitution* for December 4, 1945, was entitled "We've Known All That for Years." "As month after month passed, and press and public lost interest in the case as a 'spectacle,' the judicial foundations of the trial were strengthened by this very fact. . . ." Taylor, "Nuremberg Trials," p. 262.

22. Thirty-one newspapers have been selected for analysis on the basis of their political, territorial, and reader diversity. *Atlanta Constitution, Baltimore Sun, Boston Herald, Brooklyn Eagle, Charlotte Observer, Chicago Daily Tribune, Dallas Morning News, Detroit Free Press, Detroit News, Los Angeles Times, Miami Herald, Milwaukee Journal, New York Daily Mirror, New York Daily News, New York Journal American, New York Times, Newark Evening News, Oregonian, PM, Philadelphia Inquirer, Rocky Mountain News, San Francisco Chronicle, St. Louis Post-Dispatch, Times-Picayune, Wall Street Journal, Washington Evening Star, Washington Post, Washington Telegram, Washington Times-Herald, Worker, World Telegram.*

Rave reviews contained such statements as "a cause for pride," "a Magna Carta," "the greatest single accomplishment on the side of civilization since the war ended," "the longest and most significant trial in the annals of history," "a shining landmark in the moral development of mankind and for peace," and a "great landmark in the history of civilization." [23]

On the other hand, critics in the newspapers described the Tribunal as "an advance to barbarism." Papers opposing the trials decried the proceedings "as a supreme example of self-righteous hypocrisy" and contended that the legal action was merely the conquerors' "kangaroo court" butchering the losers.[24]

All the newspapers which repudiated the trials reiterated the view that a victor judging the vanquished could not be impartial, but each paper added its own specific reasons for condemnation. They stressed that the trials had not dealt with the basic psychological causes of modern war, that no existing international organization was competent to judge national leaders, that Nuremberg's principles could be abused, and that the victor's verdicts would motivate the losing side in any future war to fight to the death.[25]

The arguments of these dissident papers revealed some unexpected variations from the reasoning which appeared in other media. The newspapers condemning the trials paid minimal attention to the charge that the court employed retroactive law, and they had little interest in the "crimes" of the Allies. The Soviet's presence at the trials hardly occasioned comment.[26] One anti-Nuremberg paper broke the usual pattern which joined approval of the trials with endorsement of international organizations. The *Dallas Morning Sun* condemned the Tribunal, maintaining that only a superpowered United Nations could supply an unbiased court for international disputes.[27]

23. Respectively, *Brooklyn Eagle*, October 8, 1946; *New York Times*, September 29, 1946, 4:10; *Los Angeles Times*, October 2, 1946; *Philadelphia Inquirer*, October 6, 1946; *Washington Evening Star*, October 17, 1946; *Oregonian*, October 6, 1946.

24. *Chicago Daily Tribune*, November 21, 1945.

25. In order, *New York Daily News*, October 2, 1946; *Dallas Morning News*, October 2, 1946; *Rocky Mountain News*, October 2, 1946; *World Telegram*, October 1, 1946; *Wall Street Journal*, October 4, 1946; *New York Daily Mirror*, October 2, 1946.

26. Except for the *New York Journal American*, October 5, 1946.

27. *Dallas Morning News*, October 2, 1946.

Were there any common denominators among papers which disapproved of the Tribunal? It may seem at first glance that all dissenting newspapers were conservative or Republican.[28] However, most newspapers in America in 1946 were Republican; yet, most newspapers were in favor of the trials.[29] Some conservative Republican papers were among those which eulogized Nuremberg. The "isolationist impulse" also was not an absolute criterion. Every "American First" paper did not oppose Nuremberg, nor did all the "internationalist" press approve the trials. As was just noted, the *Dallas Morning News* was so much a "one worlder" that it was willing to surrender a part of United States sovereignty to the United Nations, yet it condemned the Tribunal.

Nor can one say that the anti-Nuremberg papers were following the lead of Robert A. Taft. They expressed their dissenting views before the senator from Ohio made his famous speech. How much these papers influenced the senator is open to question, but Taft's stand was so typical of him that no writer ever suggested that he was merely mouthing the opinions of the anti-Nuremberg press.[30]

The only generalization that can be made about papers which disapproved of the trials were that they *tended* to be conservative or Republican. It might also be argued that this attitude was to some extent dictated by a general antipathy to the administration's foreign policy, but the political nature of their opposition was never obvious except in the *Chicago Daily Tribune*.

Closely linked with the newspapers' judgment on the trials was their view of the verdicts. As one might expect, those newspapers which condemned the trials castigated the verdicts as being victor's vengeance, plain and simple.[31] On the other hand, a paper's approval of the trials did not automatically mean that it agreed totally with the sentences. Granted that for some pro-Nuremberg editors the judgments revealed a commendable

28. For example: The *Chicago Tribune, New York Daily News, Wall Street Journal, New York Daily Mirror, World Telegram, New York Journal American, Rocky Mountain News*.

29. For example: *Boston Herald, Los Angeles Times,* and The *Oregonian.*

30. William Smith White, *The Taft Story* (New York: Harper, 1954), pp. 47–48; *New York Times,* October 9, 1946, p. 17.

31. *Dallas Morning News,* October 2, 1946; *New York Daily Mirror,* October 2, 1946.

objectivity because, in their view, the judges had risen above national prejudice and decided each defendant's case on its own merits.[32] Others cried: "Too lenient! It should be Gallows for All."[33]

Was there a common bond among the newspapers which held that the verdict had been too lenient? Many were decidedly left of center in their partisanship. It is curious to note that immediately before the trials started, the *Worker* printed the Communist party's approval of Nuremberg. The information was communicated by this news release: "Pravda, *official* organ of the Communist Party central committee, in a dispatch giving *official* reaction to the opening of the Nuernberg trials, said today that they showed that the 'sound democratic conscience of nations had won.' . . . The trials show the 'inevitable fate of those who dare to raise the sword against the world and should aid in the promotion of an organization to ensure a long and enduring peace.' "[34]

The liberal papers of America agreed with this statement. They also vehemently seconded the lone dissenting vote of the Soviet judge to the acquittals. It is highly improbable that these liberal editors were following a party line, but rather that they held some basic attitudes of the Left which made them more intransigent than others toward leniency for the German defendants. Nazism had been a totalitarianism of the Right and had stood diametrically opposed to the Left, not only in its extreme form of Communism, but also in its more liberal manifestations. There was, moreover, an anticapitalist persuasion in most of these papers which gave emotional vehemence to their stand against the industrialists and financiers of the enemy regime.

Lest any false generalization be inferred, papers which are not considered liberal also opposed any mitigation of penalties for the Nazis. For example, the *Philadelphia Inquirer*, which described its allegiance as independent Republican, demanded

32. *Baltimore Sun*, October 2, 1946; *Boston Herald*, October 3, 1946; *Milwaukee Journal*, October 2, 1946; *New York Times*, September 29, 1946, 4:10; *Oregonian*, October 2, 1946; *Detroit Free Press*, October 2, 1946.
33. *Philadelphia Inquirer*, October 2, 1946; *Brooklyn Eagle*, October 7, 1946; *Daily Worker*, October 2, 1946; *Los Angeles Times*, October 2, 1946; *PM*, October 3, 1946; *Philadelphia Inquirer*, October 2, 1946.
34. *Worker*, November 23, 1945, p. 2; italics mine.

that not one of the German defendants escape the extreme penalty.[35]

The judgment of American newspapers on specific questions concerning the trials manifested a great diffusion of interest and opinion. Many theories were advanced to justify the trials' legality. Most newspapers appealed to the Kellogg-Briand Pact,[36] but some based the court's competence on an analogy between international and common law.[37] A third group founded Nuremberg's justice on what might be called a pragmatic or natural-law theory. This view often was presented in the popular terminology of "judgment of humanity," "conscience of mankind," "popular opinion," and "consensus of all right-thinking men."[38] The *New York Times* stood out as a champion of this last theory because it consistently presented the trials in its editorials, its features, and even in its news reporting and captions as being legally based upon the dictates of morality and a natural-law philosophy.[39]

Newspaper discussion of the Tribunal's legality repeated standard arguments because few editors comprehended the objection raised concerning retroactive law. Most newsmen began with the assumption that "the world's conscience cries out for justice and for punishment. It will not accord immunity to any individual on the basis of mere legal subterfuge."[40]

The second major topic of interest was the principle establishing the responsibility of individuals under international law. The

35. *Philadelphia Inquirer*, October 2, 1946.

36. E.g., *Detroit News, Boston Herald, Brooklyn Eagle, Los Angeles Times, Oregonian, San Francisco Chronicle.*

37. *New York Times, Detroit Free Press, Detroit News, Times-Picayune,* and *Washington Post.*

38. *Baltimore Sun, Philadelphia Inquirer, Oregonian, Milwaukee Journal, New York Times.*

39. *New York Times*, December 6, 1945, p. 26; October 2, 1946, p. 28; October 10, 1946, p. 8; October 3, 1946, p. 26; October 2, 1946, p. 20; October 16, 1946, p. 26.

40. *New York Times*, December 6, 1945, p. 26. Two papers did consider complicated legal questions: the *Baltimore Sun*, which discussed the relationship between the prohibition on enactments and the concept of *mens rea*, i.e., the idea of a criminal mentality, (October 1, 1946, p. 12); the *Washington Evening Star* championed a progressive doctrine of international law that would not allow the code to be held fixed in the mechanical application of a Latin tag such as *ex post facto* (October 1, 1946, p. A–10).

vast majority of editors did not realize the novelty of the decision, and none discussed the difficulties involved in inserting this
new principle into the long-established positivistic international
law pattern. They argued simply that twentieth-century war had
made imperative the punishment of heads of state if man were to
survive.[41]

Two minority reports, however, were submitted on Nuremberg's doctrine of individual accountability. The first held that
the court had not gone far enough. Some papers were outraged
by the leniency accorded the Nazi military defendants.[42] Others
wanted all enemy diplomats swinging in the Bavarian death-
house.[43]

Another section of the press sharpened its tomahawks for the
locks of the industrialists and financiers. The Communist *Worker*
devoted its full front page on three successive days to the men
acquitted at Nuremberg and had a special article on each pointing out his nefarious role in international high finance.[44] The
liberal *PM* and the *Brooklyn Eagle* reiterated this theme.[45]

The *St. Louis Post-Dispatch* offered a novel view regarding the
industrialists. It admitted that usually only the actual authors of
crimes were punished, but it asserted that war crimes were
different. "These men are not being tried entirely as individuals,"
the editorial stated. "They are being tried as representatives of
the varied groups that built the Nazi war machine and ordered
the ghastly crimes it inflicted upon Europe's people." [46] For the
Post-Dispatch editor, men became symbols. Nazi industrialists
had to be marked as "merchants of death," and letting off the
most notorious arms manufacturer of the Third Reich would not
achieve this goal.

The second group of papers which condemned Nuremberg's
principle of personal responsibility did so because they thought

41. *Times-Picayune*, October 17, 1946. For a discussion of the positivistic legal doctrine in regard to the principle of responsibility see Chapter
III.
42. *Daily Worker*, October 2, 1946; *Detroit News*, October 1, 1946.
43. *PM*, October 3, 1946.
44. *Daily Worker*, October 3, 1946.
45. *PM*, October 3, 1946; *Brooklyn Eagle*, October 3, 1946.
46. *St. Louis Post-Dispatch*, November 24, 1945. See also October 17,
1946.

that the court had gone too far. They editorialized that the
nooses which now hung over each losing leader's head would
drive future leaders of warring nations to desperate measures to
avoid surrender.[47] These papers also demanded to know exactly
what was now required of an individual citizen if his country
embarked on an evil course. If he had to resign his position and
work against his country, what happened to basic notions of
loyalty and patriotism?[48] Some papers worried about the burden of responsibility being extended to many lesser but involved
persons. For example, what about those German scientists who
were being so avidly sought after by the Allied governments?[49]
Other editors declared that it was unjust to teach the military
man "not to reason why" and then punish him for not making his
own decisions.[50]

Finally, the papers gave thought to the future as well as to the
past and present. What would Nuremberg's effect be upon the
development of international law? One paper went so far as to
say, that no matter whether the trials were right or wrong, legal
or illegal, they would be beneficial for the future.[51] Another
maintained that new strength had been given to existing international law and new statutes had been established for future
enforcement.[52]

Other newspapers, influenced by postwar internationalism,
stressed that Nuremberg's influence upon the future would come
through adoption of its principles by the United Nations Organization and through establishment of a permanent international
tribunal.[53] Editors supported such a court even if they realized
that it would place new limitations on the sovereignty of nations,
even that of the United States.[54]

The daily press, however, did not present exclusively the
editor's opinion, for often on the very next page his views were

47. *Wall Street Journal*, October 4, 1946; *New York Daily Mirror*, October 2, 1946.
48. *New York Daily News*, October 2, 1946.
49. *Oregonian*, October 2, 1946.
50. *Brooklyn Eagle*, October 15, 1946.
51. *Boston Herald*, October 1, 1946.
52. *Oregonian*, October 1, 1946.
53. *Dallas Morning News*, October 2, 1946; *Oregonian*, October 1, 1946.
54. *Milwaukee Journal*, October 2, 1946; *Oregonian*, October 1, 1946.

confirmed or challenged by the syndicated feature writers. These columnists' influence on public opinion can be particularly significant because syndication gives them a broader audience than that of any newspaper editor and because they enjoy the strong loyalty of millions of followers who have a remarkable confidence in their judgment.

The commendations and defenses of the Nuremberg trials among the columnists ranged alphabetically and emotionally all the way from the humane, thoughtful articles of Hanson W. Baldwin, the respected military expert of the *New York Times*, to the mordant essays of Walter Winchell. Between these extremes were such well-known columnists as David Lawrence, Walter Lippmann, Raymond Moley, and Edgar Ansel Mowrer.[55]

Most pro-Nuremberg columnists presented standard arguments in defense of the Tribunal. One stressed that the verdicts were military and severe but nevertheless just.[56] Others sustained the legality of the trials on the basis of the Kellogg-Briand Pact or a developing international legal code modeled on the evolution of domestic common law.[57] Nuremberg also was hailed as a glorious example of the ability of the Allies to work together.[58]

If most presentations were unremarkable, we do note three distinctive approaches in other columnists: optimism in Walter Lippmann, moral concern in Max Lerner, and emotional intensity in Walter Winchell.

No one surpassed Walter Lippmann in his eulogies of the Nuremberg trials. He told his ten million feminine fans in the *Ladies' Home Journal* as well as his newspaper readers: "For my own part, I do not think it rash to prophesy that the principles of this trial will come to be regarded as ranking with the Magna Charta, the *habeas corpus* and the Bill of Rights as landmarks in the development of law. The Nuremberg principle goes deeper into the problem of peace, and its effect may prove to be more

55. Of thirteen leading columnists, nine favored Nuremberg and four condemned the proceedings.

56. *New York Times*, October 2, 1946, p. 20.

57. David Lawrence in the *Detroit News*, October 9, 1946; Raymond Morley in the *Washington Evening Star*, October 2, 1946; Edgar Ansel Mowrer in the *St. Louis Post-Dispatch*, October 3, 1946. The conservative Lawrence's condemnation of Taft's stand again warns us against hasty generalizations concerning the relationship between political affiliations and views on Nuremberg.

58. William L. Shirer in the *Charlotte Observer*, October 6, 1946.

far-reaching than anything else that has yet been agreed to by the peoples of the world." [59]

If the novel tenets of Nuremberg for columnists such as David Lawrence and Max Lerner were those of individual responsibility and the new reign of conscience in human affairs, Walter Lippmann believed that Nuremberg's new concept was the limitation of national sovereignty by a higher law. An international code now ruled the will and actions of any and all sovereign states.

Max Lerner distinctively presented the Tribunal as a morality play. The court's proceedings were a ritual by which mankind attempted by "an immense and revolutionary effort to give utterance to a collective human conscience, to bring into being a collective standard by which gross violations of that conscience can be punished." [60] Indeed, no statutory law could reveal the enormity of the Nazi crimes. It was only by holding these outrages against the norm of the most elementary conscience of human beings that their hideous nature could be perceived.

Max Lerner finally answered an obvious objection to his interpretation by saying that "some may gibe that I am speaking of a 'human conscience' and a 'moral sense' that are vague and formless, things on which no body of law can be built. I submit they are the only things that a body of law ever rests on. The surest basis of a future world society lies in the sense of our common plight. When a Negro is lynched, all of us are strung upon that rope. When the Jews were burned in the Nazi furnaces, all of us were burned." [61]

The last but by far not the least of the Nuremberg champions, Walter Winchell, treated his audience of twenty-five million readers, the largest of any columnist, to a typical display of verbal pyrotechnics. [62] The main theme of his "Broadway" col-

59. Walter Lippmann, "The Meaning of the Nuremberg Trial," *Ladies' Home Journal* 63 (June, 1946): 32. See also *Charlotte Observer,* October 2, 1946.

60. Max Lerner, *Actions and Passions: Notes on the Multiple Revolutions of Our Times* (New York: Simon and Schuster, 1949), pp. 261–63.

61. Ibid., p. 263.

62. Charles Fisher, *The Columnists* (New York: Howell Soskin, 1944), p. 89 (hereafter cited as Fisher, *Columnists*). Although scholarly readers might take exception to an extended treatment of Walter Winchell, his writings are included because of the wide circulation of his column.

umn of October 6, 1946, entitled "Heil Hitler!" was that the trials were excellent but the acquittals were a travesty of justice. The court admitted that Schacht, Von Papen, Fritzsche, and the General Staff had aided the Nazis in their conquest, "yet they were aquitted because legalistic mumbo-jumbo came to the conclusion that they weren't responsible for waging an aggressive war. . . . But an American who parks his car on the wrong side of the street must pay a fine or go to the clink." [63]

This logical gem was followed by a Winchell witticism as the columnist took up each of the declarations of "not guilty." "The German General Staff was treated so nicely by the Allies—you'd think they were indicted as seditionists." [64] This military group was, for Winchell, the embodiment of the aggressive malice of the German people. Second, he observed: "The State department's dopelomats are probably breathing easier now that Von Papen, who was in the same racket, has been acquitted." [65]

Walter Winchell pungently capsuled his philosophy by the regret which ended his article: "Twelve Nazis will hang—instead of Twelve Million." [66]

Among the columnists, the triumvirate of Paul Mallon, Westbrook Pegler, and Dorothy Thompson headed the opposition to Nuremberg. Mallon scoffed at the idea that the trials would stop future aggressors, because the verdicts had only proved that to lose a war was a deadly crime. A victorious aggressor certainly would not hand himself over to punishment, and if he lost, Nuremberg would make no difference to him because national wartime leaders have always risked hanging "especially among the least civilized people." [67]

Westbrook Pegler brought up blustering barrages against those American leaders who had participated in the trial venture. His article, "Lynching Them at Nuremberg," claimed that by the Tribunal's endorsement of retroactive law, "the United States now stands committed to an article of Hitlerism which to Americans, in our normal frame of mind, is a monstrosity.

63. *Charlotte Observer*, October 6, 1946.
64. Ibid.
65. Ibid.
66. Ibid.
67. *New York Journal American*, October 8, 1946.

Adopted in our own domestic system of justice it would subject to the death penalty any person thinking criminal thoughts." [68]

Pegler contended that Nuremberg had committed the nation's government to an evil of which few Americans were aware. The times were confused; Americans felt too secure in their constitutional guarantee against *ex post facto* law. Even if the press had attempted to acquaint the public with the threat to their legal liberties, "it would have been futile, anyway, because the government was determined to follow Roosevelt on this rash and flippant commitment the airy impudence of which Elliott Roosevelt indicated in one of the articles by which he is recouping his fortune as a historian of unverified statement and incidents." [69]

Pegler then threw his bouquet to the courage of Senator Robert Taft and hurried on to slay his last monster for that morning, Justice Robert Jackson, cutting off the head of the liberal dragon on his backswing. "Robert Jackson, a justice of our Supreme Court, laid down the new law and conducted the prosecution in a role that placed him on the side of the lynching mobs and, to the cheers, be it noted, of those organized groups at home which invade the White House to threaten the President with race riots unless the national government take a hand against lynchers." [70]

Dorothy Thompson, very woman-like, changed her mind. In 1945 she told her eight and a half million readers that, although she knew of the objection which claimed the defendants' crimes were of dubious illegality when committed, she was not impressed with this problem. [71]

A year later in her column on the Nuremberg verdicts a new Dorothy Thompson emerged. At the beginning, she wrote, the trials had been a grandiose dream, a bright hope of establishing a new international law, but the ending was sour. "If now the people feel no great elation regarding the outcome, nothing more than a grim satisfaction that some, at least, of the wretches will get what they dished out to others, is it not because they doubt

68. *Charlotte Observer*, October 4, 1946.
69. Ibid.
70. Ibid.
71. Fisher, *Columnists*, pp. 30, 42; *San Francisco Chronicle*, November 26, 1945.

whether anything new has become established, beyond the precedent that whoever wins a war may put the leaders of the
vanquished on trial for their lives? Will this be a deterrent
to war? May it not, rather, make armies and states in any future
war incapable of compromise or surrender since every leader
will know that his own neck is forfeited to defeat." [72]

Another problem for her was the definition of aggression. She
pointed out that the prosecution had not charged the Nazis with
aggressive war against Britain and France, for these had first
declared war on Germany. The Nazi defendants were condemned for their invasion of Poland, but one of the countries
prosecuting them on this charge had participated in the attack.
Her conclusion was that unless crimes were defined in terms of
universal validity, Nuremberg was "merely a final incident in a
war, not the opening act of a new epoch of law, humaneness and
peace." [73]

These were some of the ways in which the columnists of
American newspapers delivered their judgments on Nuremberg.
Their viewpoints and arguments in general reflected the common citizen's hopes and fears rather than any novel or profound
insights into the nature of the greatest international trial in
history.

On the other hand, each of these feature writers did offer the
common fare spiced with his own personal experience, prejudice,
or philosophy. In that October of 1946 millions of Americans
learned the pros and contras of Nuremberg over their morning
coffee or riding the subway. Their favorite columnist provided
them with his unique view of the triumph or tragedy which had
taken place in the Bavarian courtroom.

The other printed sources of information and opinion readily
available to the general public, the mass circulation magazines,
also by and large seconded the public's favorable view of the
Tribunal.[74] In these publications are also found many of the
same arguments and views which appeared in the newspapers.[75]

72. *Washington Evening Star*, October 7, 1946.
73. Ibid.
74. Of twenty articles and editorials appearing in popular magazines, fifteen favored the trials, four opposed them, and one left the issue undecided.
75. Those supporting the trials; John Mason Brown, "Nuremberg—Century of Progress," *Saturday Review of Literature* 29 (August 24, 1946):
20–24 (hereafter cited as Brown, "Century of Progress"). Raymond Moley,

On the other hand, a few distinctive qualities marked the presentation of Nuremberg in these periodicals. First, unlike newspaper editorials, pro-Nuremberg magazines did not separate their general judgment of the Tribunal from their evaluation of its verdicts. Few questioned whether the sentences had been too lenient or too harsh, for these periodicals either favored the trials and the verdicts or they condemned both.

Again, unlike the diffusion of interest found in newspapers, the periodicals' treatment of the trials polarized around set questions. Foremost among these was the legal basis of the International Military Tribunal. The theories suggested by the magazines as a justification of the trials' law can be reduced to five. These were the Kellogg-Briand Pact, custom and conventions, morality and consensus of mankind, political decision, and a progressive theory of law.

These suggested bases generally were similar to those proposed in newspapers, but in the magazines the argument employed tended to be more elaborate and erudite. As we have noted, the newspapers and columnists also stressed the peace pact and customary law. The *New York Times* and Max Lerner developed at some length the trials' foundation in morality and the demands of the conscience of mankind.[76] On the other hand,

"Making History at Nuremberg," *Newsweek* 28 (September 30, 1946): 196; "Judgment Day at Nuremberg: World Law Takes a Long Stride Forward," *Senior Scholastic* 49 (November 12, 1945): 5–6; Vera Micheles Dean, "More Important than the Bomb!" *Rotarian* 29 (October, 1946): 8–10 (hereafter cited as Dean, "More Important than the Bomb!").

Those opposing the trials: "The Nurnberg Novelty," *Fortune* 32 (December, 1945): 140–41 (hereafter cited as "Novelty," *Fortune*); "The Nurnberg Confusion," *Fortune* 34 (December, 1946): 120–21, 256 (hereafter cited as "Confusion," *Fortune*); "Will Nuremberg Stop New Aggressors?" *Saturday Evening Post* 219 (November 2, 1946): 164; Genêt, "Letter from Nuremberg," *New Yorker* 22 (March 30, 1946): 76; James Marshall, Review of *The Nuremberg Trial and Aggressive War* by Sheldon Glueck, *Saturday Review of Literature* 29 (September 21, 1946): 9 (hereafter cited as Marshall, review of *Nuremberg Trial*).

76. In magazines this argument from morality was found in: Dean, "More Important Than the Bomb!", p. 10; Sheldon Glueck, "Justice for War Criminals," *American Mercury* 60 (March, 1945): 274, 280; *Life* 21 (October 14, 1946): 36; "Chalice of Nuremberg," *Time* 46 (December 10, 1945): 27 (hereafter cited as "Chalice," *Time*); "The Source," *Time* 46 (December 17, 1945): 27; "The Fallen Eagles," *Time* 46 (December 3, 1945): 29. This ethical foundation was attacked in "Confusion," *Fortune*, 120–21; Marshall, Review of *The Nuremberg Trial*, p. 9.

the periodicals' appeal to a progressive or pragmatic philosophy
of law was seldom found in other popular printed media.[77] Even
more distinctive of the periodicals was the appearance of the
theory of "political decision," which was more a substitute for a
legal foundation than a juridical justification of Nuremberg. This
interpretation held that the trials were fundamentally not an
action by a court of law but a formality enacted by executive
policy. The theory of Nuremberg as a political action in legal
trappings was confined mainly to these popular magazines.[78] The
general public and newspapers assumed the validity of outward
appearances and considered the Tribunal simply a judicial proceeding.

Other topics, compared with that of the legal basis, received
relatively limited attention in the magazines. The various writers
expressed opinions on particular aspects consonant with their
affirmative or negative judgment on the Tribunal, and then they
developed these specific subjects to prove the correctness of their
general verdict on Nuremberg.

In their evaluation of the Tribunal, the magazines were generally superior to the newspapers in both depth and penetration of
the factors involved. On the other hand, they still expressed basic
American values, attitudes, and assumptions, although dissenters
had begun to probe fundamentals and to question accepted
shibboleths of American mythology.

If we compare these judgments of American columnists, newspapers, and magazines with our findings concerning public opinion, we note many similarities. This agreement of the people and
the papers was not confined to general approbation of the Tribunal, for the popular press mirrored very accurately the heart

77. Note the labored terminology of one short sentence: "Prosecutor Jack-
son defended this pragmatic approach on the pragmatic ground that the end
justified the only practical means"; "Chalice," *Time*, p. 27. See also Heinz
Eulau, "The Nuremberg War-Crime Trial: Revolution in International
Law," *New Republic* 113 (November 12, 1945): 625; Brown, "Century of
Progress," p. 23. *Fortune* rejected this concept; "Confusion," p. 260.

78. This presentation of Nuremberg as a political act was found in Freda
Kirchwey, "Politics and Justice," *Nation* 163 (October 12, 1946): 396–97;
"Confusion," *Fortune*, p. 259; Charles E. Wyzanski, Jr., "Dangerous Prece-
dent," *Atlantic Monthly* 177 (April, 1946): 66–70. The theory was con-
demned by Thomas L. Karsten and James H. Mathias, "The Judgment at
Nuremberg," *New Republic* 115 (October 21, 1946): 512.

and mind of the average man. Seventy-five per cent of Americans polled approved the postwar trials of the German leaders. This judgment was echoed by 69 per cent of the columnists, 73 per cent of the newspapers, and 75 per cent of the periodicals.

These common views on postwar policy, war criminals, and the Tribunal raise a question as to what exactly is revealed concerning basic American attitudes? In other words, why did popular opinion give these answers? Do these sources reveal any pattern, any insight into the national character?

A legalistic-moralistic attitude toward international affairs has been described, hailed, and condemned as essentially and distinctively the American outlook.[79] The legalistic factor certainly seemed patent in popular views on Nuremberg. The American people did not spontaneously urge trials for war criminals, but support for such a program increased steadily during the war years. More significant, when the International Military Tribunal was proclaimed as United States policy, the American public overwhelmingly welcomed this solution to the war-crimes problem.

Newspapers, magazines, and columnists also revealed this legalism of the American mind in foreign affairs. They showed little interest in any alternative to the trials; only a few magazines and one paper ever considered whether the Tribunal might be, in truth, essentially a political action, not a legal process.[80] The administration policy apparently did appeal to the popular American tendency to find through law, solutions to their problems.

On the other hand, one must be careful in labeling this legalis-

79. "As you have no doubt surmised, I see the most serious fault of our past policy to lie in something that I might call the legalistic-moralistic approach to international problems. This approach runs like a red skein through our foreign policy of the last fifty years. . . . It is the belief that it should be possible to suppress the chaotic and dangerous aspirations of governments in the international field by the acceptance of some system of legal rules and restraints." George F. Kennan, *American Diplomacy, 1900–1950* (Chicago: University of Chicago Press, 1953), p. 95 (hereafter cited as Kennan, *American Diplomacy*). Dexter Perkins, *America's Quest for Peace* (Bloomington: Indiana University Press, 1962), pp. 10–11.

80. Some of the papers which rejected any alternative to a legal program were: *Baltimore Sun*, October 17, 1946; *Detroit News*, October 1, 1946; *Milwaukee Journal*, October 2, 1946; *New York Times*, January 22, 1961, p. 11.

tic attitude as something uniquely American. The British public was years ahead of Americans in its support of judicial action.[81] Nor can one shift the thesis to claim that Nuremberg resulted from the Anglo-Saxon legal tradition, at least in any exclusive sense. Franklin Roosevelt, the man who initiated action for an international tribunal, first became interested in legal proceedings from the precedent of the French trials of their "war criminals" at Riom.[82]

If the "moralism" often considered the basic American attitude toward international events could only be inferred from opinions expressed by the average citizens, it was bright and obvious in American newspapers.[83] We have noted Max Lerner's theory and how the *New York Times* was singular in its constant presentation of Nuremberg in terms of morality and natural law. Other papers also spoke of the trials in terms of the conscience of mankind, of absolute right and justice, of moral outrage, of fundamental law, of human nature violated, and of breaking the law of man and God. Some popular magazines strongly developed this theme and elaborated its ramifications for the Tribunal.

With legalism and moralism, the popular press reflected an idealism which was generally discernible among Americans.[84] Public opinion assumed that the United States was disinterestedly seeking justice for mankind at Nuremberg. The Russians might be pursuing political advantage, the French, revenge, but Americans were convinced that they approached the trials with an absolute altruism.[85]

In newspapers and periodicals the major opposition to Nuremberg seemed to have been directed against this idealism. Critics labelled the Tribunal "Victors' Vengeance" and "self-righteous hypocrisy" because they felt that the United States failed to acknowledge its darker motives for holding the trials. They

81. *Public Opinion Quarterly* 8 (Winter, 1944–45): 593.
82. William D. Leahy, *I Was There: The Personal Story of the Chief of Staff to President Roosevelt and Truman* (New York: McGraw-Hill, 1950), p. 81 (hereafter cited as Leahy, *I Was There*).
83. Perkins, *American Approach,* p. 73 and passim.
84. Almond, *American People and Foreign Policy,* pp. 60–62, 120, 121, 134, 136, 195, 242.
85. Ibid., p. 57.

argued that America was seeking selfish political goals and that administration officials were using the trials to divert the public's attention from the wartime failures of the United States political leadership.

Another American trait that the cultural and diplomatic historian might see revealed was a simplistic view of the international scene.[86] The picture reflected in the views of the general public and in popular publications was one of stark alternatives: black-white, good-bad, right-wrong. Popular opinion was much more certain concerning the guilt of the war's causation than were the experts. The ordinary citizen and editor frequently seemed to be oblivious to many of the intricate legal problems involved in a trial program and to the manifold political ramifications of the government's policy.

Not only was there an unawareness of the complexity of the situation, but the American public positively accepted a simple "devil" or "conspiracy" theory concerning World War II. The people's belief that a few wicked men had caused all the sufferings of their world was revealed in the high priority the public gave to the punishment of Nazi warlords, the clear distinction which they made between the leaders and the German people, and the low number of the enemy which Americans thought deserved execution. It is true that some notable exceptions to this simplistic approach appeared in popular magazines, but such exceptions were rare and usually written by lawyers. When the magazine editors expressed their views, they exhibited the same general proneness to oversimplification.

Popular attitudes toward Nuremberg also illustrate another suggested model of American reactions to foreign affairs, a corollary of the alleged tendency toward oversimplification. This pattern is that in long, complex international problems Americans usually switch from support of direct and decisive action to disillusionment, disinterest, and a feeling of hopelessness when the action does not quickly bring the desired results.[87] The search for a simple solution—the quick answer—certainly was

86. Paul A. L. Smith, "The Impact of International Events Upon Domestic Political Behavior" (Ph.D. diss., Princeton University, 1960), p. 40.

87. Kennan, *American Diplomacy*, pp. 95–96; Almond, *American People and Foreign Policy*, p. 76.

reflected in the "shoot them" mentality. It is also indicated by the
absorption in, and the high priority given to, the punishment of
enemy leaders rather than in coping with basic political, social,
and economic problems.

The drawn-out process of the Nuremberg trial, the complexity
of subsequent war-crime trials, and the complicated world created by the Cold War brought on the usual reaction among the
American people. Not only the United States government but
also the public apparently breathed a sigh of relief when the
occupation authority's gavel fell on the last war-crime trial. The
moral crusade against Hitler did not leave the world free for
peace; the trials that were to close the books upon aggressive
war had not ended threats and perils.

Another characteristic of Americans, illustrated by reactions to
Nuremberg, was their predilection for solving problems and
difficulties by means of American institutions and practices.[88] For
all the attempts of the lawyers to effect a legal synthesis and for
all the verbiage about the trials' being international in character,
Americans and Europeans, supporters and opponents, all considered the Tribunal essentially an American show. The people and
papers judged the actors and actions in the legal drama by
American law and American court practices. According to these
standards the precise correctness of the conduct of the trial and
its similarities with United States court procedures were of
greater moment than any abstract legal disputes. Public opinion
never acknowledged that "Americanism" of the Nuremberg court
often led to bewilderment of the other Allied prosecutors and of
the defense counsel.[89]

Finally, the public's attitude disclosed a heady American nationalism which at times shaded off into chauvinism. The popular view seems to have been that the enemy alone had been
responsible for the coming of the war, the enemy alone had
committed wartime atrocities, the enemy was naturally cruel and
brutal, and the enemy people, if not war-thirsty monsters, were

88. *Public Opinion Quarterly* 9 (Fall, 1945): 386, 532; 8 (Fall, 1944):
448, 455; 9 (Spring, 1945): 92; 9 (Winter, 1945–46): 533; 8 (Winter,
1944–45), 588; 9 (Summer, 1945), 246.
89. The *Detroit News*, October 11, 1946, was the only newspaper among
thirty that explicitly noted Nuremberg was governed by international law
standards and not the United States code.

at least too easily led to be trusted without control and punishment. The Germans must be guided, forced if necessary, to adopt the democratic American system of government as their only hope for reformation and salvation.

This nationalism appeared on the level of popular opinion. The Tribunal's legality was constantly evaluated by strictly domestic norms, i.e., the judicial principles of the United States. Moreover, in the popular mind the procedure of the court, the presentation of the American case and the wisdom of the American judge, left nothing to be desired and was a source of national pride. The public paid slight attention to Allied "war crimes" and seemed to drape the American flag over anything that might offend American sensibilities. Ernest O. Hauser perhaps presented the clearest picture of Nuremberg as a positive expression of American superiority and greatness. "From the very beginning of this joint effort, the United States carried the ball. Although the cooperation of other nations was genuine and sincere, there is ample proof to show that Nuremberg is a 100 per cent American concern. It was American initiative, American persistence, and American idealism that produced the final result in the face of serious difficulties." [90] The trials were brought about by a serious American effort to make cooperation among the United Nations a reality. Indeed, "starting from a shoestring," Hauser wrote, "American enterprise had produced a powerful machine, well equipped to hand down the historic verdict and to open a new age in international good conduct." [91]

We become conscious of this nationalism not only in eulogies of the nation's policy, but also in bitter attacks upon this supposedly naïve American patriotism or chauvinism. This dissent was peculiar to periodicals. Miss Janet Flanner, in her "Letters from Nuremberg" written for the New Yorker under the pseudonym Genêt, displayed the sophisticated attitude often associated with this magazine by attacking the myth of American superiority. She asserted not only that the United States had chosen the most difficult legal task, that of proving a conspiracy for aggressive war—a nebulous charge in the extreme—but also that the Americans had done the poorest job of any of the four

90. Hauser, "Backstage Battle at Nuremberg," p. 18.
91. Ibid., p. 138.

prosecuting teams. For her (as for a number of others), Goering was a sort of hero who ran rings around Jackson when the latter tried to cross-examine him.[92] The American lawyers, who she claimed were chosen for political considerations, were lacking in talent, and their work was further vitiated by adherence to American myths and their passion for pursuing the irrelevant.[93]

   Fortune condemned the public's "patriotism" because it thought that the people viewed the trials as a pageant of "our heroes against their villains," a simple morality play with the absolute justice of an American western.[94] On the other hand, *Fortune* itself displayed a flag-waving, Fourth-of-July nationalism unexpected in a journal of its urbanity. The editors violently defended the sacrosanct nature of national sovereignty, especially against Nuremberg's principle of universal jurisdiction which, *Fortune* pointed out, would invade America's traditional rights.[95] The magazine's position apparently was never really integrated with its endorsement of the new role of the United States in world affairs and in international organizations. *Fortune's* ambivalence was perhaps typical of the American mind of the 1940's, emotionally and intellectually committed to internationalism but with little understanding of the unpleasant ramifications that this new foreign policy might entail.

   92. "There had been no 'battle of ideas,' because Jackson seemed not to be able to think of any." Genêt, "Letter from Nuremberg," *New Yorker* 22 (March 30, 1946): 76. See also Francis Biddle, "Nuremberg: The Fall of the Superman," *American Heritage* 13 (August, 1962): 65–72.
   93. "Several of our legal men have evidenced an ignorance of Europe, politically and historically, which might have seemed patriotic back home but seems something else at what has been earnestly described as the greatest trial in history." Genêt "Letter from Nuremberg," *New Yorker* 21 (January 5, 1946): 48. See also ibid., 22 (March 23, 1946): 78–84; 22 (March 30, 1946): 76.
   94. "Confusion," *Fortune*, p. 263. *Fortune* magazine was unique among business periodicals in its interest in the war crime trials. At the time of the verdicts a few others carried articles such as Adolphe J. Warner, "What Case Against the German Bankers?" *Commercial and Financial Chronicle* 165 (January 2, 1947): 4, 17; and "Farbenindustrie Officials Indicted as War Criminals," *Rubber Age* 60 (May, 1947): 211; but in subsequent years little notice appeared in business periodicals.
   The reason for *Fortune's* articles on Nuremberg was probably the interest of its editor Herbert Solow. In an article in 1949, he recapitulated what had previously been printed in the magazine and stated his own opinion, which was basically the negative judgment which had appeared in all *Fortune* articles from the time of the verdicts.
   95. Ibid., p. 260.

If the popular judgment on Nuremberg revealed some of the fundamental attitudes of the American people in foreign affairs, it more specifically reflected opinions current in the mid 1940's. For, although this was a period of rapid transition in United States foreign policy, the era was still primarily dominated by the ideas that the nation could do business with the Russians, that peace such as the country had enjoyed in the prewar period was a definite and obtainable possibility, and that internationalism was the solution to the problems of the United States and the world.[96]

Nuremberg fitted into this pattern. If it was not actually the greatest example of friendly cooperation between the Soviets and the United States, it was at least a major proof of its possibility for those who thought that we could work with Stalin. Second, the elimination of the Axis leaders by the Tribunal was held to be a major key to the restoration of the situation before the war. The logic of this idea was as simple and appealing to the newspapers as it was to the average citizen. The German warmongers had destroyed the peace by aggressive war, but through Nuremberg the Nazi leaders were dead or imprisoned. Therefore, the peace of the world was once more intact. Simple was the logic, and perhaps fallacious, but it was strong with the hopes and dreams of the immediate postwar era.

The Nuremberg court also had its place in the theory of a peace sought through world organizations. As noted, among the newspapers there was only one exception to the linking of approval of the trials with approbation of a world society. The Tribunal often was thought of as a judicial function of the people of the world, and the hope for the survival of the Tribunal's principles was staked upon their adoption in the Criminal Code of the United Nations. The trials were also seen as the first step in the world's establishing an international criminal court.

Finally, we might consider the role of the United States government in the formation of public opinion. Did the administration merely follow the mandate of the people and the press, or did it totally disregard popular sentiment and decide what it objectively considered to be the best course? In simple terms, did the government lead the people or was it led by them?

96. Almond, *American People and Foreign Policy*, p. xii.

Although a residual good will and support of its citizens is brought to any project which the United States government adopts as its own, the administration did not depend on this benevolent attitude in regard to war-crime trials. As we have seen in Chapter II, the State Department conducted an active program of informing and molding public opinion to favor legal procedures. Is one to conclude from this governmental activity that the administration led the people like sheep to "ba-a-a" in approval? This interpretation seems to be borne out, for the people who were not in favor of or were not interested in the trial method, before its official adoption, changed their positions completely and gave full approval to the Tribunal when the administration established its program. Superficially it does seem that the government piped and the people danced.

On the other hand, the study of basic American attitudes toward foreign affairs has shown how closely Nuremberg fits in with the supposed idealistic, moralistic, and legalistic assumptions of the American people. Rather than casually concluding that the government dominated the national intellect, a sophisticated judgment might be made that the administration leaders, consciously or unconsciously, were forced to operate within a framework of possibilities allowed by and acceptable to the American public. These patterns of response of the American people did form firm barriers that limited the alternatives for government officials. While the American people were led down the road to Nuremberg, they were not duped, deceived, or betrayed. They were guided along a way compatible with their attitudes and aims, a path ultimately of their own choosing.

This was the judgment on Nuremberg of the American public as expressed through individual opinions and popular media. The large majority approved Nuremberg and all its works; a minority was intensely opposed to the proceedings. The general approval was based not only on the event in Bavaria, but more fundamentally on Nuremberg's consonance with the traditional presuppositions of Americans in regard to foreign policy. These factors evolved in the context of the dominant forces of the mid 1940's—internationalism and wartime hatred of the enemy.

6

Men of God Judge the Justice of Men

The judgment on Nuremberg of the religious communities in the United States is of particular interest and value because church and synagogue always have taken as their prophetic duty the role of placing the activities of men and nations under the judgment of God. They have claimed a clearer vision than others because their commitment to God placed them apart from secular considerations of expediency and self-interest. Churchmen also have argued that their principles and values supply norms and standards necessary to evaluate accurately and impartially.

Churchmen, as critics, had a special interest in Nuremberg. The trials engaged the religious mind with ultimate questions: life and death, guilt and punishment, vengeance and atonement, a higher law and the "conscience of humanity." If the church's role is usually conceived in terms of charity and mercy, still, because of the enormity of the crimes and the defendants' lack of repentance, the men of God were torn between forgiveness and retribution. This conflict was greatest in human terms since religious bodies had themselves been victims of the accused. Catholics and Protestants suffered seriously, but their persecution pales into insignificance when compared with the ordeal of the Jewish people. As the evidence at Nuremberg irrefutably documents, six and a half million Jews were sacrificed upon the altar of "racial purity" and "aryan superiority." [1]

Although diversity of judgment existed among the three major religious communities, each group did have a certain unity within itself created by interest in one particular facet of the trials.

1. Edmund A. Walsh, S.J., *Total Power: A Footnote to History* (Garden City, N.Y.: Doubleday, 1949), pp. 99, 100, 102, 119, 137–38.

The typical opinion of the Jewish community devoted little attention to Nuremberg's legal and political ramifications. There was an assumption that anything which was an instrument of righteous retribution against the Nazi monsters had to be legally valid.[2] Only one magazine, *Commentary*, the semi-official voice of reform Jewry, expressed a dissenting judgment by printing articles and editorials stating that the Tribunal's law was retroactive and that social scientists most likely would find that starvation, chaos, and hopelessness rather than the deeds of the indicted Nazi leaders provoked the persecution of minorities and the desire for aggression.[3]

The decisive and distinctive Jewish concern was the verdicts. Did the court, as far as humanly possible, make the criminals pay for their atrocities? Had the moral sense of mankind, outraged for so long, found satisfaction in the sentences rendered upon the Nazi leaders?

The answer of the Jewish community to these questions was loud and clear. The verdicts were greeted by cries of anguish, wrath, and outrage. Twelve German monsters swinging on the gallows was the least that was expected. The Jewish people were aghast to find other defendants receiving only prison terms and three German leaders acquitted. Jewish newspapers and periodicals, the Yiddish press, the rabbis of major synagogues, as well as Christians interested in Jewish questions, reacted with disgust to the judges' leniency which seemed so disproportionate to the crimes of the defendants and to the sufferings that the Jewish community had endured.[4]

2. *Jewish Examiner*, November 30, 1945, p. 1, December 7, 1945, p. 1; *B'nai B'rith Messenger*, October 4, 1946, p. 4; *Youngstown Jewish Times*, October 25, 1946, p. 3; "The Nuremberg Trials," *Opinion* 16 (December, 1945): 5 (hereafter cited as "Trials," *Opinion*); "Can Human Rights Be Enforced?" *Menorah Journal* 25 (January–March, 1947): 85–91.

3. Milton R. Konvitz, "Will Nuremberg Serve Justice?" *Commentary* 1 (January 9, 1946): 6–12 (hereafter cited as Konvitz, "Will Nuremberg Serve Justice?"); Milton R. Konvitz, *"Ex Post Facto* at Nuremberg," *Commentary* 1 (July, 1946): 91–92; Sidney Herzberg, "The Month in History," *Commentary* 2 (November, 1946): 457.

4. *Jewish Examiner*, October 4, 1946; *B'nai B'rith Messenger*, October 4, 1946; *Jewish Times*, October 11, 1946; *Jewish Advocate*, October 10, 1946; *National Jewish Post*, October 10, 1946. In contrast, Richard L. Stokes presented in the *St. Louis Post-Dispatch* an opinion diametrically opposed to the views of Jewish papers on the verdict. "The most shocking of all the

Jewish opinion condemned the judgments at Nuremberg not only because of the clemency shown to some of the German defendants but also because the Nuremberg judges had decided that they did not have the competence to punish the accused for any atrocity against a minority unless this offence had been committed as part of aggressive war. In light of the unheard-of sufferings in prewar Germany, the deep anguish of the Jewish community to this apparently rigid legalism (which was almost totally overlooked by other opinion media) can well be imagined.[5]

Although most Jews expressed anger, grief, or sorrow over the deficiencies of the verdicts, their general opinion of the Tribunal's influence upon the future was enthusiastic. With a few exceptions they voiced the belief that Nuremberg's real significance had been the trials' creation of a precedent in international law which declared aggression to be the supreme crime and those who carried out the nefarious orders of a state engaged in unjust war to be criminals.[6]

One of the most optimistic statements of Nuremberg's impact on the future was Harry L. Golden's declaration in the *Carolina Israelite* that "the historical significance of the forthcoming trial at Nuremberg cannot be overestimated. It constitutes a noble departure in international law. The verdict will affect not only the fate of the twenty-four miserable individuals responsible for the agony and suffering of millions of human beings but will, it

---

verdicts was the death sentence passed upon Julius Streicher. His condemnation was clearly a political and not a judicial act. He was acquitted of conspiracy to which he pleaded guilty and convicted ostensibly for crimes against humanity of which he was not proved to have committed a single one, unless a demolished synagogue may be so rated. He is to die solely for the expression of anti-Semitic opinion. It would be almost as just to strangle Henry Ford for the diatribes of the *Dearborn Independent*. Whether or not by design the judgment brought reassurance to five of the greatest modern forces—high finance, propaganda, the Vatican, world Jewry and the military and naval caste of all countries"; October 4, 1946.

5. *Jewish Examiner,* October 4, 1946, p. 1; *Intermountain Jewish News,* October 10, 1946, p. 4; *National Jewish Post,* October 10, 1946, p. 5; *Jewish Times,* October 11, 1946, p. 6.

6. *B'nai B'rith Messenger,* October 4, 1946, p. 4; *National Jewish Post,* October 10, 1946, p. 5; *Youngstown Jewish Times,* October 25, 1946, p. 3; *Jewish Exponent,* October 4, 1946, p. 4; *Jewish Advocate,* October 10, 1946, p. 1.

is hoped, represent the beginnings of a new morality, which says that no state or power may commit crimes against its citizens and go unpunished, and that, it is the duty of civilized society as a whole, to take action against criminals who wear the cloak of state authority." [7]

Protestants were primarily concerned with the legal foundation of the London Agreement and Charter and the Tribunal. The reason for the emphasis on this aspect, which was not the pivotal interest of other religious groups, was perhaps that Protestants were not as personally and emotionally involved as Jews and not as disturbed by the Russian specter as were the Catholics. Nuremberg was for them essentially another step in the long and hard road which men of good-will were traveling in order to arrive at a world without war.

From this Protestant viewpoint it was of crucial importance that men recognize the legality and competence of the Nuremberg court, for if the judicial foundations of the trials could be doubted and questioned, the principles which Nuremberg created could not become a precedent for actions furthering the goal of peace on earth. Protestant spokesmen therefore defended the legality and necessity of the Tribunal by declaring that all suggested alternatives were inadequate, that the Kellogg-Briand Pact was applicable to the Nazi leaders, and that the nations had subscribed to other customs and conventions which could condemn the enemies' crimes.[8] The Germans, moreover, had out-

7. Harry L. Golden, "Justice Jackson Will Unfold Nazi Tragedy," *Carolina Israelite* 2 (December, 1945): 10.
8. "The Nazi Trials," *Christian Century* 63 (August 15, 1945): 926–28; "Was It a Trial by Victors?" *Christian Century* 63 (October 30, 1946): 1300; "The Crime of War," *Information Service of the Federal Council of Churches of Christ in America* (June 23, 1945), p. 4. Some special problems are involved in establishing the attitudes of the religious press. Most Protestant papers and magazines at that time dealt strictly with religious topics, only infrequently alluding to national or international affairs. Consequently, most contained little or no mention of Nuremberg.

Catholic diocesan weeklies, on the other hand, were and are, in the words of one study, "Newspapers serving the Catholics of their dioceses, or of a group of dioceses in much the same way that small-town weeklies serve their communities. They included many features of the secular newspaper— local, national and foreign news, editorials. . . ." Consequently, we do find items on the trials. The problem here is that "most of the columns are syndicated by the National Catholic Welfare Conference or one of the national Catholic organizations associated with it. . . . In addition . . . several diocesan weeklies, notably the Denver *Register* and *Our Sunday Visitor* are is-

raged the moral sensibilities of all men, and therefore humanity itself should judge the culprits. This, indeed, was held to be the significance of Nuremberg, because for the first time the "voice of civilization" had had its say in the condemnation of aggression and crimes against humanity; mankind had declared that law, not national sovereignty, was supreme.[9]

Some Protestant periodicals did point out facts which flawed the effects of the trials. Two Lutheran papers are noteworthy in this regard. *Lutheran Outlook*, in spite of its general commendation of the trials, waxed eloquently on the Communists' association with Hitler during the invasion of Poland and found valid the charge which the *Christian Century* had rejected: "When did criminals qualify to act as judges over their fellow transgressors?"

What made the *Outlook*'s editorial unique among Protestant publications was the prominence it gave to the question of American guilt. "And when we are reminded," the magazine stated, "that the Nurenberg indictments include such crimes as the killing of defenseless civilians and the enslavement of entire populations, our feeling of discomfort begins to take on more of the sense of shame. The ominous clouds of the atomic bombs dropped on Hiroshima and Nagasaki rise like ghosts to haunt us, and from the hoarse throats of millions of German soldiers held as slaves in Allied concentration camps we seem to hear the cry, 'Hypocrisy!' "[10]

Lutheran Youth centered its misgivings on the suicide of Hermann Goering. It cited a secular journal's report that, for many

sued in a number of different editions for other cities." Therefore, the articles on Nuremberg were often reprints rather than the expression of an individual paper's editorial policy. "A Study of the Roman Catholic Press in America," Ibid., 25 (June 22, 1946): 1 (hereafter cited as "Roman Catholic Press," *Information Service*).

9. "Majestic Justice," *Christian Century* 63 (October 16, 1946): 1238–40. Reiteration of the almost universal Protestant affirmation of the legality of the trials appeared also in denominational publications which shared a common faith with interdenominational periodicals in Nuremberg's justice. David de Forest Burrell, "The New International Law," *Presbyterian* 116 (October 17, 1946): 11 (hereafter cited as Burrell, "New International Law"); "Guilty," *Christian* [the Methodist] *Advocate*, October 10, 1946, p. 1284.

10. "Nazi Leaders Hang for War Crimes," *The Lutheran Outlook* 15 (October, 1946): 294–95 (hereafter cited as "Nazi Leaders Hang," *Lutheran Outlook*).

Germans, the death of this Nazi bigwig was a snatching of triumph from defeat and commented: "Göring's one sharp breath-taking act wiped away the months of painstaking work. . . . could it be that the whole psychological effect of the Nuremberg trial was on such a flimsy footing that a single poison capsule . . . could destroy it? Only time can tell, but it has a 50–50 chance of answering with a roaring 'yes.' " [11]

Although some Protestant critics censured individual aspects of the Tribunal's activity, only one publication absolutely condemned the legality of the Nuremberg proceedings. This voice was *Christianity and Crisis,* a biweekly journal founded by Reinhold Niebuhr in 1941 to arouse American churches from isolationism in the face of Nazi atrocities. In "A Report on Germany," Niebuhr stressed German realization of their guilt, their hatred for the former Nazi leaders, and the danger for the conquerors because "the greatest evil of history is the vindictive passion of men." [12]

In a secular magazine, *Common Sense,* Niebuhr developed his evaluation of Nuremberg under the title "Victor's Justice." "One of the saddest aspects of human history," he began, "is the inevitable taint with which victorious nations tarnish the justice of their cause by the manner in which they exploit their victory." [13]

Niebuhr considered attempts at postwar justice to be necessarily vitiated by the blindness of the victors toward "the moral hazards involved in the business of being "judges in [their] own case.' " [14] The Allies could not see that their own crimes were imitative of the Nazi outrages, nor would they admit that, even in their case, absolute power breeds injustice. "If we did not so easily distill illusions of omniscience from our military omnipotence we would also practice greater circumspection in the criminal trials which are now proceeding." [15]

11. "News and Notes," *Lutheran Youth* 11 (November, 1946): 4.
12. Reinhold Niebuhr, "A Report on Germany," *Christianity and Crisis* 2 (October 14, 1946): 13 (hereafter cited as Niebuhr, "Report on Germany").
13. Reinhold Niebuhr, "Victors' Justice," *Common Sense* 15 (January, 1946): 6.
14. Ibid., p. 7.
15. Ibid.

Niebuhr held that no law or court existed to try the Nazis for aggression and that they should be punished only for "crimes against commonly accepted standards of humanity." He also doubted Nuremberg's justice because, even if Justice Jackson enunciated "hollow promises" that all nations would be judged by this new law in the future, the United Nations charter had not incorporated any such decision.[16]

A distinctive aspect of Reinhold Niebuhr's presentation is his open attack upon the "liberals" who detected an anti-Russian policy in all those who desired "a sane and healthy Germany." A study of newspaper attitudes reveals a generally liberal approbation of Nuremberg and of a harsh occupation policy, but few writers noted this interrelation. The only other presentation of this connection appeared in the vitriolic charges of anti-Nuremberg congressmen.

If Protestant concern for the world peace movement influenced its opinion on the legal basis for the trials, this consideration also colored its hopes for future benefits from Nuremberg. In those expectations Protestants agreed with Jewish writers that the judges' decision declaring aggression to be the "supreme crime" in international law and leaders of nations engaged in such a war to be criminals was perhaps "the most significant verdict ever handed down by a court of law."[17] Mankind had translated his moral hatred of unjust war into a legal principle which could aid the development of peaceful relations between states.

If the *Christian Century's* appellation of "Majestic Justice" for Nuremberg might be considered a slight exaggeration, it did indicate the general Protestant evaluation of the Nuremberg trials.

The Catholic reaction to the Tribunal also revealed some definite characteristics, but no rigid uniformity of opinion.

The question of the Tribunal's legality was not the major concern of Catholics, but discussion of this topic did reveal a

16. Ibid., p. 8.
17. *Christian Advocate,* October 10, 1946, p. 1284. See also "The Nuremburg Judgment," *Living Church* 113 (October 13, 1946): 18; *Christian Science Monitor,* October 17, 1946, p. 3; Burrell, "New International Law," p. 11.

distinct Catholic viewpoint. Presentation of strictly legal questions were seldom advanced. The *ex post facto* charge interested few; the Kellogg-Briand Pact was rarely cited; analogies between international and common law were infrequently found. What was unique in the Catholic consideration of Nuremberg's legality was the frequent appeal to the natural law as a justification for the London Charter and the Tribunal.

Other groups appealed to this concept of a natural law or moral code. Protestant authors made vague reference to a rule of morality and employed the terminology of just and unjust war, but the impression was conveyed that the writers were not conscious of the philosophical substructure underlying these concepts in their more precise meanings. Writers of other religious denominations used the terms in a strictly religious, even evangelical, sense rather than with technical significance.

Many Catholic commentators, on the other hand, obviously were conscious of the philosophical implications of these terms when they assumed, stated, or developed the idea that the Nuremberg court was a valid application of a natural or moral law.[18] Indeed, one editor almost seemed to believe that the whole Nuremberg procedure was undertaken to prove Thomistic theses, for he maintained that at "Nuremberg the natural law was established more clearly, emphatically and on a higher plane than by any other secular tribunal in history. Its universal quality, its pervasion everywhere and at all times, was re-affirmed. At Nuremberg the nations of this earth publicly and solemnly acknowledged that nations are subject to the law of God." [19]

Although Catholic thought was distinguished by an emphasis on the natural-law philosophy, the most controversial characteristic was the concern of one large segment of Catholics with the nations presiding in judgment. The major reason for this interest was, of course, this subgroup's preoccupation with the evils of

18. Edmund A. Walsh, S.J., "Comments and Corollaries," *America* 76 (November 9, 1946): 153 (hereafter cited as Walsh, "Comments and Corollaries"); "World Judgment on Persecutors," *America* 76 (October 26, 1946): 93–95; National Catholic Welfare Council, 46–3371; *Pittsburg Catholic*, October 10, 1946, p. 6; *Catholic News*, October 12, 1946, p. 11.

19. *Boston Pilot*, October 5, 1946.

Communism and Russian imperialism.[20] In their eyes our Red
Ally should have been the foe in World War II, and Stalin and
the other Communist leaders should have been the accused at
Nuremberg.

The archetype of this opinion was expressed in the *Brooklyn
Tablet*, whose verdict on the Tribunal was "Hypocrisy!" Repeatedly this newspaper declared that Russia, although one of the
nations sitting in judgment, was at least equally guilty and an
associate in crime of the accused.[21] The editor expressed his
wonderment that "von Ribbentrop should be executed as helping
to cause the war when Molotov, who was co-signer with him for
the invasion of Poland . . . was not on the gallows with him." [22]
He also raised the question whether the publicity given to Nuremberg was not created to take attention from the failures of
the post-World War II Paris Peace Conference.

This concern about the judges of the Nuremberg court was not
confined to a few conservative diocesan newspapers. It also
appeared in some national Catholic publications, both conservative and liberal.[23] A magazine most dogmatic in its stand was
Ave Maria which declared that these juridical processes had
brought shame to the average American because the trials were
based on retributive justice by a court which, because of the
varying democratic and totalitarian doctrines of the presiding

20. Thomas A. Bailey, *America Faces Russia, Russian-American Relations
from Early Times to Our Day* (Ithaca: Cornell University Press, 1950), p.
287. It should be noted that this author finally concluded that the key to
over-reaction to Russia was not religion, politics, class, occupation, race, but
education. Ibid., p. 294.

21. *Brooklyn Tablet*, October 5, 1946; October 19, 1946. This view also
appeared in the letters to the editor September 21, 1946; October 19, 1946;
October 26, 1946.

22. Ibid., October 19, 1946.

23. Some diocesan newspapers which condemned Nuremberg because of
Russia's presence were the *Catholic Transcript*, October 17, 1946, p. 4; *San
Francisco Monitor*, October 12, 1946, p. 8. There is little evidence of Catholic papers circulated in German-American areas generally opposing the
trials. This can be attributed to the fact that most editors in these regions
used the standard *Register* (or in some Wisconsin dioceses the *Catholic
Herald-Citizen* of Milwaukee) to cover world news and only added a section on items of local interest. The *Register* had little on the trials; the
Herald-Citizen reprinted Fr. Edmund Walsh's favorable explanation as its
editorial.

nations, possessed no single ideological norm and judged with no international law by which to appraise guilt. "Thus did America express an apostolate of retribution in a judicial gesture of futility." [24]

The two most important liberal Catholic weekly magazines also discussed the crimes of the nations sitting in judgment, but both concluded that the composition of the court did not invalidate its actions. Christopher Emmet in *Commonweal* asserted that evil judges did not illegitimatize the trials, but he maintained that they destroyed their moral value.[25] Father Edmund A. Walsh in *America* answered the objections against the presiding nations by responding that one judge did not nullify the integrity or judgment of the majority. He also argued from a religious analogy, pointing out that, as an unworthy minister did not invalidate the sacrament, so Nuremberg should not be evaluated by the character of the judges but rather by the justice or injustice of their verdicts.[26]

We have noted that a stress on the role of natural law and on Russia's acting as judge at Nuremberg distinguished Catholic opinion. These two views can be better understood if we realize that this religious community was divided into two clearly discernible groups. One faction affirmed the legality of the Tribunal; some among them questioned the constitution of the court, especially the Soviet's presence on it, but this was a tangential consideration. They declared that the verdicts were just, and they had almost no interest in the acquittals. Nuremberg's effect on the future, they thought, would be salutary, especially if the victors would submit to the same legal order as the vanquished. They stressed the moral implications of the juridical process.

The second group attacked the legal basis of the Tribunal, not so much from the idea of Nuremberg as an application of retroactive law but from the absolute partiality of the judgment. They objected to the powers that sat in judgment, particularly Russia.

24. "We Furnish the Hangman," *Ave Maria* 64 (November 7, 1946): 581. See also "The Nuernberg Trials," *Ave Maria* 67 (March 31, 1946): 323; "Recalling Nuernberg Trials," *Ave Maria* 70 (April 26, 1952): 514.
25. Christopher Emmet, "Verdict on Nuremberg," *Commonweal* 45 (November 22, 1946): 139–41.
26. Walsh, "Comments and Corollaries," p. 153.

They felt that one could not do business with the Communists without being infected by their vices. These Catholics had almost no interest in the specific verdicts, Senator Taft's criticism, or the trials' future effects on international law. The one point on which this faction agreed with their opponents was their emphasis on the moral and ethical considerations of Nuremberg.

Any rigid application of labels such as conservative or liberal would be invalid. The views of both groups were found in conservative magazines. At most, one can say that the majority of conservative Catholic spokesmen were against the trials. The reason is not hard to find. This was the postwar period which was marked by the emergence of what critics would call the "Catholic Red hysteria," "the kind of fanatical religious campaign against Russia and Communism that we associate with the Roman Catholic Church." [27] The presence of Russia at Nuremberg and the need to cooperate with the "satanic Soviet" and its "perfidious pattern of Communist godlessness, barbarism and enslavement" was considered working with the devil.[28]

On the other hand, we must call attention to the fact that concern for Russia was not limited to anti-Nuremberg publications. Catholics who supported the Tribunal also took exception to Russia's role in judgment. Moreover (again in warning against oversimplification), the trials were condemned by the liberal *Commonweal*, the one Catholic magazine singled out by the *Information Bulletin* of the Federal Council of Churches as being untainted by this extreme obsession with Communism and a magazine that was most fearful of this movement's manifestations and consequences for American Catholicism.[29]

Commonweal announced its verdict with the caption, "Our Law Was Broken." The editor noted that the procedures used at Nuremberg were essentially American and British law practices, not French or Russian. Therefore, Nuremberg was indeed "our" law. *Commonweal* maintained that no matter how many Ameri-

27. John C. Bennett, "Some Impressions from Geneva," *Christianity and Crisis* 6 (October 14, 1946): 5.

28. *Catholic News*, October 12, 1946, p. 1. See also Samuel Lubell, *Revolt of the Moderates* (New York: Harpers, 1956), 82.

29. "A Study of the Roman Catholic Press in America," *Information Service of the General Council of Churches of Christ in America*, June 22, 1946, p. 6.

cans approved of the Tribunal the trials were wrong because the court created new laws and then applied them retoactively. "You broke a law (in the past) we are now making (in the present)." [30] The result of such a retroactive manufacturing of law was that the whole legal code became dubious and uncertain.

Finally, we might observe that there was independence of thought in the Catholic community. This freedom was revealed in the divergence of its views, its use and nonuse of semiofficial declarations, and its presentation of individualistic viewpoints. Some may be surprised to learn that, although among the three major religious communities one finds widespread condemnation of Nuremberg only by Catholics, it was this religion's spiritual leader, Pope Pius XII, who publicly and repeatedly voiced his approbation of the war-crime trials. [31]

In conclusion a few generalizations might be made concerning the judgment on Nuremberg by the three religious communities taken as a unit. First, opinion given in a religious context generally used many of the accepted American norms and thought patterns when evaluating the Tribunal. Many interests, opinions, attitudes, and prejudices displayed by religious writers could be found in their secular counterparts. Still, as has been noted, there were distinctive themes which set off religious opinions from American public reaction in general.

Second, religious writers revealed a greater willingness to

30. "Our Law Was Broken," *Commonweal* 45 (October 18, 1946): 5.
31. Speaking to the Sixth International Congress on Penal Law on October 3, 1953, Pope Pius XII declared that "unjust war is to be accounted one of the very gravest crimes that international law must proscribe," and he called upon all civilized nations to elaborate a code of international law that would provide punishment for persons who initiate unjust wars or wage them with excessive cruelty. He called too for tribunals impartially constituted to pass judgment upon "unprincipled criminals who, in order to realize their ambitious plans, are not afraid to unleash total war." Whitney R. Harris, *Tyranny on Trial: The Evidence of Nuremberg* (Dallas: Southern Methodist Press, 1954), p. 567, citing John P. Kennedy, *Moral Aspects of Nuremberg* (Washington: Dominican House of Studies, 1949), p. viii; *Catholic Action* 27 (January, 1946): 26–27; *New York Times*, November 16, 1945, p. 19; *Michigan Catholic*, October 19, 1946, p. 4; Louis Gallagher, *Edmund A. Walsh* (New York: Benzinger, 1962), p. 146. Some American prosecutors made a point of having conferences with the Pope before the trials started.

champion unpopular stands and to exercise self-criticism. Examples of this were the *Watchman-Examiner's* condemnation of the Christian religious leadership of the period between the wars, the *San Francisco Monitor's* open declaration of American guilt because of the atomic bomb and other violations of the laws of war, the *Lutheran Outlook's* accusation of hypocrisy not only because of the bomb but also because of the enslavement of German prisoners of war, and the stand of *Commentary* as a lone Jewish voice crying out against the trials in general.[32] One will look long in the secular writings before finding such criticism of entrenched and accepted values, myths, and prejudices.

Finally, the religious leaders in pulpit and press did fulfill the function that their listeners and readers expected and desired. Church and synagogue judged the justice of men in the language of God. They presented the trials as a moral and ethical question. Judgment was made implicitly or explicitly from the viewpoint of a definite religious commitment. This was true no matter what the final verdict. Thus, religious spokesmen presented Nuremberg as: a search for the virtue of justice, or a violation of the rights of the defendants; a proclamation of the conscience of mankind, or the evil vengeance of the victors; the glorious implementation and exaltation of the moral law, or a sinful violation of that rule; the striving of good men for peace through law, or a degrading act of hypocrisy enacted by a court as guilty as the men it sentenced.

32. "End of an Evil Epoch," *Watchman-Examiner*, October 10, 1946, p. 1036; *San Francisco Monitor*, October 12, 1946, p. 8; "Nazi Leaders Hang," *Lutheran Outlook*, p. 295; Konvitz, "Will Nuremberg Serve Justice?" *Commentary*, pp. 6–12.

7

American Lawyers Judge Nuremberg

All scholarly fraternities indulge in "shop-talk." Lawyers are no exception, and, therefore, when the Nuremberg trials caught the attention of the nation, the lawyers of America showed a constant and intense interest in the proceedings far beyond that of any other group. They discussed the Tribunal among themselves, and many lawyers expressed their judgments in legal journals throughout the land.

If the legal profession's interest was not unexpected, neither was it surprising that their verdict in the main coincided with the favorable judgment on Nuremberg by the people and the popular press. The distinctive factor determining this expressed attitude of many American lawyers was their personal involvement in the trials of the alleged Axis criminals. As one of the Tribunal's most vitriolic critics pointed out, if one eliminated all the lieutenant colonels and all the War Department judges and prosecutors, those lawyers writing on the trials would separate into two almost equal groups, pro and con.[1]

This attack, however, contained only a half truth. For although the participating lawyers did have a personal stake in the approval of the proceedings, their involvement did not automatically invalidate their arguments or make their evaluation a hypocritical one. Still, the list of legal writers who participated in the war-crime trials is impressive. A partial roster would include Robert Jackson, Telford Taylor, Murray Bernays, Edward Daly,

1. Gordon Ireland, "*Ex Post Facto* from Rome to Tokyo," *Temple Law Quarterly* 21 (July, 1947): 53–54 (hereafter cited as Ireland, "*Ex Post Facto*"). If involvement with the prosecution is not considered, the division of opinion would be 75% favorable to the trials, 25% against. The basis for this estimate is the views expressed in over seventy-seven articles on the Nuremberg trials which appeared in forty-one American law journals.

Robert Stephens, Thomas Dodd, Benjamin Frencz, Sidney Alderman, Ben Bruce Blakeney, Morris Kolander, Victor Swearinger, Winfield Hale, Robert Storey, Calvin Behle, James Morris,
Bernard Meltzer, Joseph Keenan, James Brand, Willard Cowles,
Charles Pegler, and P. F. Gault. Of these, only three—Calvin A.
Behle, Major Ben Bruce Blakeney and Lt. Col. P. F. Gault—were
critical of the trials, and they distinguished carefully between
the Nuremberg principles and their own personal activities.

This participation in the trials resulted in lawyers who specialized in American domestic law stressing the practical aspects of
the Tribunal's principles and proceedings rather than more philosophical or theoretical considerations. Emphasizing these pragmatic considerations, they clearly differed from experts in international law.

Foremost among American jurists were the members of the
United States Supreme Court. Their individual opinions on the
Tribunal were of importance not only because of their position
and the respect customarily accorded to their views, but also
because of the roles that some of the justices played in the
government's activity concerning Nuremberg.

A legal question of the magnitude of the International Military
Tribunal certainly could not escape the notice of the justices, but
the discovery of their opinions presents us with a historical
detective story where clues must be ferreted out and evidence
evaluated in the attempt toward valid inference and conjec-
tures.[2]

We are most certain of Justice Robert H. Jackson's judgment
on Nuremberg. The dedication and zeal which he brought to the
prosecution revealed a man sincerely committed to the undertaking. Yet, even in this champion of the accusers we find complexity, for Robert Jackson was not always committed to either the

2. That this "detective" work is absolutely necessary is proved by the
fact that the biographer of Chief Justice Harlan Stone has no knowledge of
any direct statements on Nuremberg by any of the justices who are pre-
sented as doubtful in this study. Letter of Alpheus T. Mason to the author,
October 11, 1965. The members of the Supreme Court at the time of the
Nuremberg trials were Chief Justice Harlan F. Stone and Associate Justices
Robert H. Jackson, Hugo L. Black, Frank Murphy, Wiley B. Rutledge, Jr.,
William O. Douglas, Stanley Forman Reed, Felix Frankfurter, and Harold
H. Burton.

principles or the general policy of war-crime trials. If at Nuremberg Jackson charged the German generals as legally accountable for their actions, in his dissent in *Korematsu* v. *U.S.* he maintained that it was fatuous to place any hope in the judge's words against the warrior's might. "The chief restraint upon those who command the physical forces of the country," Jackson declared, "in the future as in the past, must be their responsibility to the political judgment of their contemporaries and to the moral judgments of history." [3]

Once the trials started, Jackson placed all doubts and hesitations behind him and devoted himself completely to the promotion of the prosecution.[4] Jackson himself said "that the hard months at Nuremberg were well spent in the most important, enduring and constructive work of my life." [5] The associate justice indefatigably upheld the new developments in international law, not only in the courtroom but also by a number of speeches, press interviews, periodical articles, and by prodding the executive for action on subsequent trials.[6]

If Jackson's ultimate position on Nuremberg was clear, so was that of Justice William O. Douglas. In 1954 he published his diary, *An Almanac of Liberty,* which included his declaration that Nuremberg proceedings violated the long-established American tradition against vengeance, a tradition which had been preserved even in the most trying times. "No matter how many books are written or briefs filed, no matter how finely the lawyers analyze it," Douglas wrote, "the crime for which the Nazis were tried had never been formalized as a crime with the definiteness required by our legal standards, nor outlawed with a death penalty by the international community. By our standards that crime arose under an *ex post facto* law. Goering et al. deserved

3. Glendon A. Schubert, *Constitutional Politics, The Political Behavior of Supreme Court Justices and the Constitutional Policies That They Make* (New York: Holt, Rinehardt, and Winston, 1960), p. 358 (hereafter cited as Schubert, *Constitutional Politics*).

4. *New York Times*, April 14, 1945, p. 16; Robert H. Jackson, "The Rule of Law Among the Nations," *American Bar Association Journal* 31 (June, 1945): 290.

5. Eugene C. Gerhart, *America's Advocate, Robert H. Jackson* (Indianapolis: Bobbs-Merrill, 1958), p. 453.

6. *New York Times*, May 30, 1945, p. 3; June 7, 1945, p. 8; June 8, 1945, p. 4; July 7, 1945, p. 5; August 2, 1945, p. 8 and passim. Jackson, "Final Report," pp. 774–76.

severe punishment. But their guilt did not justify us in substituting POWER for PRINCIPLE." [7]

Chief Justice Harland Fiske Stone's judgment on Nuremberg was also certain. Privately, and not too privately, the chief justice was bitter in his condemnation of the Nuremberg trials because he thought that the German leaders should be dealt with by executive action.[8] "Jackson is away conducting his high-grade lynching party at Nuremberg," Stone wrote to a correspondent. "I don't mind what he does to the Nazis, but I hate to see the pretence that he is running a court and proceedings according to common law." [9]

Less privately the chief justice refused former Attorney General Francis Biddle's personal request that Stone swear him in as judge of the Nuremberg court. Stone explained, "I did not wish to appear, even in that remote way, to give my blessing or that of the Court on the proposed Nuremberg trials." [10] He also wrote to the editor of Fortune, William D. Geer, complaining that the magazine's December 1945 article seemed to leave the reader with the impression that Jackson represented the United States Supreme Court. Stone wanted the editor clearly to understand that the "Supreme Court had nothing to do, either directly or indirectly, with the Nuremberg Trials, or the governmental action which authorized them. I was not advised of Justice Jackson's participation until his appointment by the Executive was announced in the newspapers." [11]

The conclusion that we might draw from this evidence is that the chief justice was totally adverse to Nuremberg and its principles. This is not true. In every case presented to the Supreme Court which in any way concerned postwar trials, Harlan Stone always decided for the legality of both the punishment and principles of these tribunals.[12]

Stone's biographer, Alpheus T. Mason, suggests that the rea-

7. William Orville Douglas, An Almanac of Liberty (Garden City, N.Y.: Doubleday, 1954), p. 96.
8. New York Times Magazine, January 1961, p. 11.
9. Alpheus Thomas Mason, Harland Fiske Stone, Pillar of the Law (New York: Viking, 1956), p. 716 (hereafter cited as Mason, Stone).
10. Ibid., p. 715.
11. Ibid., p. 715.
12. Trial of War Criminals Before the Nuernberg Military Tribunals Under Control Council Law No. 10, 15 vols. (Nuernberg: International Military Tribunal, 1949), 15:1192 (hereafter cited as TWC).

son for the chief justice's opposition to Nuremberg was more personal than theoretical. Justice Jackson's going to Germany presented Stone with annoying problems. The head of the bench had to appoint another member of the court as justice for the Second Circuit; a number of cases were stymied by a four to four vote; and Jackson was not on the bench to write his share of the opinions. According to this authority these vexations, rather than any intense conviction of the illegality of the proceedings of the Tribunal, were the real cause of the chief justice's irascible condemnation of Nuremberg.[13]

Hugo Black was another justice to whom personal considerations may well have been important in his judgment on Nuremberg. The personal vendetta between Justice Jackson and Black was well known and culminated in the Nuremberg prosecutor demanding a congressional investigation into his colleague's alleged unethical conduct.[14] Whether personal animosity caused Black to oppose Nuremberg is locked in this justice's silence. The only indication of his negative vote appeared in his dissenting opinion in the case of *Oswald Pohl* v. *Acheson et al.* Hugo Black was the justice who with William O. Douglas favored the request for *certiorari* in the case of the German defendant.[15]

We are tempted to list Justices Rutledge and Murphy among anti-Nuremberg critics because of their dissenting opinions in the case of General Yamashita. Similarities between the trial of the Japanese general and those at Nuremberg obviously did exist. Both were concerned with high ranking enemy leaders; both stressed enemy atrocities; both employed new legal principles.

13. Harlan Fiske Stone's son attempted to clarify his father's apparently contradictory views in a letter to Mason. "I am not at all sure that Father's view regarding the Nuremberg trials [and] his opinions in the Saboteur and Yamashita cases are inconsistent. It was Father's thought from the beginning that the Nazi defendants could be dealt with through a military rather than a judicial trial—the very thing that eventually occurred in the Yamashita case. . . . There seemed to be no basis for using a judicial trial to carry out a matter of military or national policy." Letter of Lauson H. Stone to A. T. Mason, cited in Mason, *Stone*, p. 719.
14. John P. Frank, *Marble Palace, The Supreme Court in American Life* (New York: Knopf, 1958), pp. 258–59; John P. Frank, *Mr. Justice Black, The Man and His Opinions* (New York: Knopf, 1949), p. 131.
15. *TWC*, 15:1192.

Beneath these external likenesses, however, the trials essentially differed, and any facile analogy is suspect. If we examine the dissenting opinions in Yamashita's trial, we see that most of the judges' technical objections were not germane to Nuremberg.[16] The Tribunal in Germany, unlike the court trying the Japanese general, did exercise the utmost diligence to prove the personal nature of the guilt of the twenty-one defendants and did use extreme care that due process be observed.

A convincing case, on the other hand, can be constructed for the dissenting justices' approval of the Nuremberg trials because they explicitly affirmed fundamental principles often employed to undergird the Tribunal. Both Justices believed in a dynamic, progressive philosophy of law in which the courts must not be emasculated by uncompromising demand for precedents.[17] The acceptance of such a natural-law philosophy usually coincided with approval of Nuremberg.[18]

If the evidence concerning the opinions on Nuremberg of Justice Rutledge and Murphy is not certain, the affirmative judgment of the other three judges of the Supreme Court—Reed, Frankfurter, and Burton—must be inferred from their decisions supporting the majority in the cases of Yamashita and Oswald Pohl.[19] Certainly these justices made no dramatic revelation of any opposition to the Tribunal at Nuremberg.

Other lawyers throughout the land also found the trials an intriguing study. These legal minds naturally tended to concentrate on the strictly judicial questions of Nuremberg and in particular on the precise point of the legal foundation of the assize. The search for justification of the court's law and jurisdiction was spurred on not only by the very human motives arising from the writers' participation in the trials, but also from a sincere desire for justice and a total dissatisfaction with suggested alternatives to the Tribunal. The American lawyer typically was repelled by the suggestion that these Nazi moral monsters should go unpunished. The establishment of a neutral

16. A. Frank Reel, *The Case of General Yamashita* (Chicago: University of Chicago Press, 1949), Appendix, *In Re Yamashita*, 327, US 1., pp. 286, 287, 289 (hereafter cited as Reel, *Case of Yamashita*).
17. Ibid., p. 289.
18. Ibid., pp. 272–73.
19. *TWC*, 15:1192.

court seemed unfeasible; to shoot them, un-American. Most lawyers argued that by the end of the war no true neutrals were left and that a neutral court was neither demanded nor customary in international law. The appeal for summary execution with or without action by an ordinary military court fell on deaf ears.[20] It was not the American way but rather the Nazi method.[21] The final result of such shooting would be to make martyrs of the victims.[22] As John Parker, the alternate United States judge at Nuremberg, wrote: "The argument frequently made that, in the absence of an international criminal code, the accused should have been shot summarily, without trial or judicial process, had nothing to commend it in law, in morals, or in common sense." [23]

Lawyers supporting the trials based their justification for its law primarily on two foundations, preexisting statutes or customary international law. The first basis was presented in terminology that varied from the most simple to the most scholarly. Some lawyers thought that all objections were answered if one merely pointed out that the Nazis' actions were always considered crimes, or that the Kellogg-Briand Treaty outlawed war.[24] Other writers, however, realized that the treaty's authors had explicitly rejected the term "aggressive war," the pact had established no sanctions for individuals, and repeated violations of the treaty's provisions had occurred without any serious repercussions.[25]

20. P. F. Gault, "Prosecution of War Criminals," *Journal of Criminal Law and Criminology* 36 (September–October, 1945): 180–82 (hereafter cited as Gault, "Prosecution").

21. Biddle, "Nurnberg," p. 681.

22. Charles Pegler, "War Crimes and War Criminals," *Journal of the Bar Association of the District of Columbia* 13 (September, 1946): 391; Sheldon Glueck, "The Nuernberg Trial and Aggressive War," *Harvard Law Review* 59 (February, 1946): 398 (hereafter cited as Glueck, "Aggressive War").

23. John J. Parker, "The Nuernberg Trial," *Journal of the American Judicature Society* 30 (December, 1946): 113 (hereafter cited as Parker, "Nuernberg"). Since Judge Parker was the alternative American Judge at Nuremberg and Francis Beverly Biddle (cf. note 21) was the presiding judge at the trials, these statements might be taken as a semi-official declaration of American policy in regard to alternatives to trials for the war criminals.

24. Florence E. Allan, "Nuremberg Trial Implements World Law," *Women Lawyers Journal* 34 (Winter, 1948): 6–7; "Indictment of War Criminals," *American Bar Association Journal* 31 (December, 1945): 645; Tappan Gregory, "The Nuremberg Trial," *Illinois Bar Journal* 34 (June, 1946): 478–79 (hereafter cited as Gregory, "Nuremberg").

25. Calvin A. Behle, "The War Crime Trials," *Nevada State Bar Journal* 13 (April, 1948): 64 (hereafter cited as Behle, "War Crime Trials").

In response to these criticisms, some lawyers argued that the pact had an evolutionary history so that a significance which perhaps was not present in the beginning had been imparted to it by developing attitudes and demands of humanity. Francis B. Biddle, the American judge at Nuremberg, urged the binding power of the pact, basing his arguments on the interpretation of Henry L. Stimson of 1946 rather than on that of Henry L. Stimson of 1928.[26] The secretary of war's earlier statements that the treaty's force was only moral gave place to his belief in its legal potency.

Others found their preexisting statutory jurisdiction in more erudite, or at least less well known, precedents. For some the trial of the German saboteurs who landed on the eastern coast of the United States supplied a model for the International Military Tribunal. These spies were put to death by an American military court which ruled out such defenses as "act of state" and "superior's orders."[27] One authority made a strong case for the use of the fourth part of the Hague convention of October 18, 1907 as a statutory foundation. This document had stated that besides signed agreements between states there were also "principles of the law of nations, as they result from the usages established among civilized peoples, from the laws of humanity, and the dictates of the public conscience. . . ."[28] This statement was interpreted thus: "In precise words, democratic public opinion has been received as a source of law through Hague Convention IV, and is translated into a force through successful belligerent action."[29] Lawyers also stressed that the law of the nations had evolved from the Roman legal tradition and not the Anglo-Saxon, and, consequently, interpretations or limitations based on the latter code were misleading.

The legal basis which most often appealed to American lawyers was an analogy with English common law. Using this argument writers followed a regular pattern which started with the fact that international law was not as well developed as national law. Because of this condition they argued that it was impossible to expect such refinements as prohibition of retroac-

26. Biddle, "Nurnberg," pp. 686, 695.
27. Cowles, "Trial of War Criminals," p. 330.
28. Franklin, "Sources of International Law," p. 156.
29. Ibid., p. 157.

tive law or rigid limitation of the law of the nations to statutory enactments. International law, like common law, must leave a great deal to the discretion of the judge, the dictates of equity, and the needs of society.[30]

One distinctively American variation on this analogy with common law was the theory that the Nuremberg code was like the vigilante law of the nineteenth-century western frontier. As the settlers' improvised legal system had been the necessary and effective answer to lawless conditions, so Nuremberg, it was maintained, was the necessary legal code to bring international gangsters and desperadoes to justice.[31]

An unusual defense of Nuremberg's law based its analogy on a mixture of one-half common law and one-half similarity to the old English chancery court. The latter tribunal tried any case for which no adequate legal remedy existed. It was thought that this condition could be easily proved concerning Nuremberg.[32]

The American lawyers who urged these positive legal foundations to justify the Nuremberg proceedings were indirectly answering the charge that the trial applied retroactive law, but many lawyers felt that a more detailed refutation of this legal objection to Nuremberg was necessary. Consequently they dissected the principle to show that it was not applicable to the event in Germany and that the trials' adversaries were using a Latin phrase in a mechanical way that destroyed its intent.

Against those who declared Nuremberg to be a retroactive application of law, a "kangeroo court," these lawyers argued that the *ex post facto* principle, of its very nature, demanded good faith on the part of the one performing the deed; that is the

30. Robert Gier Stephens, Jr., "Aspects of the Nuremberg Trial," Part III, *Georgia Bar Journal* 9 (August, 1946): 64; Edward F. Carter, "The Nurnberg Trials: A Turning Point in the Enforcement of International Law," *Nebraska Law Review* 28 (March, 1949): 373; G. R. McConnell, "The Trial of War Criminals at Nuremberg," *Wyoming Law Journal* 1 (December, 1946): 12; Sack, "Superior Orders," p. 11; Robert B. Walkinshaw, "The Nuremberg and Tokyo Trials: Another Step toward International Justice," *American Bar Association Journal* 35 (April, 1949): 302 (hereafter cited as Walkinshaw, "The Nuremberg and Tokyo Trials").

31. James T. Brand, "Crimes Against Humanity and the Nürnberg Trials," *Oregon Law Review* 28 (February, 1949): 98 (hereafter cited as Brand, "Crimes Against Humanity"); Willis Smith, "The Nuremberg Trials," *American Bar Association Journal* 32 (July, 1946): 394–96.

32. Max Radin, "International Crimes," *Iowa Law Review* 32 (November, 1946): 43 (hereafter cited as Radin, "International Crimes").

action must have appeared good, or at least indifferent, when it was committed. This condition obviously was not true in regard to the Nazi atrocities, for even the Nazis must have realized that the wonton seizure of neighbors' territory and the killing of six million Jews was morally and legally reprehensible. It was not the London Charter which had made Nazi wickedness criminal; that document had merely declared what all knew to be the case.[33]

Another argument against the *ex post facto* charge, besides the perpetrator's consciousness of criminality, was the contention that this principle was not a rule of law, but of justice. The *ex post facto* dictum would then not be bound to a rigid technical application but would be employed according to the rules of equity.[34]

Another defense against the charge of retroactivity was the claim that for the opponents to demand statutory law to cover all contingencies in a society so primitively organized as the international community, and one without any legislative body, was to demand that there be no law at all. The consequence of the adoption of the anti-Nuremberg lawyers' theory would be a savage, lawless international jungle.[35] Critics of the Tribunal were also condemned for demanding written laws when they were the very ones who in the past had consistently blocked all attempts at a codification to cover these crimes, who had condemned the use of the common law analogy in international judication, and who had opposed the enactment of any general laws which a court could interpret through analogy.[36] If the court's law was retroactive, this was the critics' own doing.

33. William Allen Zeck, "Nuremberg: Proceedings Subsequent to Goering et al.," *North Carolina Law Review* 26 (June, 1948): 377; Tappan Gregory, "Nuremberg Trials," *Connecticut Bar Journal* 21 (January, 1947): 18 (hereafter cited as Gregory, "Trials").

34. Office of the U.S. Chief of Counsel, *Nazi Conspiracy and Aggression* (Washington: U.S. Government Printing Office, 1947), p. 49.

35. Biddle, "Nurnberg," p. 686; A. Frederick Mignone, "After Nuremberg, Tokyo," *Texas Law Review* 25 (May, 1947): 478 (hereafter cited as Mignone, "Tokyo"); Sidney E. Jaffe, "Natural Law and the Nuremberg Trials," *Nebraska Law Review* 26 (November, 1946): 94 (hereafter cited as Jaffe, "Natural Law"); Brand, "Crimes Against Humanity," p. 115.

36. Nicholas R. Doman, "The Nuremberg Trials Revisited," *American Bar Association Journal* 47 (March, 1961): 261 (hereafter cited as Doman, "Nuremberg Trials Revisited"); Franklin, "Source of International Law," p. 169; Brand, "Crimes Against Humanity," p. 115; Bernard D. Meltzer, "A

On more factual grounds anti-Nuremberg arguments based on the absolute universaliy of the retroactive law prohibition (i.e., that all people everywhere have always had enactments against *ex post facto* law) were answered by the affirmation that this limitation was in no way comprehensive. Many nations in the past had no such rule, and many countries in the modern world did not have it.[37] In fact, it was urged that the principle apparently was a major fetish only of American lawyers; European legal experts who opposed Nuremberg did not give great weight to the principle. Other lawyers pointed out that it was neither enforced in common law courts nor a necessary rule in international law.[38]

Finally, the Nuremberg defenders tried to lay to rest the specter which haunted the minds of such men as columnist Westbrook Pegler and Senator Robert Taft who feared that the use of retroactive law by an international tribunal would be used as a precedent in national law by which governments could perpetrate unheard-of outrages against their citizens. The trials' advocates offered the refutation that historically the stream of influence has always been exclusively from national law to international law, from the more developed code to the less developed.[39] One might as well worry, they would hold, about the United States adopting the legal principles of the Hottentots.

Authors who defended the trials' legality hailed their future effect upon international law, claiming that the Tribunal was the first step toward a new world criminal law code.[40] In particular they approved the Nuremberg court's declaration that aggressive war was the "supreme crime." Some American lawyers even perceived that the Tribunal's decision on this question was a

Note on Some Aspects of the Nuremberg Debate," *University of Chicago Law Review* 14 (April, 1947): 45 (hereafter cited as Meltzer, "Note on the Nuremberg Debate").

37. Franz B. Schick, "Crimes Against Peace," *Journal of Criminal Law and Criminology* 38 (January–February, 1948): 460 (hereafter cited as Schick, "Crimes Against Peace"); Jaffe, "Natural Law," p. 94.

38. Brand, "Crimes Against Humanity," p. 114; Biddle, "Nurnberg," p. 686.

39. Glueck, "Aggressive War," p. 452; Gregory, "Nuremberg," p. 474.

40. Robert H. Jackson, "Nuremberg in Retrospect: Legal Answer to International Lawlessness," *American Bar Association Journal* 35 (October, 1949): 887.

return to the medieval theory of "just" and "unjust" war and that the Tribunal was reintroducing natural-law concepts into international affairs.[41]

These lawyers also heartily endorsed the court's establishment of individual responsibility, arguing that legal sanctions were effective only when they fell upon persons.[42] They cited the relative effectiveness of the United States government under the Articles of Confederation and the Constitution as historical proof of their contention.[43] These writers also maintained that the Nuremberg court was correct in disallowing the pleas of "head of state" and "superior orders" since the acceptance of these defenses would create the anomaly in which, by an almost infinite shifting of responsibility, all accountability would be placed on those holding supreme power, and these men, as heads of state, would be completely immune from punishment. The consequence of the admission of these pleas, therefore, would mean that individuals would avoid sanctions precisely because of the enormity of their crimes and their power to do evil.[44]

One element on which the attitude of the pro-Nuremberg lawyers and popular opinion differed was the power of the Tribunal's verdicts to inhibit potential international criminals. Lawyers had much less confidence in the deterrent effect of outlawing aggressive war than did the ordinary citizen. Perhaps this resulted from the lawyers' perception that international

41. F. Blaine Sloan, "Comparative International and Municipal Law Sanctions," *Nebraska Law Review* 27 (November, 1947): 12–13, 21–22; Radin, "International Crimes," p. 41; C. P. Phillips, "Air Warfare and Law," *George Washington Law Review* 21, Part I (January, 1953): 313; Part II (March, 1953), 40 (hereafter cited as Phillips, "Air Warfare"); Jaffe, "Natural Law," pp. 90–95; Miriam Theresa Rooney," "Law Without Justice?—The Kelsen and Hall Theories Compared," *Notre Dame Lawyer* 23 (January, 1948): 141.

42. John Foster Dulles, "International Law and Individuals: A Comment on Enforcing Peace," *American Bar Association Journal* 35 (November, 1949): 912–13 (hereafter cited as Dulles, "International Law"); Ernest Schneeberger, "The Responsibility of the Individual Under the International Law," *Georgetown Law Journal* 35 (May, 1947): 489.

43. Dulles, "International Law," pp. 912–13.

44. Glueck, "Aggressive War," p. 419; Sack, "Superior Orders," p. 11; Doman, "Nuremberg Trials Revisited," p. 261; Biddle, "Nurnberg," p. 689; Gregory, "Trials," pp. 18–19; Lawrence Lauer, "The International War Criminal Trials and the Common Law of War," *St. John's Law Review* 20 (November, 1945): 24.

events subsequent to the trials had belied any hope that Nuremberg would be a spectacular barrier to aggressive action and from the lawyers' knowledge that laws were ineffectual without proper enforcement.

Implicit in our consideration of the defenses of Nuremberg's legality is the fact that most attacks on the Tribunal from American lawyers were based on the objection that the Tribunal's law was retroactive. The prohibition against *ex post facto* law is clearly stated in the United States Constitution (Sec. XX, Art. 3) and has been a principle strongly upheld by the American judiciary. It was logical, therefore, from historical reasons as well as a sense of justice that many whose minds had been formed in the American legal tradition would see Nuremberg as an illegal process which violated the rights of the accused. Not that these lawyers wished the Nazis to escape punishment, but their protest condemned the use of legal procedures instead of some political or military means.

The basic idea behind this legal objection was that there existed no precedent for the trials in all of modern history. The Nuremberg court and law were novelties which had no natural development but were the *ad hoc* creation of the four victors to wreak vengeance upon the conquered.[45] Critics asked: What foundation did the composers of the London Charter have to make law except the military power that stood ready to crush any opposition to their new decrees? What right did the conquerors have to declare actions, which most nations considered legitimate at the time of their commission, to be criminal?[46] War was not a crime. All the codes of international and national laws governing the conduct of belligerency attested that, prior to Nuremberg, war was never considered illegitimate.[47] Nor was killing in war considered murder. If the Tribunal declared it so, all belligerents of necessity must be guilty.

45. Walkinshaw, "The Nuremberg and Tokyo Trials," p. 300; McIntyre, "Nuernberg Trials," p. 91.
46. Behle, "War Crime Trials," p. 64; Ireland, *"Ex Post Facto,"* pp. 47, 56; Arthur Nussbaum, Just War—A Legal Concept," *Michigan Law Review* 42 (December, 1943): 178–79.
47. Ben Bruce Blankeney, "International Military Tribunal, Argument for Motion to Dismiss," *American Bar Association Journal* 32 (August, 1946): 477 (hereafter cited as Blankeney, "International Military Tribunal").

For these reasons anti-Nuremberg lawyers noted that in suggesting guidelines for postwar punishment the American Bar Association's Committee on Prosecution of War Criminals had laid down three salutary principles: the court should not aim at revenge but justice; *ex post facto* laws should be sedulously avoided; and no enemy leaders should be tried for crimes within their own boundaries and against their own citizens.[48] Mankind's moral sensibilities might be anguished by adherence to such legal technicalities, but care for such judicial principles would in the long run achieve verdicts generally accepted as just and within the framework of the laws of the nations.

The Executive Board of the National Lawyers Guild adopted a like admonition for those who would be the planners of postwar punishment. These legal experts stated that Axis criminals should be tried only on violation of the accepted rules and customs of war. Such indictments "should not be confused with the war-guilt questions or with violations of the Treaty of Versailles and the Pact of Paris. To do so would be to introduce complicated legal issues and in effect draw a red herring across the whole problem. The Axis has been guilty of enough definite and well-recognized crimes to make it unnecessary to invent new offenses."[49]

A basic argument offered by critics of Nuremberg to illustrate that the Tribunal's law was of necessity retroactive was presented as a logical conclusion from existing legal and political factors of modern life. "[With] no World-State there can be no world law; and because there is no world law, there can be no world crime. An act which is not a crime, is not justiciable before a judicial tribunal."[50] Without a world legislature to codify law for the nations the declaration that wars were unjust was an ethical judgment without legal validity, and the Tribunal's verdicts, therefore, were not a rendering of justice but a ritual used by the victors to convince others of their moral superiority over

48. Gault, "Prosecution," pp. 180–81.
49. Executive Board, "The Punishment of War Criminals," *Lawyers Guild Review* 4 (November–December, 1944): 23.
50. Nathan April, "An Inquiry Into the Juridical Basis for the Nuremberg War Crime Trial," *Minnesota Law Review* 30 (April, 1946): 328 (hereafter cited as April, "Inquiry Into the Juridical Basis").

the fallen adversary.[51] The justices merely had declared that the "supreme crime" was losing a war.

A specific aspect of the court's principles which anti-Nuremberg lawyers attacked was that of personal accountability which, they held, violated the accepted legal axiom that only nations possessed rights and duties in international law. These lawyers held, consequently, that the defenses of "act of state" and of "superior orders" should create immunity for defendants because the law of the nations had no jurisdiction over the individual citizens of a sovereign state unless the state explicitly ceded this power.[52]

A further problem was created by the judges' verdicts on the military. The court's decision implicitly demanded that the ordinary soldier evaluate the legality and morality of every command of his officer before obeying. This would create an impossible burden because, if international lawyers in the calm of their studies had difficulties determining what was permissible under the laws of war and what was not, how could one expect the average soldier in the tensions of wartime always to make the right decisions.[53]

These then were the judgments of the lawyers trained in American jurisprudence upon Nuremberg. Most of these American lawyers, it has been pointed out, had contact with international law on the practical level of conducting or participating in war-crime trials or of doing the research for prosecution or defense in such cases. As a consequence, they stressed practical considerations rather than theoretical questions and used analogies and concepts derived from a background in American law to arrive at their verdict on the Tribunal. Most American lawyers approved of the work that they had done.

51. McIntyre, "Nuernberg Trials," p. 110; Blankeney, "International Military Tribunal," p. 475; April, "Inquiry Into the Juridical Basis," p. 327.
52. Hans Kelsen, "Collective and Individual Responsibility in International Law with Particular Regard to the Punishment of War Criminals," *California Law Review* 31 (December, 1943): 538–39; Hans Kelsen, "Sanctions in International Law under the Charter of the United Nations," *Iowa Law Review* 31 (May, 1946): 523.
53. McIntyre, "Nuernberg Trials," p. 88, 112–13; Franklin, "Sources of International Law," pp. 165–66.

8

Realism or Idealism?
Historians and Foreign Affairs Writers
Evaluate Nuremberg

We have earlier seen that the attitudes of international lawyers toward Nuremberg illustrated the fundamental
truth that pre-existing assumptions, not the objective event,
largely determined judgments on the International Military Tribunal. We find this also in the views advanced by diplomatic
historians and writers on foreign affairs.

The two basic doctrines in international relations are usually
designated as "realist" and "idealist." Once more we must note
that labels such as these, used in regard to Nuremberg, are
oversimplifications and do not lend themselves to precision.
There are schools of interpretation which would prefer not to be
identified with either of these major divisions.[1] Nor do these
names indicate the still greater number of theories which eclecti-
cally choose between or synthesize these systems.[2] Still, when all
qualifications are noted, a hard core of basic assumptions re-
mains which differentiates two basic mentalities among most
writers on foreign affairs.

1. Stanley Hoffman, "International Systems and International Law,"
World Politics 14 (October, 1961): 232–33 (hereafter cited as Hoffman,
"International Systems").
2. Percy E. Corbett, "National Interest, International Organization, and
American Foreign Policy," *World Politics* 5 (October, 1952): 46–56 (hereafter cited as Corbett, "National Interest"); Josef L. Kunz, "The Swing of
the Pendulum: From Overestimation to Underestimation of International
Law," *American Journal of International Law* 44 (January, 1950): 135–40
(hereafter cited as Kunz, "Swing of the Pendulum"); Reinhold Niebuhr, "A
Protest Against a Dilemma's Two Horns," *World Politics* 2 (January, 1950):
338–44.

The diversity among these authors was indeed more striking than that among international lawyers. While the contest between the idealists and realists was not of as long duration as that between positivists and natural-law adherents, the struggle had a special immediateness and practicality because it had a direct bearing on the choice of a postwar American foreign policy. Consequently, these two basic attitudes divided men into rival factions, not only in the universities but also in the halls of Congress and in the conference rooms of the State Department. The conflict of ideas had a special vehemence because both sides were obsessed with the conviction that between the systems existed an irreconcilable cleavage and that their opponents' tenets would lead the United States to destruction.[3] Even the contest between isolationists and interventionists, these two theories contended, started with an essential agreement on the nature of the American tradition in foreign affairs, the desired goals of United States policy, and acceptance of common values. But in the disagreement between the realist and idealist, aptly christened by Senator Vandenberg as the "Great Debate" in foreign affairs, the "two different conceptions of the basis of international organization carry with them underlying assumptions of the nature of man, of the possible rôle of human institutions as well as implicit attitudes toward the democratic process."[4]

Before analyzing the judgment on Nuremberg of foreign affairs experts, we should note that those concerned with international relations reversed the pattern found in other groups. Many writers on foreign affairs in the period since Nuremberg have failed even to mention the Tribunal; others have made only passing reference to the trials. But of those who did evaluate the

3. The intensity of conviction in this debate is implied in Frank Tannenbaum's statement: "The fact that so erudite a scholar as Professor Hans J. Morgenthau, of the University of Chicago, and so subtle a mind as George F. Kennan are the chief proponents of this dreadful doctrine in the United States will add zest to the debate. The appointment of Mr. Kennan as Ambassador to Russia gives his views immediate significance in American foreign policy. But the American people will not take this advice, for they cannot act upon it without ceasing to be both a Christian and a democratic people." "The Balance of Power Versus the Coordinate State," *Political Science Quarterly* 67 (June, 1952): 175 (hereafter cited as Tannenbaum, "Balance of Power").
4. Ibid.

proceedings, two-thirds condemned the trials or proposed serious objections to the assize. Historians and experts in international relations were the only groups in which a majority disapproved of Nuremberg.[5]

The reasons for the lack of interest in Nuremberg and the negative votes on the Tribunal will be examined shortly, but we might observe here another distinctive characteristic. While international lawyers seem to be turning more to natural law for the basic principles governing international relations, the writers on foreign affairs seem to be traveling in the opposite direction —toward a political philosophy kindred in spirit to the waning judicial theory of legal positivism.

Perhaps one explanation of this development can be found in the psychological attachment almost any scholar has to his own discipline. Such an involvement frequently makes it almost impossible for him to declare that his study has little or no relevance to the real world and to the solving of mankind's problems.

This hypothesis' application to Nuremberg was that the theories which were gaining favor with jurists endowed law and the lawyer with a crucial role in the achievement of a just peace. These legal philosophies tended to relegate diplomacy and politics to ephemeral variables coursing about the constant pole star of the law. On the other hand, the realist in foreign affairs who condemned Nuremberg belittled juridical attempts to solve world problems and placed the world's hope in the lessons to be learned from his own specialty—in politics and diplomacy.

Realism, the first system adopted by foreign affairs experts, had as its cornerstone the primacy of the state and power. These two factors must be taken together for, although in the realist system states were important rather than organizations, theoretical international governments, or ideological movements, this

5. Newspapers, popular periodicals, "domestic" law journals, and the writings of international lawyers align themselves in a ratio of approximately three to one, 75% who approved of the Nuremberg trials against 25% who disapproved. Writers on postwar diplomacy reversed this proportion. A survey of almost a hundred books published since the end of World War II on general international relations and on America's role in the world showed that thirty-five authors devoted some significant attention to the Nuremberg trials. Of these thirty-five, eight writers were in favor of the proceedings, twenty proposed serious objections, and seven related the event in a chronological fashion or limited themselves to printing documents.

political theory rejected the idea that all nations were equal merely because they were sovereign and independent. States had importance only in so far as they had power.[6]

The primary dynamic of these two fundamental realities of the state and power was national self-interest. This latter element was often so narrowly defined as to be identified with the state's security and preservation, but it also was explained in more inclusive terms. A more general definition would be that national self-interest is composed of the relatively constant aims and values of a nation which include its preservation, security, welfare, and its honor among the countries of the world.[7]

The realist maintained that this activating principle of international evolution could not be bound by the thin threads of legal statutes or moral exhortations. Nations would live in peace only when their national interests were satisfied or when these were made commensurate to the state's power.

The application of the realist theory to the international scene had many facets. First, world organizations were not condemned, but they were viewed as instruments having value only insofar as states found the associations an effective tool for satisfying national self-interest.[8]

Another tenet of some realists was that international law did not exist because, they insisted, only enforceable and enforced rules were law. A code of the nations broken with impunity had no legal value. A voice of the military, a group which frequently adopted the philosophy of diplomatic realism, tersely presented this view; "If there were such a thing as international law, Mr. Jackson might be justified in making this claim, but as World War II confirmed, belligerents are not guided by any law and act only as their interests command." [9]

Other realists stated their positions on international law in less

6. Kennan, American Diplomacy, p. 97.
7. Corbett, "National Interest," p. 47. See also John Gange, American Foreign Relations: Permanent Problems and Changing Policies (New York: Ronald, 1959), pp. 24, 259 (hereafter cited as Gange, American Foreign Relations).
8. George Frost Kennan, Realities of American Foreign Policy (Princeton, N.J.: Princeton University Press, 1954), pp. 45–46 (hereafter cited as Kennan, Realities of American Foreign Policy).
9. Army and Navy Journal, October 19, 1946, p. 160.

absolute terms but maintained that the code's injunctions were valid and effective only if agreed to by the power forces in international affairs and only as long as these rules did not conflict with important national interests.[10]

If international organizations and law were not the means to secure order and tranquility, how then did the realist suggest that men should seek peace? His answer was through politics and power. The world's savior, for the realist, was not the lawyer but the diplomat. The latter realized that world tensions arose basically from conflicting national interests and tried realistically to eliminate the points of friction.[11] Further, peace came from the balance of power, or, if one wishes, the "balance of terror" which bridled the ambitions of strong nations and checked the irresponsible and inordinate dreams of the weak. Peace through power not peace through law was the realist's solution to modern world problems.

How were the realist's principles and his objections to the idealist's system germane to the Nuremberg trials? The Tribunal was for him the culmination of an orgy of political idealism and the epitome of all the fallacies of Allied and American diplomacy. The trials embodied a destructive legalistic-moralistic approach to international relations because the Tribunal attempted to answer political questions by legal solutions. "The end of the Second World War witnesses in the trial of war criminals according to the rules of Anglo-American procedure a revival of this legalistic approach to essentially political problems. The rule of law has come to be regarded as a kind of miraculous panacea which, wherever applied, would heal, by virtue of its intrinsic reasonableness and justice, the ills of the body politic, transform insecurity and disorder into the calculability of a well-ordered society, and put in the place of violence and bloodshed the peaceful and reasonable settlement of social conflicts."[12] The

10. Gerard J. Mangone, *The Idea and Practice of World Government* (New York: Columbia University Press, 1951), pp. 185–86; Kennan, *Realities of American Foreign Policy*, pp. 18, 38–39.

11. Kennan, *Realities of American Foreign Policy*, p. 36; Hoffman, "International Systems," p. 237.

12. Hans J. Morgenthau, *Scientific Man* vs. *Power Politics* (Chicago: University of Chicago Press, 1946), p. 112 (hereafter cited as Morgenthau, *Scientific Man*).

Nuremberg judges, they held, acting upon an invalid analogy between personal and national behavior, established absolute norms of right and wrong conduct for states. With doubtful cogency, at least to the realist's mind, the court claimed to possess the wisdom needed to declare which wars were just and which were unjust and thus conferred upon neutral facts, such as war and power, an ethical and legal value.[13]

Other realists condemned Nuremberg because of specific aspects which were of particular interest to experts in foreign affairs. Although in the ideal order personal accountability for government leaders might be a bewitching concept, the realist condemned this innovation. Some denounced this decision because responsibility in modern government was so divided that participants scarcely realized the full import of their actions.[14] Some objected because they felt that the principle furthered the myth that wars were the product of a few enemy leaders' "insane ambitions" and obscured the dominant role played by national self-interest in the initiation of belligerent actions. As long as men beguile themselves with this myth, said the realists, it will be difficult to motivate them to necessary political and military actions against objective evils.[15] Other realists thought that the principle of personal accountability was unjust when applied to aggression because at the time of commission this political decision could not have been reasonably regarded as criminal by those who committed it nor by public opinion.[16] Indeed the Allies by their prewar appeasement policy earlier acquiesced in what they were now denouncing as criminal.

The exceptional and unacceptable character of Nuremberg's principle of personal responsibility was clearly illustrated for the realist by the fact that even after the trials the United Nation's

13. Hans J. Morgenthau, Eric Hula, and Moorhouse F. X. Millar, S. J., "Views on Nuremberg, A Symposium," *America* 76 (December 7, 1946): 266–67 (hereafter cited as Morgenthau, "Views on Nuremberg").

14. Franz Neumann, "The War Crimes Trials," *World Politics* 2 (October, 1949): 140 (hereafter cited as Neumann, "War Crimes Trials").

15. Morton A. Kaplan and Nicholas de B. Katenbach, *The Political Foundations of International Law* (New York: John Wiley, 1961), pp. 45–46 (hereafter cited as Kaplan and Katenbach, *Political Foundations*).

16. Max Radin, "Justice at Nuremberg," *Foreign Affairs* 24 (April, 1946): 379, 380–81 (hereafter cited as Radin, "Justice at Nuremberg").

International Court of Justice allowed only sovereign nations to propose cases; never did it give hearing to individuals.[17]

The personal punishment of leaders also brought to the fore the realist's specific objections to the indictment for waging unjust warfare. First, some opponents to Nuremberg stressed that the complexity of aggression was such that no court could possibly ravel its manifold causes. The Tribunal's inability to provide a definition of what it declared to be the "supreme crime" stood witness to the intricacies involved.[18]

A more novel objection raised by some realists to the court's charge of aggression was that the accusation that Germany initiated unjust war was an Allied myth rather than a criminal indictment. The creation by World War II propaganda of the "good" and "bad" nation fallacy—that some nations by their natures were peace-loving and others were aggressive—was seen as the basis of the Nuremberg verdicts. The realist argued that no inherent differences existed between nations, and what idealists labeled as immoral policies usually were nothing but irrational acts performed by nations caught in predicaments they could not solve diplomatically.[19]

If novelty and diversity keynoted many realists in foreign affairs arguments against Nuremberg, almost all these authors agreed that the fundamental indictment of the Tribunal could be summarized in one word—hypocrisy. This accusation was presented in vivid language: "International hypocrisy probably reached its highest point in the trials of thousands of Germans and Japanese for alleged war crimes"; Nuremberg was an "all-time low point in the prostitution of the forms of law to the purposes of political revenge"; it was "pseudo-legalized vindictive retribution"; and "gratifying it may have been to wartime passions of hatred, revenge and self-righteousness, [it] seems in

17. Edith Wynner and Georgia Lloyd, *Searchlight on Peace Plans: Choose Your Road to World Government* (New York: Dutton, 1949), p. 540 (hereafter cited as Wynner and Lloyd, *Searchlight on Peace Plans*).

18. Roland N. Stromberg, *Collective Security and American Foreign Policy* (New York, Praeger, 1963), p. 183 (hereafter cited as Stromberg, *Collective Security*). Hoffman, "International Systems," p. 228.

19. Louis J. Halle, *Dream and Reality, Aspects of American Foreign Policy* (New York: Harper, 1958), pp. 322–23.

retrospect a colossal blunder, morally, legally and politically." [20]

Three reasons were given for this harsh judgment, but these arguments were basically interdependent: the Allies had committed the same crimes, the trials were "victors' vengeance," and the Tribunal's lesson was that henceforth losers paid with their lives.

Professor Charles C. Tansill, one of the revisionist historians who presented the extreme statement of the realist position, went so far as to claim that the Allies were not only hypocritical but were the real criminals at the trials. Germany, he maintained, by means of World War II had only attempted to break the cruel chains of Versailles. If Henry L. Stimson and Cordell Hull were outraged because "a wild German bull was breaking the choicest dishes in the china shop of world peace, at Nuremberg men were hanged because they had planned to break these vessels filled with national hatreds. Nothing was said of the pseudo statesmen who prepared at Paris the witches' brew that poisoned German minds." [21]

Realists had a field day enumerating Allied war crimes and the victors' moral blindness to their own misdeeds. The litany of Allied atrocities ranged from ruthless saturation bombing of German cities, the invasion of Finland, Russian atrocities in Poland and the Baltic states, the Katyn Forest massacre, the postwar deportation of Germans from central Europe for the crime of their nationality, to the atomic slaughter of Japanese after their

20. In order, William Henry Chamberlin, "The Bankruptcy of a Policy," in Perpetual War for Perpetual Peace, ed. Harry Elmer Barnes (Caldwell, Idaho: Caxton, 1953), p. 533 (hereafter cited as Chamberlin, "Bankruptcy of a Policy"); Ibid., p. 535; Gange, American Foreign Relations, p. 258; William Henry Chamberlin, Beyond Containment (Chicago: Regnery, 1953), p. 73 (hereafter cited as Chamberlin, Beyond Containment).
21. Charles C. Tansill, "The United States and the Road to War in Europe," in Perpetual War for Perpetual Peace, ed. Harry Elmer Barnes (Caldwell, Idaho: Caxton, 1953), p. 96–97. A journalist of the revisionist school, Miss Freda Utley, presented by far the most vehement exposition of that stand. She added to the list of alleged allied crimes the conduct of the war crime trials themselves. Miss Utley asserted that the prosecution used "beatings and brutal kickings; knocking-out teeth and breaking of jaws; mock trials; solitary confinement; torture with burning splinters; the use of investigators pretending to be priests; starvation; and promises of acquittal." The High Cost of Vengeance (Chicago: Regnery, 1949), p. 162 (hereafter cited as Utley, High Cost of Vengeance).

government had started negotiations for surrender.[22] All this evidence indicated to some anti-Nuremberg authors that the trials were merely a catharsis for war-weariness and frustrations. The trials, they contended, were a resurrection of the long discredited "aggressor myth" and "devil theory," the attempt to create the idea that the Allies were angels because the enemy was the embodiment of evil.[23] The Tribunal, for them, was sheerly an imposition of the conquerors' punitive will on the vanquished.[24] It was all "too easy to mistake the voice of the victor for the voice of Divine Justice." [25] The more radical asserted that, because of the alleged Allied aggressions and atrocities, mankind should have convened the Tribunal in Washington and not Nuremberg. The real war criminals were in the Allied capitals.[26]

The realist's conclusion from the alleged Allied hypocrisy at Nuremberg was that it would lead to a ferocious barbarism in future wars. Since the declaration of guilt had no relation to the truth, the practical conclusion to be drawn by nations was that a war must be won by all means.[27] As a consequence, this reasoning continued, Nuremberg's idealism and moralism brought new ruthlessness to a world already terrified by mankind's ingenuity for destruction.

22. In order: Stromberg, *Collective Security*, p. 183; Chamberlin, "Bankruptcy of a Policy," p. 503; Chamberlin, *Beyond Containment*, p. 74; Wynner and Lloyd, *Searchlight on Peace Plans*, p. 540; Charles C. Tansill, "Japanese-American Relations, 1921–1941, Pacific Back Road to War," in *Perpetual War for Perpetual Peace*, ed. Harry Elmer Barnes (Caldwell, Idaho: Caxton, 1953), p. 298 (hereafter cited as Tansill, "Japanese-American Relations").

23. Harry Elmer Barnes, "Revisionism and the Historical Blackout," in *Perpetual War for Perpetual Peace*, ed. Harry Elmer Barnes (Caldwell, Idaho: Caxton Printers, 1953), p. 64.

24. Sisley Huddleston, *Popular Diplomacy and War* (Rindge, N. H.: Richard R. Smith, 1954), p. 190 (hereafter cited as Huddleston, *Popular Diplomacy*); Joseph P. Morray, *From Yalta to Disarmament, Cold War Debate* (New York: MR Press, 1961), p. 74; Stromberg, *Collective Security*, p. 184.

25. Morgenthau, "Views on Nuremberg," p. 267; D. A. Graber, *Crisis Diplomacy, A History of United States Intervention Policies and Practices* (Washington, D.C.: Public Affairs Press, 1959), p. 336 (hereafter cited as Graber, *Crisis Diplomacy*); Gange, *American Foreign Relations*, p. 258.

26. Tansill, "Japanese-American Relations," p. 298.

27. Huddleston, *Popular Diplomacy*, p. 190; Barnes, "Revisionism," pp. 10, 64; Chamberlin, *Beyond Containment*, p. 74.

One charge a few realists added was that the trials were a naïve participation by the other allies in a Communist conspiracy. The prosecution's indictment of financial and industrial leaders proved to Freda Utley that the real objective of the United States policy was to help the Soviets who "were endeavoring to destroy not the Nazi but the pre-Nazi social structure of Germany, based on private property, free enterprise, and the European tradition." [28]

Eugene Davidson, president of the Foundation for Foreign Affairs, in a more moderate and scholarly presentation partly concurred with her thesis, affirming that "for Stalin the successful revolution could come to Germany or any other country only by rooting out the representatives of the old order and their sources of power in industry and land." [29]

Another basic charge against Nuremberg's law by those in foreign affairs was utopianism. The realist asserted that his opponent, in his inordinate seeking after an ideal world, was creating new principles based on the faulty premises of the existence of a stable world order, ideological homogeneity, the positive foundation of a basic likeness in political systems, and an ability of public opinion and "world parliamentarism" to limit the scope of international conflicts.[30] All these assumptions being invalid, then building a foreign policy upon such "sand" would lead only to wasted efforts, disillusionment and possible destruction because of neglect of the actualities of the world situation.

Finally, the realist took one last hard look at Nuremberg and decided that its effect upon the future would be nil. This was one of the basic explanations for the great number of books on post-World War II foreign affairs which were not concerned with the Tribunal. The hope of Nuremberg establishing a deterrent to aggression evaporated quickly when, in the decade after the trial, hostilities blazed forth in many parts of the world.[31]

According to the realist Nuremberg scarcely affected interna-

28. Utley, *High Cost of Vengeance*, p. 183.
29. Davidson, *The Death and Life*, pp. 104–5.
30. Gerhart Niemeyer, "Relevant and Irrelevant Doctrines Concerning International Relations," *World Politics* 4 (January, 1952): 282–92; Kunz, "Swing of the Pendulum," p. 140; Hans Morgenthau, *In Defense of National Interest: A Critical Examination* (New York: Knopf, 1951), pp. 95–99.
31. Gange, *American Foreign Relations*, p. 259.

tional relations because the Tribunal did not fit into the United States' Cold War foreign policy in which the Germans were no longer hated enemies but necessary allies and because the trials did not deal with the fundamental problems between nations. On the international scene, "our first appeal is always to the law and lawyers, and since the questions which the law and lawyer can answer are largely irrelevant to the fundamental issues upon . . . which the peace and welfare of nations depend, our last appeal is always to the general. *Fiat justitia, pereat mundus* became the moth of decadent legalistic statescraft." [32]

The conclusion as well as a basic assumption of the realist philosophy and its judgment on Nuremberg was this affirmation: "The Second World War was a war for survival, undertaken by individual nations in their own national interest, not the punitive war of a morally united humanity for the purpose of making eternal justice prevail." [33]

The relevance of Nuremberg to the "Great Debate" was manifested not only in the realist's mordant condemnation but also by the idealist's vigorous approbation of the Tribunal. The most fundamental concept of the idealist theory was that ideas have consequences. In this context "ideas" must be understood in its most inclusive sense including psychological assumptions, intellectual reasonings, and moral convictions. For the idealist the power of these intangibles was that they were not only great motivating and determining factors in the affairs of men and nations but also the factors giving value to men's deeds and to their very existence. Man's life, not his mere brutish ability to wield power, was endowed with significance by ethical considerations.[34]

A direct consequence of this theory's affirmation of the importance of ideas, convictions, and morals was that it placed the utmost significance upon the difference between right and wrong. The world was not all dull or neutral gray as the realist contended; there were "blacks" and "whites." The world was

32. Morgenthau, *Scientific Man*, p. 121.
33. Morgenthau, "Views on Nuremberg," p. 267.
34. Thomas I. Cook and Malcolm Moos, *Power Through Purpose: The Realism of Idealism as a Basis for Foreign Policy* (Baltimore: Johns Hopkins University Press, 1954), p. 146 (hereafter cited as Cook and Moos, *Power Through Purpose*).

essentially moral, for actions were good and bad; men were honorable or evil. Although virtue and vice were mixed in any given event or person, the idealist believed that men could make valid, ethical judgments on national leaders and their policies.

If ideas constituted the ultimate forces in the world, if right and wrong were of paramount importance, what was to be the criterion of good and evil? The idealist answered simply and directly that his theory considered the values of Western Civilization to have universal validity. This heritage and criterion consisted of "first, the Graeco-Roman concept of man the social-political animal and of law as restraining and enabling principle for his realization. Second, it comprises the Hebraic-Christian revelation of man the essential person, endowed with ultimate dignity and worth, and never to be fully cabined and confined in the matrix of earthly institutions, which are his necessary servants but never his final and all-inclusive masters." [35]

The idealist based the application of his philosophy of international relations on two fundamental analogies: the rules of private behavior were also the rules of state conduct, and the ideal for international affairs was a federalism of equal nations modeled on the parity of the individual states within the United States. These analogies followed from his principle that the world of international relations was a moral world and from the primacy ascribed to national independence and equality. [36]

The conclusions drawn from these concepts of morality and federalism were the absolute necessity for new organizations as instruments of cooperation between nations and the need for an effective international law. A juridical code was essential to the smooth operation of international relations, to the elimination of intimidation by mighty states, and to the promotion of equality, right conduct, and confidence between nations. This international law, for the idealist, must be based on the natural law and must legally enforce a universal morality which the nations of the West claimed to be theirs and which they wished to share with all mankind. [37]

35. Ibid., p. 206.
36. Ibid., pp. 175, 176, 177, 179, 194–95.
37. "Our deeper concern is that international law be based on natural law. A world of justice can be realized only through the securing of men's

Nuremberg embodied the idealist philosophy because the Tribunal dramatically affirmed almost every principle of the theory which we have just examined. The trials were expressly not only the legal but also the moral answer to international crimes.[38] The court clearly proclaimed that a moral code existed and that it was valid for all mankind because the conscience of mankind could make valid and objective the judgments enforcing the accepted standards of western civilization.[39]

The idealist theory, which emphasized the importance of the individual in international law, was affirmed by Nuremberg's establishing the personal accountability of governmental leaders and by asserting that transnational law protected individual men's rights and dignity. That these principles constricted national sovereignty did not trouble the Tribunal or the idealist, for they believed that the world was progressing toward an era in which the law of the nations would be the shield of human rights everywhere.

Consistent with these tenets, the idealist rejected the anti-Nuremberg argument which declared that the law of the Tribunal was retroactive by appealing to a "higher law," a moral code for nations which unequivocally condemned aggression and atrocities. In particular, the idealist urged the validity and applicability of the principle of *mens rea*, holding that "the injustice of *ex post facto* punishment consists in making penal an act which

---

natural rights." Cook and Moos, *Power Through Purpose*, p. 146. See also Dexter Perkins, *America's Quest for Peace* (Bloomington: Indiana University Press, 1962), p. 11 (hereafter cited as Perkins, *America's Quest*); Perkins, *American Approach*, p. 106.

38. "The victors could, of course, have subjected the vanquished to the same type of summary punishment that the Nazis could have been expected to employ, but they would thus have sunk to the moral level of the Nazis." Hollis W. Barber, *Foreign Policies of the United States* (New York: Dryden, 1953), p. 552–53. "The zeal behind the measures is commendable but to many observers it appears they are expressions more of idealism than a realistic grappling with the facts of international life." Gange, *American Foreign Policy*, p. 259. "The defenders of the trials said that the Nuremberg precedent would force the leaders of nations to observe moral and humanitarian principles." Alexander De Conde, *A History of American Foreign Policy* (New York: Scribner, 1963), p. 656 (hereafter cited as De Conde, *History of American Foreign Policy*). See also William E. Jackson, "Putting the Nuremberg Law to Work," *Foreign Affairs* 25 (July, 1947): 564.

39. Taylor, "Nuremberg Trials," pp. 247–48.

when committed seemed innocent or at least indifferent. Can
that be said of the crimes against humanity? And since it cannot,
can there be any injustice for punishing what the consensus of
civilized nations has regarded as punishable?" [40]

If the Tribunal's and the idealist's affirmation of the moral
nature of foreign affairs reminds us of the natural-law philosophy among international lawyers, the insistence that Nuremberg
must fulfill the needs of mankind re-echoed the doctrine of the
legal pragmatist.[41] The idealist affirmed that for survival the
complicated modern world demanded codification of laws which
would embody and preserve man's attempt to solve the perplexing problems which confronted humanity. Not that the establishment of a new international law would be the total solution, but
it was at least a necessary element in man's search for the way
out from the dark world of brutality and ruthlessness. Mankind
must not go down to destruction clutching the ineffectual straws
of sterile nationalism and outmoded legal positivism.

The pragmatic emphasis of the idealist was further revealed in
his championing Nuremberg's principle of individual responsibility. Experience had proved the inefficacy of sanctions upon
nations. Their opponents' objections to personal accountability,
based on the dicta that only states were subjects of international
law and that acts of state created legal immunity for government
leaders, were, for the idealist, "absurd" in the modern day.[42] Such
defenses were a "vestige of the sacrosanctity of an anointed
monarch," a concept straight from the age of the Divine Right of
Kings but meaningless in a world of genocide and totalitarian
states.[43]

40. Radin, "Justice at Nuremberg," p. 375.
41. James R. Shotwell, Preface to "Nuremberg Trials" by Telford Taylor;
International Conciliation no. 450 (April, 1949): 241; Vera Micheles Dean,
The United States and Russia (Cambridge, Mass.: Harvard University Press,
1947), p. 270.
42. Winifred H. Handsel, "Allied Military Rule in Germany," *Foreign
Policy Report* 21 (November 1, 1945): 229; Jackson, "Putting the Nuremberg Law to Work," p. 555; John G. Stoessinger, *The Might of Nations,
World Politics in Our Time* (New York: Random House, 1964), p. 242;
Wynner and Lloyd, *Searchlight on Peace Plans,* p. 540.
43. Radin, "Justice at Nuremberg," p. 370; Richard W. Van Alstyne,
American Diplomacy in Action, 2d ed. (Stanford: Stanford University Press,
1947), p. 477.

The idealist among the experts in foreign affairs did not deny that the Tribunal's enforcement of law by personal punishment limited the absolute nature of national sovereignty. He felt that these new restrictions on governments were required to provide effective means to defend men's rights against the encroachment of the all-powerful state and to protect weaker nations against their more potent neighbors. Nor did the idealist gloss over the obvious ramification of an international court's new ability to call individuals to account. He recognized that it was indeed a giant step toward world government because the principle of personal accountability promoted an international judicial system which could pierce the shield of national sovereignty and touch the citizen directly.[44] He welcomed this development as a necessary advance in international relations.

In response to the extreme realist contention that international law did not exist because of nonobservance of regulations, the idealist maintained that nations of the world did comply with these rules. It was fallacious to judge the law only by sensational violations of its injunctions and to overlook the daily, ordinary compliance with its regulations.[45] He granted that fulfillment of the code's injunctions had not been universal, and consequently a widespread cynicism toward international law was rampant, especially among ordinary citizens, but this resulted from exaggerated expectations of the law's ability to eliminate war. These ill-founded hopes overlooked the fact that international law consisted of a body of rules and regulations which no one could expect to be able to prevent aggression by themselves. Law could make contributions to peace, but to be effective it had to be joined with strong machinery for enforcement and with adequate agencies for settlement of disputes.[46] On the other hand, progress had been made: "We should recall that Members

44. For a negative view see Edgar Ansel Mowrer, *The Nightmare of American Foreign Policy* (New York: Knopf, 1948), p. 25. More positive statements will be found in Quincy Wright, *The Study of International Relations* (New York: Appleton-Century-Crofts, 1955), p. 261; De Conde, *History of American Foreign Policy*, p. 656.

45. Perkins, *America's Quest*, p. 11; Corbett, *Morals, Law and Power*, pp. 24–25.

46. Norman Hill, *International Relations* (New York: Oxford University Press, 1950), p. 124.

of the United Nations did agree to renounce the use of force in international affairs, except to defend against an armed attack— and have, in practice, generally abided by this renunciation." [47]

The idealist maintained that the realist in his attack on supposed "quixotic adventurism and the doctrinaire pursuit of utopias," tilted with a straw man. "Americans are not in great danger of having their national feet lifted off the ground by moral balloons. Their bargain-driving habits (which incidently, they share with the British and the French) guarantee adequate attention to the material aspects of any plan or proposal. Intensive and disillusioning experience since the end of the war is rapidly teaching them to apply their native shrewdness to the problems of world politics." [48] On the other hand, the idealist asserted, the realist's crass espousal of power and his limited concept of national interests made a reality out of the "ugly American" myth by trying to convert the country into a vulgar, might-mad, spartanistic state.

By arguing that "there is probably no human contrivance, however beneficent in design, which cannot be used or misused in unlawful and wicked pursuits," the idealists responded to their opponents' objection that Nuremberg was a dangerous precedent that might boomerang on its creators. "We cannot forego the rule of law in international society because there are those who, at some future date, might seek to pervert it to our detriment." [49]

By these arguments the idealist in foreign affairs supported the action against the German defendants and answered realist objections. If the trials were an anathema to the realist, to the idealist they were a harbinger of constructive efforts to achieve an orderly and law-abiding world. He contended that the court voiced the judgment of mankind's conscience on international criminals and man's will to strive for a better world, not to despair before the power of the state and the power of his own perverted genius for destruction.

47. Richard A. Falk, "The Reality of International Law," *World Politics* 14 (January, 1962): 362. John C. Campbell, *United States in World Affairs, 1945–1947* (New York: Harper, 1947), p. 445.
48. Corbett, "National Interest," pp. 52–53.
49. Taylor, "Nuremberg Trials," pp. 353–54.

After presenting this summary of the attitudes of the realist and idealist toward Nuremberg, we must once more warn the reader that few experts in foreign affairs and political science presented a complete, orderly development such as we have synthesized. Some scholars touched upon only one aspect of Nuremberg. Some applied only one principle of these diplomatic theories in making their judgment. Some were not consistent in employing the system they chose.

Two exceptions to our general presentation are of particular importance. Perhaps the most incisive treatment of Nuremberg by any writer was Otto Kirchheimer's *Political Justice: The Use of Legal Procedures for Political Ends*, which employed law, history, political science, and sociology as tools with which to study the trials. The author adopted a norm of flint hard realism, and yet, unlike the typical realist, supported the Nuremberg experiment. He considered the International Military Tribunal not as a precedent but as the culmination and crown of a long tradition of the use of legal forms to achieve political justice. Kirchheimer categorized Nuremberg as a "successor trial," although he noted that the Tribunal differed from the prototype of this judicial action because it was not a domestic successor discrediting his fallen foe but rather four foreign powers, having come to world supremacy, foisting the evils of the world upon their predecessor in world hegemony.[50]

Designating Nuremberg as a "successor trial" established for Kirchheimer a complete, new criterion for judging the proceedings. On this standard the author maintained that the Allied nations were correct in uniting political and criminal proceedings against the Nazis, for these factors in the practical order were intimately connected with each other. Furthermore, if Nuremberg created the precedent that aggressive war was criminal, its efforts were justified, for this was the paramount political goal of the trials.

In his final verdict on Nuremberg, Kirchheimer arrived at a comprehensive and scholarly evaluation which reflected his realism, his political preoccupation, his concern with national my-

50. Otto Kirchheimer, *Political Justice: The Use of Legal Procedure for Political Ends* (Princeton, N.J.: Princeton University Press, 1961), p. 322 (hereafter cited as Kirchheimer, *Political Justice*).

thology, and his intellectual honesty which at times approximated cynicism. "Yet while the [usual political] trial may enter history," the Princeton Professor declared, "only rarely will it become part of history's own verdict. In an exceptional case, such as the Nuremberg trial, the record of the defunct regime may be so clear-cut that the image produced in court could not but appear a reasonably truthful replica of reality. While the methods, the preoccupations, and the competency of prosecution and court may be endlessly taken to task, the criticism will neither efface nor materially rectify the permanency of the image. But while it retained many overtones of the convenience type of trial, did the Nuremberg trial, with all the hypocrisy and grotesqueness deriving from its very subject, not belong very profoundly in the category of a morally and historically necessary operation?" [51]

Eugene Davidson's *Trial of the Germans* is a second exception to our survey of the two positions in foreign affairs. In this detailed study Davidson presents almost every criticism of the trials urged by the realists, but he seems to have concluded with many reservations that Nuremberg was necessary. "A trial had to take place for political and for psychological reasons; what the Nazis had done was no matter of lurid propaganda. . . . Shocking crimes had been committed, war crimes and murder on a large scale; the question was how their perpetrators were to be dealt with so that victors and those of the vanquished capable of reeducation would see at long last that justice had been done." [52]

Even more than Kirchheimer, Davidson concluded his study of the Tribunal by stressing the complexity and ambiguity involved in the trials and in their effect on subsequent history. He wisely implies that too many simple judgments on Nuremberg have done limited justice to the reality in all its intricacy.

Now that we have surveyed the attitudes of foreign affairs experts, we will briefly consider the views of a group of scholars closely united to these, the American historians. In general the scholars dealing with the history of the United States or Ger-

51. Ibid., p. 423.
52. Eugene Davidson, *The Trial of the Germans* (New York: Macmillan, 1966), p. 586 (hereafter cited as Davidson, *Trial*).

many in the post-World War II period are not noteworthy because of the originality or profundity of their thought. However, they provided an interpretation of the Nuremberg trials which reached an exceptionally large audience. Many Americans, especially students, have obtained their information and views of the Tribunal from these sources.

Most historians of the United States since 1945 tended to leave evaluation and interpretation to scholars in foreign affairs, to popularizers, and to eye-witnesses. These professors realized that because this period was so immediate they lacked the necessary historical perspective and were too emotionally involved in events to evaluate them objectively. Most writers who did not avoid treating this era catalogued occurrences or presented both sides of the interpretational conflict. Some, however, did evaluate Nuremberg, and the majority of these were critical of the trials.[53]

Professor Arthur Link's statement was typical of those textbook writers who condemned Nuremberg: "The Tribunal," he wrote, "tried hard to avoid the appearance of a kangaroo court and observed some of the forms of justice. Even so, the trial violated nearly every tradition of Anglo-American jurisprudence. . . . Above all, the trial of defendants for war crimes and atrocities in a special military court instead of by regular courts established the principle that, as Churchill put it, 'the leaders of a nation defeated in war shall be put to death by the victors.'"[54]

Of interest is Professor Link's view of the Tribunal as one aspect of a short-lived postwar "utopianism" which flowed forth from American messianic efforts to reform other nations.[55] Other authors of American history surveys placed Nuremberg in the

53. Of seventeen authors of textbooks covering the post-World War II period, eight gave a simple objective account or patently balanced arguments for and against the Tribunal. Only three historians favored the trials or some specific aspect of them; six condemned the proceedings.

54. Arthur S. Link, *American Epoch: A History of the United States Since 1890's*, 2d ed. rev. (New York: Knopf, 1963), pp. 693–94 (hereafter cited as Link, *American Epoch*). See also Frank Freidel, *America in the Twentieth Century* (New York: Knopf, 1960), pp. 470–71; Thomas Neville Bonner, *Our Recent Past: American Civilization in the Twentieth Century* (Englewood Cliffs, N.J.: Prentice-Hall, 1963), p. 316.

55. Link, *American Epoch*, p. 693.

context and spirit of the "Morgenthau Plan," a policy of a harsh peace for defeated Germany.[56]

Most textbook writers who favored the trials arrived at their judgment for standard reasons. They maintained that the important aspect was that justice had been accomplished and that the Kellogg-Briand Pact had been enforced by the Tribunal.[57] Samuel Eliot Morison and Henry Steele Commager declared that, although questions might be raised against the entire trial concept, all recognized the beneficial effects of the court's action because aggressive war had been declared criminal and the Tribunal's verdicts prompted the United Nations to adopt the Declaration of Human Rights.[58]

Although these arguments appealed to the textbook writers who defended Nuremberg, the majority of American historians who wrote histories of postwar Germany condemned the trials or ignored the proceedings. The probable reason for the latters' attitude was that they concurred in many judgments and attitudes with their colleagues who specialized in current foreign affairs. Nuremberg was not of prime interest for these historians. It was an incident inserted between the large movements of Hitler's rule and the rising tension of the Cold War. They de-emphasized the trials because they did not fit easily into the pattern of postwar German affairs. The Tribunal exemplified Allied peaceful cooperation which contrasted sharply with subsequent disunity and hostile confrontation. Nuremberg, moreover, symbolized for these writers a harsh peace agreed upon in wartime passion, a policy which was dramatically reversed when Germany became a sought-after prize in a bipolarized Cold War world.[59]

56. John M. Blum et al., *A History of the United States, The National Experience* (New York: Harcourt, Brace and World, 1963), p. 733. See also Harry J. Carman, Harold C. Syrett, and Bernard W. Wish, *A History of the American People*, 2d ed., vol. 2 (New York: Knopf, 1961), p. 863.

57. Dwight Lowell Dumond, *America in Our Times, 1896–1946* (New York: Holt, 1947), pp. 672–73.

58. Samuel Eliot Morison and Henry Steele Commager, *The Growth of the American Republic*, 5th ed. 2 vols. (New York: Oxford University Press, 1962), 2:883.

59. T. L. Jarman, *The Rise and Fall of Nazi Germany* (New York: New York University Press, 1956), pp. 340–41; Drew Middleton, *The Struggle for Germany* (Indianapolis, Ind.: Bobbs-Merrill, 1949) pp. 54–55 (hereafter cited as Middleton, *Struggle for Germany*).

The difference in attitude between American historians of postwar Germany and the foreign affairs experts was the limited, particular, and concrete view of the former. The variety of topics which engaged the interest of the diplomatic writer was not found among the historians whose attention tended to be riveted upon the trials' effect on the conquered enemy and the future of Europe rather than upon a philosophical debate on realism as opposed to idealism.[60] Still, most historians did at least implicitly embrace realist principles by viewing Nuremberg as one event in a momentous political chess game played by the rules of *Realpolitik*.[61]

These, then, were the judgments on Nuremberg of foreign affairs scholars and historians writing on postwar America and Germany. Realism was their dominant creed; their vote on the International Military Tribunal was negative.

60. Henry Cord Meyer, *Five Images of Germany, Half a Century of American Views on German History* (New York: Macmillan, 1960), p. 49.

61. William Henry Chamberlin, *The German Phoenix* (New York: Duell Sloan and Pearce, 1963), p. 42; John Anspacher, "The German Guilt," in *This Is Germany*, ed. Arthur Settel (New York: William Sloan, 1950), pp. 120–22 (hereafter cited as Anspacher, "The German Guilt"); Middleton, *Struggle for Germany*, p. 56.

9

"Theirs Not to Reason Why, Theirs but to Do . . .": Nuremberg and the Military

Hermann Goering, commander in chief of the Air Force, was sentenced to death by hanging; Wilhelm Keitel, chief of the High Command of the Armed Forces, was sentenced to death by hanging; General Jodl, chief of the Operations Staff of the High Command of the Armed Forces, was sentenced to death by hanging; Grand Admiral Raeder, commander-in-chief of the Navy, was sentenced to imprisonment for life; Admiral Doenitz, commander-in-chief of U-Boats, was sentenced to ten years imprisonment.[1]

In solemn, staccato tones the Nuremberg court hammered out in terms of death and confinement new principles affirming that military leaders were legally accountable for crimes against peace and humanity. Never had victorious powers created a tribunal to judge enemy military chieftains, for previously the conquerors had summarily executed opposing commanders or had viewed war as a game played by members of the "honorable profession of arms." At the conclusion of this contest the winner shook hands with the loser. Nuremberg proclaimed that henceforth mankind would hold as legally responsible the warriors who plotted aggression or violated the accepted laws of war.

Professional soldiers were not easily converted to Nuremberg's new military morality.[2] A few weeks after the prosecution's opening remarks, the *New York Times* reported that American

1. *TMWC*, 1:365–66.
2. "Chalice" *Time* 46:26–27; "One for Fifteen," *Time* 46 (December 10, 1945): 28.

army officers objected to the proceedings against their German counterparts, asserting that the military man's fidelity to his oath of obedience provided him with immunity from prosecution.[3] The military defendents at Nuremberg, for whom the question was literally one of life or death, eloquently seconded this thesis and welcomed the moral support of various American members of their fraternity.[4]

At the beginning of the trials a certain cleavage appeared in the ranks of the military. Soldiers whose primary function was leading troops in battle or planning the tactics of combat tended to express fear of Nuremberg's effect on their profession. On the other hand military "executives," whose task was the formation of policy or grand strategy, usually endorsed the Tribunal and the principle of army and navy leaders' legal accountability.[5] In the front ranks of the latter stood Secretary of War Henry L. Stimson, who by pleading and planning had determined that the trials rather than an alternative method be adopted for dealing with war criminals.[6] As Colonel Murray C. Bernays related, the officers of Personnel Division G-1 of the War Department General Staff were the lawyers who took the secretary of war's idea and worked out the methods of indictment, the courtroom procedures, and the manner of conducting the cases.[7] The Navy

3. *New York Times,* December 6, 1945, p. 26. For additional assumptions of the soldier's opposition to trials see: C. Arnold Anderson, "The Utility of the Proposed Trial and Punishment of Enemy Leaders," *American Political Science Review* 37 (December, 1943): 1089 (hereafter cited as Anderson, "Utility of Proposed Trial"); "Nuremberg Tribunal Verdicts Due Next Week," *Army and Navy Bulletin* 2 (September 21, 1946): 10 (hereinafter cited as "Nuremberg Tribunal Verdicts," *Army and Navy Bulletin*).

4. "The professional soldiers among the 22 prisoners were ready to maintain that orders are orders in any army. Keitel sniffed enough support for this theory to observe: 'I am sure there are lots of sympathizers to my way of thinking. I am told that the *Army and Navy Journal* (whose contents he studies) tends to agree with me.' Said Gross-admiral Doenitz' lawyer: 'My client would have a good chance to be acquitted if the judges were Allied naval officers.'" "Indefensibles' Defense," *Time* 47 (March 18, 1946): 29 (hereinafter cited as "Indefensibles' Defense," *Time*).

5. *New York Times,* December 5, 1945, p. 3.

6. Stimson and Bundy, *On Active Service,* p. 584; *Cong. Rec.,* 80 Cong., 2 Sess., 94:A-1082.

7. Murray C. Bernays, "The Legal Basis of the Nuremberg Trials," *Survey Graphic* 35 (January, 1946): 4–9, and (November, 1946), 390–91; *New York Times,* December 16, 1945, 4:8.

Department under Secretary James V. Forrestal also actively cooperated in the trial program.[8]

Two notable indications of the professional military man's opposition to Nuremberg occurred during the trials. One received little publicity; the other had brief notoriety. The first was the simple fact that an American admiral sent encouraging notes to Raeder and Doenitz while they were in the dock.[9] The other incident was the appearance of a critical editorial in the December 1, 1945 *Army and Navy Journal.*[10]

The *Journal's* attack on the Tribunal centered around the prosecution's attempt to obtain a declaration of "a principle of international law under which professional soldiers, sailors and air men shall be convicted as criminals on the mere grounds of membership in High Commands or General Staffs."[11] The editorial insisted that the new principle went against the practice of all civilized nations as well as international conventions governing warfare.[12] A more valid norm, the military weekly maintained, would be "that policy is the responsibility of political government, and in obedience to directives thereunder the military must obediently carry it out. Officers and men going beyond that policy or these directives, and perpetrating outrages as the Germans and Japanese did, properly are subject to punishment."[13] Since the United States armed forces always have taken meticulous care to prosecute any member's violation of law, the editor suggested that Justice Jackson "should be given instructions by the President to abandon a course that has no basis of justice, or the War and Navy Department should condemn it, else gentlemen of ability and experience will not be disposed to hold or seek commissions, and our defense thereby will be gravely impaired."[14]

8. "Navy Department Participation in the Prosecution of War Crimes," *Journal of Criminal Law and Criminology* 36 (May–June, 1945): 39, 40.

9. Anspacher, "The German Guilt," p. 129. For a number of reasons, Mr. Anspacher is unable to name the American admiral involved. Letter of John Anspacher to the author, May 26, 1965.

10. Shirer, *End of Berlin Diary*, p. 325.

11. *Army and Navy Journal*, December 1, 1945, p. 468.

12. Ibid.

13. Ibid.

14. Ibid. The *Journal* cited as examples of adverse criticism of Jackson's views Senator Wherry's request for an investigation into alleged conflicts

The reaction to the *Army and Navy Journal*'s editorial was sharp and dramatic.[15] In a hastily called press conference, Prosecutor Robert Jackson angrily repeated his argument that the German military leaders were not being indicted or tried because of their mere membership in a "profession" but for inhumane and monstrous outrages and for conspiring to bring on an unjust war which had consumed many innocent lives. "The position of the author [of the editorial]," Jackson added, "and those for whom he speaks so inaccurately seems to be that it is alright to punish somebody for illegal war-making, shooting American prisoners of war and murdering and enslaving civilians—so long as you don't get the men who actually did it. This makes nonsense to me."[16] Correspondent William L. Shirer noted in his *Diary* that Justice Jackson's distinction between starting and losing a war was "something that you would have thought would be self-evident even to our brass hats."[17]

A month after the start of the trials in Germany, an *Army and Navy Journal* editorial evaluating General Yamashita's condemnation shed light on the precise objection of the magazine to Nuremberg's principle of organizational guilt. The *Journal* lauded the United States Army court at Manila for sentencing the Japanese leader to hang, and it hailed General MacArthur's approval of the verdict. The editor believed that Yamashita had disgraced the military fraternity and had "profaned the profession of arms, threatened the very fabric of international society, and failed utterly the soldier's faith."[18]

---

between the State Department and army and navy personnel concerning policy in occupied territories and the fact that three of the leading army lawyers withdrew from the trials. Two of the three lawyers mentioned by the *Journal*, General William J. Donovan and Murray I. Gurfein, publicly denied that they left the trials because of any conflict over policy. "I am sure that the *Army and Navy Journal* editorial was written in good faith, but based on a misconception." Letter to the author from Murray I. Gurfein, April 22, 1965.

15. The *New York Times* thought that the *Journal* had "brought out into the open criticisms, heard from time to time, by American colonels and generals in Europe of the trial of military men. This talk, however, has not been echoed by the top American commanders, such as Gen. Dwight D. Eisenhower and Gen. Omar N. Bradley. December 5, 1945, p. 3.
16. *Army and Navy Journal*, December 8, 1945, p. 520.
17. Shirer, *End of Berlin Diary*, p. 325.
18. *Army and Navy Journal*, February 9, 1946, p. 744.

The exact point of the *Journal's* statement was that Yamashita and other commanders should not be punished because they held high positions but because of their abuse of authority and failure to assume responsibilities.[19] The *Journal's* plea for immunity was restricted to the military profession and did not extend to soldiers who allegedly committed the crimes.

The October 1, 1946 announcement of Nuremberg's verdicts of stiff penalties for military men renewed and intensified military reaction to the trials. As soon as the verdicts were read the editor of the *Army and Navy Journal*, LeRoy Whitman, reiterated both his attacks upon Justice Jackson and his principles of organizational guilt. Joy was taken in the judges' acquittal of the German General Staff, the acquittal being based on a legal technicality, and in the frustration of Jackson's attempt to obtain blanket punishment of military organizations and groups.[20] The periodical's basic theme that guilt must be personal also reappeared in the article. In accord with this tenet the *Journal* approved the German military leaders' sentences by ascribing their punishment to criminal commands and cabals rather than to battlefield exploits.

Finally, the editor announced Nuremberg's lesson for the military: "The best way to avoid prosecution and the horrors of defeat is to win a war."[21] This principle was repeated in the *Journal's* "Service News and Gossip" column which, after a gen-

19. Legal experts almost universally disagree with the judgment of the *Journal* on the very point of individual culpability. These lawyers contend that at Manila the prosecution never proved any personal guilt against the Japanese general. Yamashita had been indicted, sentenced and executed not for participating in, ordering, condoning or even knowing about the commission of crimes, but merely for being in command of an area in which outrages had been perpetrated. Many maintain that if ever a military officer were condemned merely because of his membership in the upper echelons of the enemy's military establishment and because of national and personal vindictiveness, Yamashita was that victim. Reel, *Case of Yamashita*, pp. 1, 2, 6, 8, 16, 17, 25, 246–48. Hanson W. Baldwin, "Nuremberg Trial Upholds Our Justice," *New York Times*, October 2, 1946, p. 20.

20. The legal point which frustrated the prosecution's attempt to have the General Staff declared criminal was that the court decided that these military leaders did not have the cohesiveness necessary for them to constitute technically a "group" in the sense of the London Charter.

21. *Army and Navy Journal*, October 5, 1946, p. 112.

eral eulogy of Nuremberg's justice, noted that other modern aggressors were not in the dock. Subsequently a soldier's conclusion was reached: "The moral would seem clear—if wars are imminent, pick the winning side. And if that is the need, there is a corollary moral—maintain such force and such readiness for action if trouble comes, that you WILL be on the winning side." [22]

The man caught in the middle of the personal and official military views of Nuremberg at the time of the verdicts was Army Chief of Staff Dwight David Eisenhower. His immediate reaction to the verdicts displayed an unguarded amazement, although he did not condemn the judgment at Nuremberg, for the General expressed profound surprise at the ease with which the judges dealt with the military defendants. Eisenhower believed their cases were complicated and contained many mitigating factors.[23]

When reporters asked him whether he thought he would have been hanged if the United States had lost the war, the general charmingly replied: "Such thoughts you have!" Eisenhower asserted that two basic facts differentiated his service to his country from that of Keitel: "First, we don't have dictators, thank God, and second, I was in the field." [24] General Keitel had been at the center of decision making.

These were the general's words for publication, but Drew Pearson reported that the commander privately expressed another view to his superiors in Washington. "The War Department isn't saying anything about it but General Eisenhower and Field Marshal Montgomery, both now in Europe, got nervous over the results of the Nuremberg trials. What they didn't like was the conviction of their opposite numbers in the German army, especially Field Marshals Jodl and Keitel and Nazi Admiral Doenitz. Eisenhower sent some rather strong though confidential representations back to the War Department from Europe." [25]

22. Ibid., p. 166.
23. "Morning after Judgment Day," *Time* 48 (October 14, 1946): 32.
24. *New York Times*, October 3, 1946, p. 15.
25. *San Francisco Chronicle*, October 18, 1946.

It might be intimated from the commander's further lucidations of his remarks that the War Department was not completely happy with Eisenhower's original statement to the press. When the general reported to newsmen on his tour of the European theater, he attempted to clarify his former words. Eisenhower explained that he did not question the wisdom of trying high German military leaders. "What I said was that it was none of the Army's business, but that of the International Tribunal. . . . The Nuremberg decision was reached after serious consideration." [26]

This was not the general's last word on Nuremberg. If the International Military Tribunal had not condemned the German General Staff as a criminal organization, it had stated that they were a "disgrace to the honorable profession of arms." On January 22, 1951 authors remembered this verdict when General Eisenhower, newly appointed commander-in-chief of SHAPE, "announced in a public statement at Bad Homburg that he did not consider German military honour to have been sullied." [27] Times and coalitions had changed.

Not all reaction to the verdicts was qualified or uncertain. Many hailed the Nuremberg court's sentences for the generals and admirals as a step toward peace and held the military men's anti-Tribunal attitudes to be based on lack of precise knowledge of the court's decisions or on narrow professional provincialism. [28]

Justice Robert H. Jackson, chief American prosecutor at Nuremberg, provided the Tribunal's most authoritative defense against army critics during the period immediately following the verdicts. After citing the four charges of the indictment as defined in the London Charter, Jackson listed the five defendants connected with the military. Most soldiers would accept the justice's summary of the case against Goering because few military

26. "Eisenhower Reports on ETO Tour," *Army and Navy Bulletin* 2 (October 26, 1946): 2.
27. John W. Wheeler-Bennett, *The Nemesis of Power: The German Army in Politics, 1918–1945* (New York: St. Martin's Press, 1954), p. 44 (hereafter cited as Wheeler-Bennett, *Nemesis of Power*).
28. Harry S Truman, "Reply of President Truman to Justice Jackson," *Department of State Bulletin* 15 (October 27, 1946): 776; Cecil F. Hubbert, "Nuremberg—Justice or Vengeance," *Military Government Journal* 1 (March, 1948): 11–14; Colonel David George Paston, *Superior Orders as Affecting Responsibility for War Crimes* (New York: H. G. Publishing Co., 1946), pp. 1–32 (hereafter cited as Paston, *Superior Orders*).

men considered him to be primarily a soldier.[29] Then Jackson brought forward the case against Keitel. Here again the armed forces would make few objections to his conviction, for Keitel was a contemptible man, a cowardly lackey ever-ready to fawn upon and shout agreement with his Führer. However, few military men wished to consider Keitel representative of the professional soldier.

When Jackson presented the prosecution's evidence against Jodl, Doenitz, and Raeder, facts became few, assertions became vague, and the author seemed to wander continually to the acts of Keitel. Jodl's real crime seemed to have been his knowledge that "incidents" would give Germany an excuse for military action.

The chief prosecutor concluded by maintaining that the real significance of the Nuremberg trials for the armed forces was that "instead of fearing the fact that you might have a trial if you lose a war—and I hope to God you never will—I think the military profession ought to feel grateful that hereafter if this precedent is followed men will not be shot merely because they have lost a war; they will be brought in, given an opportunity to explain their relations and positions, and at least before they are executed will have had an opportunity to be heard." [30]

Military opposition to the principles of Nuremberg did not end with the verdicts. Army officers as leaders of the occupational forces controlled the trials which followed those of the major Nazi leaders, and in this capacity they effectively opposed further applications of the Tribunal's precepts.[31] Some notorious Nazis, many of whom were military men, were not brought to trial, others were not transferred to the country which had jurisdiction over their crimes, perpetrators of atrocities against the Jews were released, and others received ridiculously light

29. Exception might be taken to Jackson's personal opinion that Goering "Was a much more influential and potent man than Hitler himself. He was the focus around which many men rallied who could not have rallied to Hitler, who after all was a vague sort of demogogue and a mystic." Robert H. Jackson, "The Significance of the Nuremberg Trials to the Armed Forces," *Military Affairs* 10 (Winter, 1946): 6 (hereafter cited as Jackson, "Significance of Nuremberg Trials").
30. Ibid., p. 15.
31. Delbert Clark, "Bubble, Bubble, Toil and Trouble," *Saturday Review of Literature* 35 (December 6, 1952): 29, 38.

sentences.[32] The army leaders' policy was aided by a changed political situation. With the coming of the Cold War two rivals were wooing Germany, and the one which pressed too zealously for punishment of former German leaders would not win the hand of the now fair Fraülein.[33]

The conflicting opinions that we have considered regarding Nuremberg's treatment of the military can be reduced to certain basic points of dispute. Those who condemned the Tribunal's new principles urged three fundamental arguments or objections: the problem of "superior orders"; the charge of aggressive war; and the verdict's effect on the future of the military profession. In response to Nuremberg's attempt to establish the principle that a soldier may not comply with a command that is obviously illegal, military men answered that soldiers should not be punished for doing their duty.[34] Concerning the principle of "Theirs not to reason why, theirs but to do, . . ." "Who is to say whether or not the given order is lawful? Is the subordinate required to go back to his bunk, look up the law on the subject, and if he believes the order is not lawful, so report back to his superior and decline to obey? Of course, the fact that he probably would be shot for not obeying the order cuts no figure with the honorable court." [35] The rules and laws of international society constitute an intricate study, because those regulations forbid what might seem to be legal and permit many practices which at first glance appear to be criminal. Consequently, the argument goes, it is impossible for the ordinary soldier to be certain that in any given instance the order he has received should not be obeyed.

Further, changes in warfare made previously illegal actions permissible. The Nuremberg judges refused to punish Nazi admirals for blatant violations of the statutory law of submarine warfare mainly because American Admiral Chester William Nimitz had issued orders for United States submarines to sink enemy ships on sight without any respect for international con-

32. Hobbs, "Indecent Burial," p. 534.
33. Ibid., p. 535.
34. *New York Times,* November 19, 1946, p. 30; *Worker,* October 6, 1946, p. 3.
35. *Brooklyn Eagle,* October 15, 1946.

ventions.[36] British naval policy had endorsed the same principle. The Nuremberg court's verdicts therefore recognized that a legal development had arisen without any international conference, formal treaty, or explicit declaration of a change in the rules. Men asked whether, in such a nebulous legal world, it was just to demand that every soldier master the latest changes or possible changes in the war code.

Prosecutor Robert Jackson was a surprising supporter of the contention that the written laws of war were often relative or obsolete and therefore no sure guide for legal and moral military action. Even more surprising was the authority he cited for his view, Reichsmarshall Hermann Goering. "The Hague Convention was for land warfare," Goering had testified. "When I scanned it over on the eve of the Polish campaign I was reading the articles and I was sorry I had not studied them much sooner. If I had done so, I would have told the Fuehrer that with these rules as they had been put down paragraph by paragraph a modern war could not be waged. . . ."[37]

Jackson suggested that United States officials should seriously consider Goering's opinion. "I think it is a serious question," the Justice wrote, "whether these rules should be allowed to stand in their present conditions in the face of the challenge which Goering throws out, and Goering is not the only man who has the same view of the impossibility of waging total war within these obsolete rules."[38] Although Jackson added many criticisms concerning the existing rules of war, it must be assumed that this judgment did not create for him an impossibility in enforcing a minimum standard of conduct for the military.[39]

36. *Washington Post*, April 14, 1948; *TMWC*, 1:312, 313; Samuel Flagg Bemis, *The United States as a World Power, A Diplomatic History, 1900–1955* (New York: Henry Holt, 1955), p. 875; Harris, *Tyranny on Trial*, pp. 506–7.

37. Goering's testimony as cited in Jackson, "Significance of Nuremberg Trials, p. 11.

38. Ibid., p. 12. Indeed, Justice Jackson could have cited Winston Churchill's famous declaration that he would not be restricted by "legal decisions or neutral rights," and also his statement that "it would not be fair, if in the fight for life and death the Western Powers adhered to legal agreements." Speech of March 30, 1940, as cited in Alfred Vagts, *Defense and Diplomacy: The Soldier and the Conduct of Foreign Relations* (New York: King's Crown Press, 1956), p. 317 (hereafter cited as Vagts, *Defense and Diplomacy*).

39. Ibid.

Armed forces professionals had many objections to Nuremberg's principle which established that generals and admirals were accountable if they plotted or waged aggressive war. First they argued that, although the final belligerent act which broke the peace was indeed a military operation, the forces which impelled such a course were a matrix of social, economic, ideologic, and diplomatic considerations totally outside the competence or control of armed forces commanders.[40] Let political leaders be brought to trial as symbols of the justice or injustice of the nation's decision for war, but let not the generals be tried merely for being the instrument employed to affect decisions made on another level by another authority.

Samuel P. Huntington in *The Soldier and the State* presented in its most sophisticated form the relationship between military and political responsibility. He questioned the validity of the basic premise of those men, technically termed "fusionists," who asserted that any commander in military matters must also be an expert and involved in political considerations.[41] Huntington claimed the fusionist theory dominated civilian thinking in the Cold War administrations and manifested itself in two basic principles or policies. First, it demanded that military leaders incorporate political, economic, and social factors into their thinking. "A second manifestation of fusionist theory was the demand that military leaders assume nonmilitary responsibilities. . . . It was impossible, it was argued, to rely upon the political neutrality of military leaders and their simple obedience to state institutions. . . . One of the most notable manifestations of fusionist theory was the argument that the German generals shared the moral and political guilt of Hitlerism by not openly and energetically opposing the domestic and foreign programs of the Nazi regime." [42]

The attitudes of Justice Robert Jackson on the relation of the military and civilian are interesting in the light of this fusionist theory. At Nuremberg, Jackson was most vehement in his de-

40. "Nuremberg and Tribunal Verdicts," *Army and Navy Bulletin*, p. 10.
41. Samuel P. Huntington, *The Soldier and the State: The Theory and Politics of Civil-Military Relations* (Cambridge: Harvard University Press, 1959), p. 353 (hereafter cited as Huntington, *Soldier and the State*).
42. Ibid.

mand that the generals and admirals be held legally responsible for planning and waging aggressive war and for violating national, international, or natural law. On the other hand, in his dissenting opinion in *Korematsu v. United States*, which dealt with the wartime evacuation of Japanese-Americans from the west coast, he held for a "suspended constitution in wartime" or, more exactly, a "dormant court." "It would be an impractical and dangerous idealism," Jackson declared, "to expect that each specific military command in an area of probable operations will conform to conventional tests of constitutionality. When an area is so beset that it must be put under military control at all, the paramount consideration is that his measures be successful rather than legal. . . . No court can require such a commander in such circumstances to act as a reasonable man. . . ."[43] Louis Smith commented on this opinion: "In his varied capacities as Attorney-General, Justice of the Supreme Court, and prosecutor of war criminals at the Nuremberg trials, Justice Jackson has appeared to act on varied premises as to the rule of law in regard to the conduct of military command in wartime."[44]

Second, military men objected to the indictment for aggression because they felt that an enemy could always picture strategic planning done in peacetime as a conspiracy to wage unjust war.[45] For example, army leaders worried that a maneuver such as "Operation Muskox," the joint United States and Canadian military exercise conducted to explore the difficulties of arctic warfare, might subsequently be depicted as an aggressive scheme against Russia.[46]

Another argument against the aggression charge was that a nation's assertion that it was fighting a defensive war involved highly intricate and subjective political and military factors. Alfred Vagts, an American expert on army affairs, accepted the validity of the Nazi generals' defensive statement that they were fighting a preventive war in the sense that Vagts believed the

43. Louis Smith, *American Democracy and Military Power: A Study of Civil Control of the Military Power in the United States* (Chicago: University of Chicago Press, 1951), p. 297.
44. Ibid., p. 357.
45. Vagts, *Defense and Diplomacy*, pp. 263, 319.
46. *San Francisco Chronicle*, October 18, 1946; *New York Times*, November 19, 1946, p. 30.

German military leaders were sincere in holding this opinion. The Nazi chieftains' logic was that the conflicts of World War II were inevitable, and that, as the Wehrmacht was numerically inferior, waiting for the attack would be suicidal.[47]

The soldier's final major objection to Nuremberg's new law for military men looked to the pragmatic effects upon the profession's future. Army leaders first argued that the Tribunal's attack upon the technical plea of "superior orders" would demoralize the Allied armies. This prospect cast terror not only into military leaders but also deep into the hearts of United States congressmen. Congressman George A. Dondero of Michigan considered that the most sinister idea of the "left wingers and ideologists" who influenced the United States' German policy was the opinion of the war-crimes tribunal: "The obedience of a soldier is not the obedience of an automaton. A soldier is a reasoning agent. It is a fallacy of widespread consumption that a soldier is required to do everything his superior orders him to do. The Subordinate is bound only to obey the lawful orders of his superior."

Dondero commented on this decision: "Follow the implications of this statement through to a logical conclusion. In effect, it encourages mass disobedience to superior officers within our armed forces. Implied therein is the threat that if the forces of international communism are victorious, ruthless vengeance will be meted out to those who dare defend their country and its interests. . . . The person or persons who are responsible for this formulation should be severely disciplined."[48]

Senator Burton K. Wheeler, democrat from Montana, raised a similar fear, and Admiral William Leahy, chief of staff under Presidents Roosevelt and Truman, also was apprehensive about the disintegration of army morale and judged that the Tribunal was grossly unfair to military personnel because now a conquering nation could label any soldier of the defeated nation a "war criminal" merely for opposing it in war.[49]

47. Vagts, *Defense and Diplomacy*, p. 319.
48. *Cong. Rec.*, 80 Cong., 2 Sess., 94:A-2369.
49. Ibid., 79 Cong., 1 Sess., 91:11019; Leahy, *I Was There*, p. 315. See also Nicholas Doman, "Political Consequences of the Nuremberg Trial," *Annals of the American Academy* 216 (July, 1946): 87 (hereafter cited as Doman, "Political Consequences").

Lieutenant Colonel P. F. Gault, who served in the Judge Advocate General's Department and was a member of the committee on military and naval law of the American Bar Association, presented a slight variant on the idea of the disastrous effect, upon military leaders, of the precedent for wholesale retribution. The author, perhaps epitomizing the military mind, contended that the trials were bungled because civilians were allowed to dominate the proceedings and because "for the orderly trial and punishment of war crimes as defined and established and commonly accepted [as] law the army needs neither advice nor instruction from civilians." [50] Gault added at another time that "the basic difficulty with the whole procedure is that Nuremberg is entirely a civilian show and strictly amateur at that." [51] For the Lieutenant Colonel, the Tribunal's verdicts on military leaders resulted from noncombatants working out their hatred and frustrations upon soldiers whose only crime was defending their country. [52]

The military's attacks on Nuremberg were not placidly accepted. Anne O'Hare McCormick's *New York Times* column noted that professional soldiers were especially forceful in opposition to the condemnation of organizations as criminal, "but others believe that one of the most hopeful results of the trials is to put powerful governments on record in agreeing that organizations like secret police forces, military associations, parties or even armies can be responsible instruments of oppression or terrorization." [53]

Some newspapers, in fact, denounced the court's failure to declare the German General Staff and the High Command to be criminal organizations. [54] Other writers claimed hypocrisy or naïvete were expressed in the military's protestations that their profession had no part in political decisions. Critics maintained

50. Gault, "Prosecution," p. 180.
51. *Army and Navy Journal*, December 15, 1945, p. 522.
52. Gault, "Prosecution," p. 180. "The entire Jackson program has been arbitrary and ridiculous from the beginning"; *Army and Navy Journal*, December 15, 1945, p. 522.
53. *New York Times*, October 2, 1946, p. 28. See also the *Brooklyn Eagle*, October 7, 1946.
54. *Philadelphia Inquirer*, October 2, 1946; *St. Louis Post-Dispatch*, October 1, 1946; *New York Post* as cited in the *Army and Navy Journal*, October 19, 1946, p. 15.

that "the prosecution has shown that members of these groups
were not purely military technicians; they were informed of, and
initiated in, political and diplomatic considerations and schemes.
. . . No responsible military leader can contend that his role is
merely that of a concierge or custodian of the war machine
under his command and that he bears no responsibility for the
use to which that machine is put. . . . They are on trial not
because they lost the war but because they started it. And if
recognition is given to the claim of the prosecutors, then this will
mean that the collective security of world society attained supremacy over the personal security of the militarists." [55]

One of the most systematic studies of the active military
intrigue for Nazi aggression was Commander Anthony Talerico,
Jr.'s article "Operation Justice" in the semiofficial *United States
Navy Institute Proceedings*. This professor at the Naval College
summarized Nuremberg's verdicts against each of the German
officers and indicated that the court condemned them primarily
for initiating aggressive action against Denmark and Norway.
Talerico's summary is worth a careful reading because we might
wonder if the evidence adduced against the military leaders by
the author justified the court's stern sentences. "Admiral Raeder,"
Talerico writes, "who claimed that he did nothing that the Allied
Admirals would not have done, is shown in conference with
Hitler, Goering, and Quisling, while preparing the invasion.
Admiral Raeder was also the originator of the armament plan for
attaining readiness for war which would enable the Nazis to
initiate war without an alert. For these non-professional operations he was sentenced to life imprisonment. Admiral Doenitz
issued the operational order for the invasion of Norway and
Denmark, but this was done in a professional status which
caused his final judgment to include only ten years imprisonment." [56]

In the light of Justice Jackson and Commander Talerico's
difficulties in proving a conclusive case against some of the
German war leaders, the general indifference or acquiescence of
many military writers regarding the Nuremberg convictions and

55. Doman, "Political Consequences," p. 88. See also *Detroit News,* October 19, 1946; *Army and Navy Journal,* December 15, 1945, p. 522.
56. Anthony Talerico, Jr., "Operation Justice," *United States Naval Institute Proceedings* 73 (May, 1947): 519.

punishments might seem amazing. Military journals, letters, and books usually repeated vague generalizations that the defendants were not convicted for their acts as soldiers but for their influence upon diplomacy or for atrocities. The verdict condemning Admiral Doenitz to prison for ten years because he issued a military order implementing a program decided on by political leaders should have touched a sore spot. This was especially true because the main crime of the admiral was the invasion of Denmark and Norway, a military operation which preceded by a few weeks, an identical British expedition.[57]

Why were not more questions asked, more objections raised? Much can be explained by the unavailability of the transcript of the Tribunal's proceedings at the time when most military men made their comments. When the record was published it provided a more substantial basis for punishment than that indicated by Talerico and Jackson. A less technical but perhaps more persuasive influence was the temper of the times. The public reaction to Senator Taft's criticism of Nuremberg stood as a warning to anyone who would object to the trials. The American people were unable or unwilling to distinguish legal and political difficulties from moral and emotional considerations.

Pro-Nuremberg writers answered by factual arguments the soldier's problem with the court's refusal to accept the defense of "superior orders." Some authorities pointed out that, in the past, military courts frequently declared that such a plea gave no automatic immunity. Others noted that the purported orders for violations often had never been issued or that the criminal aspect of a policy was an addition of the individual commander.[58] Others claimed that the military codes of almost every army, including Germany's, allowed the soldier to refuse to comply with any order that was obviously criminal.[59]

The *Detroit News* printed a popular answer to the military men's objection that the verdicts threatened their profession's future. An editorial stated "They That Take the Sword Shall Perish with the Sword." The *News* noted military opposition to Nuremberg's judgment but indicated its support for the court's

57. Vagts, *Defense and Diplomacy*, p. 317.
58. *Army and Navy Journal*, December 22, 1945, p. 579.
59. *New York Times*, December 16, 1945, 4:8 and October 26, 1945, p.. 18; Jackson, "Significance of Nuremberg Trials," p. 13.

ruling because "Joe Doakes, the little guy who goes to war because he is sent, will not complain at the creation of this hazard for those engaged as political or military planners in the business of promoting war. If losing a war is to constitute a capital offense, there will, he will be inclined to think quite simply, be fewer wars."[60]

Some antimilitary newspapers presented a final criticism of the soldiers' attitude toward Nuremberg. The papers did this by expressing their concern because the army personnel did not seem to have their hearts in the proceedings. These presses dramatized the military's lack of righteous indignation by reporting the champagne party which was held by wives of the defendants and attended by United States officers on the prosecution staff.[61]

Nuremberg's significance for the military does not end with eleven bodies swinging from the Bavarian gallows in 1946. The Tribunal had come to grips with basic problems concerning conduct in war, ultimate responsibility for decisions, and the conscience, or lack of conscience, of every military man. New circumstances and new personalities developed ramifications undreamed of by the Nuremberg judges as they handed down their decisions.

At 4:00 A.M., June 25, 1950 invading forces swept out of North Korea and new factors crowded upon the world scene. What was the relevance of Nuremberg to the Korean conflict? The United Nations' condemnation of North Korea as an aggressor nation certainly expressed the spirit of the judgment given October 1, 1946. Nuremberg's meaning was, however, even more dramatically portrayed in the contest between President Harry S Truman and General Douglas MacArthur. The following questions became urgent and crucial: What was the responsibility of a military commander when he was fully convinced that the policy of his country was against the nation's true interests? How far was he limited to a blind obedience to civilian policy makers? When must he choose his conscience's dictates over his commander-in-chief's orders?

After his removal from command in Korea because of his

60. *Detroit News,* October 1, 1946.
61. Ibid., October 10, 1946, p. 1.

conflict with presidential policy, General Douglas MacArthur developed at length his philosophy of military obedience in his speech before the Massachusetts legislature July 25, 1951. Mac-Arthur said: "For example, I find in existence a new and heretofore unknown and dangerous concept that the members of our armed forces owe primary allegiance and loyalty to those who temporarily exercise the authority of the executive branch of government, rather than to the country and its constitution which they are to defend. No proposition could be more dangerous. None could cast greater doubt upon the integrity of the armed service. For its application would at once convert them from their traditional and constitutional role as the instrument for the defense of the Republic into something partaking of the nature of a pretorian guard owing sole allegiance to the political master of the hour. . . . Yet so inordinate has been the application of the executive power that members of the armed service have been subjected to the most arbitrary and ruthless treatment for daring to speak the truth in accordance with conviction and conscience." [62]

Although more immediate and sensational aspects of the Truman-MacArthur controversy overshadowed this speech of the general, a few newspapers did take issue with the former commander's statement. The *Washington Post* called attention to this paragraph of the speech in its July 28, 1951 editorial and held that the real peril for the republic was not the phantom spectors of doom enumerated by the general but MacArthur's own doctrine of military disobedience. Although the army leader said he never questioned the chief executive's authority, the paper contended that his principle "comes close to saying that the President should not have final control over the military." [63] The *Post* solved MacArthur's problem of soldier's allegiance by asserting the principle that faithful service to the country must be manifested by absolute fidelity to the president, who was in turn responsible to the people.

62. Douglas MacArthur, *Revitalizing a Nation: A Statement of Beliefs, Opinions and Policies Embodied in the Public Pronouncements of General of the Army Douglas MacArthur*, correlated and captioned by John M. Pratt (Chicago: Heritage Foundation, 1952), p. 61.

63. *Washington Post*, July 28, 1951.

The complexity of the problem of military obedience was indicated clearly by the fact that many who had demanded that the German generals follow their conscience, even to death, now demanded just as vehemently that American military leaders should leave all decision to the civilian branch of the government and concern themselves exclusively with fighting war as they were paid to do. Samuel Huntington castigated just such attitudes as an illustration of the illogical nature of the fusionist theory: "Some supporters of this critique rather brazenly defied logic by supplementing their denunciations of von Runstedt in 1945 with an equally vehement attack on MacArthur in 1951." [64]

The MacArthur controversy created some interest in the principles and law of Nuremberg, but from the trials' end to America's involvement in Vietnam, Nuremberg was not a major concern of America or other nations. The growth of opposition to the United States' action in southeast Asia, however, resurrected the memory of the World War II Tribunal. Behind the war protestors' burning of draft cards, behind their spread fingers, and behind their chant of "Hell, No! We won't Go!" were the language and arguments popularized in World War II and crystallized at Nuremberg: "The war is illegal and criminal"; "American is the aggressor"; "Green Berets commit war crimes"; "The Government is guilty of genocide and crimes against humanity." Supporters of the administration in rebuttal constantly brought the debate back to the points that "North Vietnam is the aggressor"; "It has perpetrated crimes against peace"; "Ho Chi Minh is another Hitler"; "The Viet Cong commit atrocities and war crimes."

With these passionate words Nuremberg, as law and precedent, moved toward center stage. No single incident brought about this new development; it took shape gradually. Usually the motion consisted of two steps forward, then—with a realization of what Nuremberg's application would mean—one step backward. It was as if men and nations realized that the Tribunal must be fitted in somewhere, but also that the world was not yet ready to handle its full implications.

64. Huntington, *Soldier and the State*, p. 353.

The movements forward centered about three incidents: the proposed trial of American airmen, Lord Russell's Stockholm tribunal, and the case of Captain Levy.

On June 19, 1966 Nguyen Hoa, counsel general of North Vietnam, announced in New Delhi that American pilots held in North Vietnam were "war criminals" and that Hanoi had the right to put them on trial. The Counsel General justified his statement by saying that the aviators were classified as criminals under the statutes of the Nuremberg Charter.[65] "The charges made against the fliers were that their missions, in themselves, constituted aggressive war and were crimes against the peace, and that the numerous bombing raids had resulted in war crimes (wanton destruction of villages) and crimes against humanity (inhumane acts committed against a civilian population)."[66] The irony of this situation was that by Hanoi's action Nuremberg had been brought into conflict with the Geneva Convention for war prisoners and with regulations similar to those for which the Tribunal had tried to provide effective sanctions.[67]

World reaction was immediate, violent, and negative. U Thant, secretary general of the United Nations, Pope Paul VI, British Prime Minister Harold Wilson, and officials of the International Red Cross appealed directly and indirectly to President Ho Chi Minh not to go through with the proposed trials. Ho Chi Minh, either because he had misjudged the reaction to his idea or because he had achieved his psychological goals, immediately responded that prisoners of war held by the North Vietnamese would be treated humanely. A short while later Robert Little, an enterprising CBS official, took a wild chance by cabling Ho Chi Minh to ask if the trials would take place. The North Vietnamese president cabled back: "No trials in view."[68] A relative calm came as quickly as had the preceding storm.

65. *New York Times*, July 19, 1966, p. 3.
66. Delbert D. Smith, "The Geneva Prisoner of War Convention: An Appraisal," *New York University Law Review* 62 (November, 1967): 902.
67. George F. Westerman, "International Law Protects PW's," *Army Information Digest* 22 (February, 1967): 32–33, 39 (hereafter cited as Westerman, "International Law Protects PW's").
68. "An Instructive Episode," *Nation* 203 (August 8, 1966): 108 (hereafter cited as "Instructive Episode," *Nation*).

American attitudes toward North Vietnam's alleged application of the Nuremberg precedent were similar to those of the rest
of the world but were much more intense. This was one issue on
which "doves" and "hawks" agreed although for widely different
motives. Antiwar leaders such as Norman Thomas, Dr. Benjamin
Spock, Senator Wayne Morse, and Senator William Fulbright
(as well as other congressional dissenters from administration
policy) wrote to Ho Chi Minh that nothing would destroy
antiwar sentiment in the United States and unite the nation to
crush his government as would the execution of the flyers.[69] They
might agree with the North Vietnamese president that the American war effort violated Nuremberg's statutes, but pragmatically
his proposed policy was suicidal folly. Administration leaders
and supporters concurred that any execution would unite the
country as Pearl Harbor had done.

Some individuals attempted to answer the legal questions
raised by North Vietnam's appeal to the Nuremberg precedent.
Senator Thomas Dodd, one of the American prosecutors at the
Tribunal, called Hanoi's proposed court "legal skulduggery." The
post-World War II tribunal, he pointed out, had judged violations of accepted international standards by major war ciminals.
In the present case there was no legitimate charge because "the
American airmen in Vietnam are soldiers performing military
duties in the strictest sense of the definition."[70]

President Johnson also stressed that "military men, who
[were] carrying out military assignment in line of duty against
military targets, are not war criminals, and should not be treated
as such."[71]

Experts in military law further developed the defense of Dodd
and the president by citing the fact that the airmen were prisoners of war and therefore protected from trial by the Geneva
Convention. They asserted that contrary to Hanoi's claim these
agreements were binding even when there was no formal decla-

69. *New York Times,* July 16, 1966, p. 15; Ibid., July 20, 1966, p. 1.
70. Ibid., July 23, 1966, p. 3. For other popular defenses maintaining that
Nuremberg's law did not apply to the airmen see "Deplorable and Repulsive," *Time* 88 (July 29, 1966): 13; "If North Vietnam 'Convicts'
Captured U.S. Fliers—," *U.S. News and World Report* 61 (August 1, 1966):
20.
71. *New York Times,* July 15, 1966, p. 1.

ration of war.[72] Only a few writers pointed out that North Vietnam had made an explicit reservation to the Geneva Convention regarding war criminals. This reservation allowed prisoners to be tried for "acts committed prior to capture." [73]

Most administration officials and supporters of their policy did not indulge in any legal arguments concerning Hanoi's proposed war-crime trials. Their response was much more direct: "Execute the fliers and the American people will make you pay for it a thousand times over." When North Vietnam announced its plan Arthur Goldberg, United States ambassador to the United Nations, asked the International Red Cross to provide protection for the American airmen but also made public the statement that there would be "disastrous consequences" if the threat were carried out.[74] This was reiterated by many government officials. Vice President Hubert H. Humphrey, Secretary of State Dean Rusk, and Ambassador at Large W. Averell Harriman stated that harm to the prisoners would be an "extremely grave development." [75] Georgia's Richard B. Russell, chairman of the Senate Armed Services Committee, warned that the execution of United States fliers would "bring about the application of power that will make a desert of their country." [76] A number of American publications seconded this threat of vast retribution. Jack Anderson, writing for the Los Angeles Times, said that President Johnson "had confided to intimates" that if the trials and executions took place he might have to ask for a declaration of war and then pursue the conflict to total victory.[77]

The incident passed but thoughtful men wondered—wondered in the words and concepts of Nuremberg. The execution of

72. Westerman, "International Law Protects PW's," 33; Wade S. Hooker, Jr. and David H. Savasten, "The Geneva Conventions of 1949: Application in the Vietnamese Conflict," *Virginia Journal of International Law* 5 (Number 2, 1965): 248.
73. *New York Times,* July 20, 1966, p. 2; Clayton Fritchey, *Los Angeles Times,* July 27, 1966.
74. *New York Times,* July 19, 1966, p. 3.
75. Ibid., July 20, 1966, p. 2.
76. "Hanoi's Kind of Escalation," *Time* 88 (July 22, 1966): 26. This view was seconded by George D. Aiken, ranking Senate Republican and a member of the Foreign Relations Committee, *Minneapolis Tribune,* July 17, 1966.
77. Jack Anderson, "Reds to Decide U.S. Position," *Los Angeles Times,* July 27, 1966.

the American airmen might well be a crime, but did not the administration's "proposal to obliterate tens of thousands of noncombatant North Vietnamese in retaliation for the execution of 37 Americans—unjust though it would be—dangerously [resemble] the Nazi's retaliatory slaughter of noncombatants in Lidice and other hostage towns and villages." [78] The *Nation* also pondered: "If the flyers themselves were not war criminals, it became perfectly obvious that genocide did not repel numerous U.S. politicians and publicists. Few were willing to advocate it forthrightly—the gimmick was that the American people would unite in an irresistible demand for the nuclear destruction of North Vietnam if the flyers were harmed. . . . Congressmen, editors, and others behaved as if the prisoners had already been condemned and were on the scaffold with the noose around their necks. It was almost as if they WANTED the men to be put to death, so that their hawkish passions would be justified by the event." [79]

The *Nation's* vague hint that the government's militant indignation might be contrived and premeditated was spelled out by the *St. Louis Post-Dispatch*. It affirmed a credibility gap. Individual antiadministration leaders had been asked by U.S. government officials to appeal privately to Hanoi for the airmen on the grounds that the enemy would listen only to them. As soon as they complied with this request, government spokesmen publicly issued violent threats. The *Post-Dispatch* wondered if the administration was not deliberately inflaming public opinion to

78. *Minneapolis Tribune*, July 19, 1966.
79. "Instructive Episode," *Nation*, p. 108. A typical statement that the *Nation* might be alluding to was attributed by another publication to a senior military man in Washington who said: "If one American is tried and shot by the Hanoi government, I do not see how this country can be restrained from bombing the cities of North Vietnam until they are completely devastated." *U.S. News and World Report*, "If North Vietnam 'Convicts' Captured U.S. Fliers—," p. 21. The theme of awesome retribution was the most dominant idea appearing in the United States press. See James Reston, "Washington: The American Prisoners in Hanoi," *New York Times*, July 13, 1966, p. 42; "War Crimes Trials in Hanoi," *Los Angeles Times*, July 15, 1966; Roscoe Drummond, "Prisoners of War: Hanoi's Fateful Threat," *Washington Post*, July 20, 1966; *Chicago Tribune*, July 15, 1966; *Detroit News, Atlanta Journal, Louisville Courier-Journal* as quoted in the *New York Times*, July 24, 1966, 4:11.

unite the country behind its policies. The editor thought that the incident could have been settled by private negotiations rather than public fanfare.[80]

The *Chicago Tribune* ran a biting editorial connecting the trials of the flyers and that of Nuremberg. In contrast to the liberal press, this newspaper viewed the situation realistically and admitted that the doctrines given sanction at Nuremberg did relate to Hanoi's claims. Instead of insisting that the American flyers were not involved in war crimes and therefore could not be tried, the *Tribune* insisted that the entire Nuremberg doctrine was nonsense. "We have handed them [Hanoi] . . . a fictitious legal pretext which they threaten to turn against our fighting men."[81] The United States was thus caught in a dilemma of its own making. "Obeying military commands and yielding to superior authority were rejected as legitimate defenses by the Nuernberg tribunal. Are we to be accessories in the condemnation of our sons out of our own past follies?"[82]

The position of the *Chicago Tribune* was echoed with some difference in tone in the *National Review*. James Burnham believed that Ho Chi Minh was using the threatened trials as a political and psychological weapon. The Nuremberg principles were being employed to make the United States look like an aggressor, but "it is our nation more than any other that is responsible for the Nuremberg concepts. We have got ourselves tangled in nets largely of our own weaving."[83]

Senator Everett Dirksen concurred with the *Chicago Tribune* and *National Review*'s judgment. Commenting to a reporter Dirksen said that the Nuremberg trials "may have been a ghastly mistake" in the light of the threat to try the flyers.[84]

From the various views on the proposed trial of the airmen we can see that, although there was criticism of the bellicose attitude of certain American officials, the majority of the nation held

80. *Saint Louis Post-Dispatch,* July 19, 1966.
81. "Postscript to Tokyo and Nuernberg," *Chicago Tribune,* July 11, 1966.
82. Ibid.
83. James Burnham, "Hanoi's Special Weapons System," *National Review* 18 (August 9, 1966): 764.
84. *Chicago Tribune,* July 20, 1966.

that no matter how some might interpret Nuremberg's principles, they believed that the military man doing what he was ordered was not personally responsible for his country's decision to go to war nor for judging whether that action was aggression. Second, most citizens in a simple patriotic spirit assumed that it was impossible for Americans to commit war crimes. Third, by their endorsement of threats of retribution if the trials took place, the people implicitly acknowledged that, whatever the justice of the charges, trying military men for war crimes was feasible only when the judging nation was strong enough not to fear reprisals. Finally, the extensive discussion on the flyers and Nuremberg indicated a new American awareness of the attempts to create an international criminal law and a rather shocking realization that other nations might not see the United States's role in future international trials as exclusively that of judge of other nations' wrong doings. Americans might be the defendants in the dock.

In May 1967 European condemnations of America's action in Vietnam came to a climax with the Stockholm War-Crime Trial. Lord Bertrand Russell, a brilliant and controversial British critic for over half a century, assembled Asian and European intellectuals to formally condemn President Lyndon B. Johnson and other political and military leaders of the United States.

Russell's trial certainly recalled the name of the International War-Crime Trials. Perhaps, in some strange fashion, it renewed the spirit of Nuremberg. But the substance—the procedure, the structure, and the power—were not even sought. It was not a trial but a form; the aim was not juridical but propagandistic. The Stockholm group admitted this implicitly by the composition of the court, explicitly in their diatribes. The "court" was composed of a seventeen-man jury; there was no judge. There were three lawyers; the remaining were poets, novelists, historians, and diplomats. No testimony contradicting the predetermined conclusion was allowed. No juridical power or authority was claimed. As the court's president Jean-Paul Sartre, the renowned French philosopher and novelist, stated in inaugurating the proceedings: "What a strange tribunal: a jury and no judge. It is true: we have neither the power to condemn, nor the power to acquit anyone. Therefore, no prosecution. . . . But the judges are everywhere. They are the people of the world, and particularly the American people. It is for them that we are working." [85]

Russell's court sat for eight days and came in with the expected unanimous verdict: "Guilty. In view of international law, the U.S. Government and U.S. armed forces have committed aggression in Vietnam." [86]

Americans noted that the Stockholm trial was called a war-crimes tribunal and that Russell and his followers had attempted a "do-it yourself Nuremberg." [87] Hardly anyone, however, seriously compared the two trials, because the differences were so obvious and startling. Stockholm was not in the image of Nuremberg except by the most surrealist imagining.

Official United States policy toward the trial in Sweden was epitomized by Secretary of State Dean Rusk's comment that he did not wish "to play games with a 94-year-old Englishman." [88] This policy was eminently successful. Although the trial achieved some minor publicity in Europe and Asia, it did not have its desired impact in these areas. The Stockholm jury itself became bored after a few days because of the inevitability of the judgment.[89]

The government's policy of ignoring the trial was also successful at home. Many American publications printed nothing on Russell's trial; almost nowhere was great enthusiasm shown except among the Englishman's diehard followers.[90] The attitude of others who paid attention to the trial was scorn, ridicule, and pity. These reactions centered on Bertrand Russell the man as well as on his court.

New York Times columnist C. L. Sulzberger presented Russell as a "corpse on horseback," an empty shell tied to his mount like El Cid in his final battle against the Moors. "It is pitiable," he

85. Gosta Julin, "Evidence at Stockholm: The Judges are Everywhere," Nation 206 (June 5, 1967): 712 (hereafter cited as Julin, "Evidence at Stockholm"); Sam Rosenwein, "International War Crimes Tribunal: Stockholm Session," Guild Practitioner 27 (Winter, 1968): 22–29.

86. Julin, "Evidence at Stockholm," 712.

87. "The Trial Begins," Newsweek 69 (May 2, 1967): 54; New York Times, May 11, 1967, p. 61.

88. "The Games Men Play," Newsweek 69 (May 15, 1967): 44.

89. Ibid.

90. New York Times, May 14, 1967, 4:3.

wrote, "when a hero becomes his own tomb." [91] Journalist Bernard Levin depicted Russell as "an old man in a hurry, who has left his judgment, his reputation and his usefulness behind." [92]

Some writers declared the trial itself ridiculous because the verdict was announced before the hearings began. *Time* magazine hardly left its readers in doubt concerning its attitude when it stated that "Jean-Paul Sartre, long a Communist crony, called together a sullen séance of left-wing conjurors who had reached their verdict long before the trial started." [93]

Americans did not think that Russell's trial had done any great harm to the United States. A few thought that the Tribunal had helped the nation's cause. Among these were *Time* and *Commonweal* magazines. Their reasons differed vastly because of their attitudes toward administration policy. *Time* affirmed that the trials were beneficial because influential European papers had labelled the Stockholm production a "circus," "childishness," an excuse "for those who want to avoid thinking seriously about Viet Nam." *Time* concluded, "It finally exposed the extreme critics of the U.S. position in Viet Nam for what they are—cynical and ridiculous." [94]

Commonweal, however, thought that the profit of the trial was that it dramatized to the world and to the United States in particular the criminal course of American action in Vietnam and called men to reassess their positions. Moreover, the trial's exploration of new methods of protest exemplified the novel forms needed to dramatize problems so citizens might be "coordinated into a gigantic effort to rescue the nation and the world from what can only be described as Lyndon's folly." [95]

Reaction to the Russell trial seems to indicate that the makeshift tribunal and its foreign condemnations of American actions

91. C. L. Sulzberger, "Corpse on Horseback," *New York Times*, May 12, 1967, p. 46. For a defense of the British philosopher's view on the war crimes tribunal see Robert Scheer, "Lord Russell," *Ramparts* 5 (May, 1967): 16–23 (hereafter cited as Scheer, "Lord Russell").

92. Bernard Levin, "Bertrand Russell: Prosecutor, Judge and Jury," *New York Times Magazine*, February 19, 1967, 68.

93. "Sartre's Seance," *Time* 89 (May 12, 1967): 30. Even Scheer in "Lord Russell" agreed that the trial was ineffective, p. 22.

94. "Trial's End," *Time* 89 (May 19, 1967): 37.

95. "The Dissent Ahead," *Commonweal* 86 (May 16, 1967): 252.

did not arouse enthusiasm in the United States even among those who opposed the administration's policy. Although the prisoner of war trial controversy presented an issue that was nearly impossible for Americans to avoid, they found it relatively easy to ignore or ridicule the Stockholm experiment. Factors such as Russell's personality, the partiality of the tribunal, the philosophical estericism of the proceedings, and a basic patriotic reaction to criticism by outsiders ran counter to any renewed interest in international criminal law and the personal responsibility of the military.

Hanoi's proposed trials and the Stockholm War-Crimes Tribunal were events outside the nation which related Nuremberg to Vietnam. Within the United States, in a more constant if less sensational form, the International Military Tribunal was linked to the war in southeast Asia. The law and the rhetoric of Nuremberg were heard in antiwar speeches, accusations, and petitions, and appeared most forcefully in refusals of induction into the army and of assignment to Vietnam.

Conscientious objection has been a policy followed by a few in almost every war. The numbers of those taking this means of dissent to the Vietnam war, however, made their stand a national concern. As always the basic reason offered for such action was that one must follow his conscience rather than the nation's call to arms. For him the war effort was immoral and criminal. In the past the government had demanded that the objector must be a pacifist—one convinced that all war of its nature was wrong. Some Americans would not go as far as to condemn all conflicts but felt that serving the government's policy in Vietnam was morally impossible for them. They needed, therefore, new legal arguments to justify their attitude and action. One of these was the "Nuremberg Defense," an effort to incorporate Nuremberg's principles as a functioning part of our national law.[96]

When this argument was first introduced, judges peremptorily dismissed it by affirming the right of the government to decide

96. Mary K. Kaufman, "The Individual's Duty under the Law of Nurnberg: The Effect of Knowledge on Justiciability," *Guild Practitioner* 27 (Winter, 1968): 16 (hereafter cited as Kaufman, "Nurnberg and Justiciability").

whether the war was necessary for the nation. The court's duty was to judge according to the existing laws and not to decide whether the war was moral and legal. But insistence by defense lawyers on the relevance of the World War II Tribunal brought about a slow growth of awareness that led some to believe that Nuremberg might indeed have some role in the trials of war protestors.

On September 16, 1965 D. H. Mitchell was sentenced to five years in prison as an evader of the draft. The defendant had pleaded that the Nuremberg trials affirmed the principle of individual responsibility and guilt. Therefore, he felt that he must avoid complicity in what he alleged were the "criminal actions of the government." [97] New York Federal District Judge T. Emmet Clarie barred from evidence any facts concerning war crimes as not germane.

Mitchell's case was appealed, but the Supreme Court ruled against hearing his motion. Paradoxically, this negative decision was the occasion of Justice William O. Douglas' dissent which raised many of the questions that would vex courts concerning the Nuremberg Defense. Douglas contended that the federal courts should answer some "extremely sensitive and delicate questions." Specifically, the justice wished the courts to decide whether the London Charter, which established Nuremberg's principle of personal responsibility of the individual military man, was a treaty since it had been signed by the governments of Great Britain, Russia, France, and the United States. If it were declared a treaty, it would be part of United States law. Douglas continued his questioning: If the charter was binding as a treaty, could it be applied to the Vietnam conflict, the judicial branch determining whether the United States action there was technically a war and whether it was aggression? Finally, the justice wished the court to judge whether a private individual could raise these questions, and, if so, could the court consider the questions in defense or in mitigation of a sentence? [98] Justice Douglas in his dissent thought that Mitchell had a right to

97. *New York Times*, September 16, 1965, p. 27.
98. Ibid., May 21, 1967, p. 13. See also Kaufman, "Nurnberg and Justiciability," p. 17.

attempt to show that the United States was violating the London Charter and that he might be found guilty as a war criminal if he participated in the conflict as a soldier.[99]

While Mitchell's case of refusal of induction was being processed through the courts of appeal, three soldiers, Pvt. David A. Samos, Pfc. James A. Johnson, Jr., and Pvt. Dennis Mora, on trial for refusing assignment to Vietnam, pleaded the Nuremberg Defense. Colonel Maguire, officer of the military court-martial, agreed with the civilian judge in Mitchell's case that the legality of the war could not be debated in the courtroom. He argued that President Johnson as commander-in-chief had full authority to order men to Vietnam.[100] The soldiers were convicted, but they immediately instituted suit in the federal courts challenging the actions of President Johnson and Secretary of Defense Robert S. McNamara on the grounds that the war violated international agreements and the principles of the Nuremberg war-crime trials. This legal action was unsuccessful.

Attempts to employ the Nuremberg Defense culminated in the Fort Jackson, S.C. trial of Captain Howard Brett Levy, a Brooklyn dermatologist.[101] This medical officer was charged with disobeying a written order to train Green Berets in the treatment of skin diseases and with promoting "disloyalty and disaffection" among Army troops bound for Vietnam. Levy's lawyer, Charles Morgan, Jr., of the American Civil Liberties Union, attempted many defenses for his client, e.g., medical ethics, racial prejudice, violation of the right of free speech.

Finally, on May 17, 1967 Colonel Earl V. Brown, law officer or presiding official, was perhaps exasperated by the defense's spicing "the otherwise routine trial with dark hints that U.S. Special Forces in Viet Nam were guilty of war crimes as heinous as any

99. *New York Times*, May 21, 1967, p. 13.

100. Ibid., September 10, 1966, p. 4. "The major problem in cases raising the Nurnberg claim concerning our conduct in Vietnam is whether the courts will treat this question as a justiciable one or as a political one solely within the competence of the executive." Kaufman, "Nurnberg and Justiciability," p. 18.

101. The Defense was later raised, but unsuccessfully, in the case of Benjamin Spock and others for counseling draft resistance. Arthur L. Goodhart, "Draft Resistance and the 'Nuremberg Defense,'" *New York Times*, May 25, 1968, p. 34.

condemned at Nürnberg two decades ago." Or perhaps he
wished to clear the military of vague general charges and put the
peace movement on the defensive. Regardless of his reason
Brown told defense attorney Morgan that the Nuremberg Defense was admissible.[102] "My research discloses," Colonel Brown
stated, "the Nürnberg trials involve a rule that a soldier must
refuse an order to commit war crimes. If it can be shown that by
obeying an order Levy was abetting the commission of atrocities
the major charge against him would be dropped." [103] The defense
lawyer, therefore, was permitted to prove the United States had
committed war crimes, but he also had to prove that these were
not isolated incidents but a matter of policy.

On the appointed day Colonel Brown heard Morgan's evidence without the other members of the court-martial present.
He ruled, as was expected by both prosecution and defense, that
the charge had not been proved and that the argument was
therefore not admissible in court. The defense attorney was as
relieved as anyone with the decision. "At last I can get back to
the business of defending my client," Morgan said, "instead of
prosecuting the whole damn Army." [104] The Nuremberg Defense
had been allowed in a domestic court for the first time.

Reaction to the Levy trial showed consensus that the hearing
of the Nuremberg Defense was an interesting and significant
precedent.[105] All agreed, moreover, that the task of proving a
strict similarity between Nazi Germany and the United States

102. *Washington Post*, May 18, 1967, May 21, 1967; "Men at War," *Time*
89 (June 2, 1967): 15.
103. "Nürnberg & Viet Nam," *Time* 89 (May 26, 1967): 20; *Washington
Post*, May 18, 1967; *New York Times*, May 22, 1967, p. 4. Benjamin B.
Ferencz, former executive counsel at Nuremberg (certainly no "hawk"),
disagreed with Brown's research. "No principle evolved during the Nuremberg war crime trials requires disobedience to either the draft or combat
in Vietnam." Letters to the Editor of the *Times*, *New York Times*, May 14,
1968, p. 17.
104. "Back to Business," *Newsweek* 69 (June 5, 1967): 30.
105. "Nuremberg Revisited," *Newsweek* 69 (May 29, 1967), 23; *Washington Post*, May 18, 1967; Elinor Langer, "The Court-Martial of Captain
Levy: Medical Ethics v. Military Law," *Science* 156 (June 9, 1967): 1347
(hereafter cited as Langer, "Court-Martial of Captain Levy"); "Nuernberg
Echoes," *Chicago Tribune*, May 22, 1967. John MacKenzie argued that the
precedent Brown set by allowing the Nuremberg Defense was not binding
on other courts in the United States: *Washington Post*, May 28, 1967.

was out of the question.[106] Beyond this factual consensus, opinion split radically. The bitter sarcasm used by both sides revealed the intensity of the division in this country.

Pro-administration speakers and writers seemed to second the views of Captain Richard Shusterman, senior prosecutor in the Levy trial, who maintained that "no man in uniform can pass on the 'wisdom and propriety' of his commanding officers' orders. To recognize such a privilege would permit every soldier to become a law unto himself." [107] He added that "personal ethics, religious feelings or medical scruples were no defense against wilful refusal to obey a lawful order." [108]

Newspapers and magazines insisted that the army must have discipline and that only the most naïve could think that a soldier's individuality and freedom of speech should not be curtailed for the necessary right order. "An army is an instrument," the *Baltimore Sun* editorialized, "which must be fused for its harsh work by subordination of the individual . . ." [109] Moreover, the army's morale was of the highest importance, and therefore Levy's advising soldiers not to fight was wrong. The *Air Force Times* calmly presented the military man's viewpoint: "It appears to us that Levy's court-martial acted with restraint and complete fairness. It found him unfit to be an officer, and the three-year sentence seems a well-deserved punishment." [110]

The most abstract and yet the most penetrating study of the connection of Vietnam and Nuremberg with respect to the Levy case was written by Martin Redish. After discussing Nuremberg's relation to national prejudice and to international law, he treated the Tribunal's principle for the military. Redish held that the concept of absolute liability of every soldier to judge the legality of all orders placed the military man in an impossible dilemma. It was his opinion that absolute liability should be

106. *Washington Post*, June 6, 1967; "The Burrowers," *Birmingham News*, May 23, 1967.
107. "Nürnberg & Viet Nam," p. 20; Nicholas von Hoffman, *Washington Post*, May 16, 1967.
108. *New York Times*, May 16, 1967, p. 8. When the Levy court adopted this view it was bitterly criticized by Nicholas von Hoffman in "The Conviction of Captain Levy," *New Republic* 156 (June 17, 1967): 11.
109. *Baltimore Sun*, June 4, 1967.
110. "Court Actions," *Air Force Times* 27 (July 5, 1967): 12.

changed to accountability for war crimes only in those cases such as the Nazi concentration camps where there was "manifest illegality." [111]

Redish saw the Levy trial as the United States beginning a trend to adopt the absolute liability rule. He was opposed to this. Only those who order crimes perpetrated should be held responsible because if we accept absolute liability the individual might become a "sacrificial lamb." The consequence of Redish's doctrine for the Levy case was that Levy would not have been able to use the Nuremberg Defense to justify his refusal to obey superior orders. [112]

Anti-Vietnam war writers, however, urged that Nuremberg had established that all men are personally responsible for their actions and that the military man could not follow the orders of superiors blindly or without any decision on the action's legality or morality. [113]

Other critics went further and claimed that the accusation that the United States had committed war crimes could be proved. Not that they had evidence of a vast campaign of genocide or of ruthless aggresssion, but they felt that in a technical sense the charge could be established. They cited the United States Army Manual, *The Law of Land Warfare:* "Every violation of the law of war is a war crime." They went on to maintain that in the Levy trial "the defense proved several such violations, including mutilation of the dead, using weapons that cause unnecessary suffering, forcible removal and transfer of civilians, assassination teams, placing a bounty on enemy heads, wanton destruction,

111. Martin Redish, "Military Law: Nuremberg Rule of Superior Orders," *Harvard International Law Journal* 9 (Winter, 1968): 169.

112. Ibid.

113. *U.S. Catholic* as quoted in "Just War," *Commonweal* 87 (December 22, 1967): 372. See also the *Los Angeles Times* June 4, 1967. It is a curious fact that although most nations of western Europe changed their military code to eliminate the defense of "Superior Orders" and establish personal responsibility, the United States manual of November 15, 1944, Section 345(1) was much more conservative than the English, Russian or French army code. In July 1956, the regulation was revised, qualified and confused. "This equivocal statement could serve as authority for the commission of almost every type of atrocity against the belligerent nations as well as, in many cases, against civilians." Alan M. Wilner, "Superior Orders as a Defense to Violations of International Criminal Law," *Maryland Law Review* 26 (Spring, 1966): 142.

summary execution of prisoners and torture."[114] Most of these charges concerned not action by Americans but complicity in the atrocities of the South Vietnamese.[115]

An unusual argument on Levy's behalf, typical perhaps of the New Left, was presented by Elinor Langer. Levy's punishment was "unsettling" to her because of the authoritarian nature of the army into which he had been drafted. This resulted in Levy's being sanctioned by a system over which he had no control, whose purpose and values were not his. She worried because he was jailed for committing a crime that was to him the opposite of a crime.[116]

One reader objected to her argument and philosophy in the following manner: If the only type justice which Miss Langer would not find "unsettling" was that in which the defendant would admit he committed a crime and would affirm the values and purpose of the system, then what of the Nuremberg war-crime trials? The reader pointed out that the defendants certainly did not consider their actions crimes, although they murdered millions, and certainly did not accept the purposes and values of their conquerors. By her norms, therefore, there was little basis for the Tribunal.[117]

The opinions expressed by Americans concerning the Levy case showed both positive and negative attitudes toward international law and Nuremberg. On the positive side Colonel Brown's action of allowing war-crime evidence to be heard in a domestic military court was a first. While a few publications regarded the introduction of such evidence as a nuisance, the general opinion was that it was in accord with international law.

Even those publications and reporters who rejoiced at Morgan's failure to prove a systematic pattern of war crimes paid an off-hand deference to the principles of international law and the Nuremberg precedent. By stating relief that Morgan could not

114. Ira Glasser, "Judgment at Fort Jackson: The Court Martial of Captain Howard B. Levy," *Law in Transition* 4 (September, 1967): 123 (hereafter cited as Glasser, "Judgment at Fort Jackson"); *Los Angeles Times*, June 4, 1967; *New York Times*, May 25, 1967, p. 1.
115. Glasser, "Judgment at Fort Jackson," p. 149.
116. Langer, "Court-Martial of Captain Levy," 1350.
117. Kurt Gingold, "Letters: Captain Levy and Army System," *Science* 157 (July 14, 1967): 140.

produce evidence, they implicitly accepted the principle that theoretically the United States could be convicted of war crimes.

Perhaps the most important comment expressed in the Levy case came as we have noted, from Martin Redish when he discussed "Nuremberg and Common Sense." While the average American and even the average reporter did not talk in terms of "absolute liability" and "manifest illegality," these concepts apparently were at the root of what the nonlegal mind was attempting to point out in regard to the Nuremberg principle of the responsibility of the military. While there was widespread sympathy for Levy and his dilemma of conscience, most negative comment on his case, at least from such liberal papers as the *New York Times* and the *Washington Post*, can be seen as an unwillingness to accept the absolute liability principle. It would be easy to interpret this as being anti-Nuremberg, but it is probably more accurate to say that it was a different interpretation of Nuremberg than that offered by Levy.

These years of debate on Vietnam and Nuremberg had their effect upon the attitudes of military men. In 1968 Admiral James Calvert's statements on assuming the position of superintendent of the United States Naval Academy reflected a new awareness shared by many American armed forces men. The Admiral said: "A policy might be doubted or even challenged—Vietnam is an example—and yet, in the case of the professional military man, the total loyalty to the American system, and willingness to serve it, remain untouched. The military obligation of every young American should rest, in other words, on an abstract value, a higher value than what might be seen as right or wrong about any given U.S. policy on any given day. I can't see how our system can continue to function effectively without acceptance of that principle—and believe me, I thoroughly understand that the shadow of the Nuremberg trials—the Achilles' heel of all nationalism—hangs over that statement." [118] Calvert further elucidated the Tribunal's ramifications by saying that "if the shadow of Nuremberg hangs over loyalty to the system, then an equally large shadow hangs over dissent which is carried too far. It is difficult and it may be impossible to define exactly what 'too

118. "A Submariner Rises to Annapolis," *Life* 65 (November 22, 1968): 60.

far' means. But I can define it for the professional military men: it's when dissent calls for change outside the American system." [119]

The principles of the Nuremberg trials were no longer a subject for calm historical study; the Vietnam debate had once more made them a matter of life or death, freedom or prison.

We have just seen that during the past decades numerous writers commented on different incidents involving the soldiers' reactions to the Tribunal's principles. General Telford Taylor, however, raised the discussion to a more philosophical level. In *Sword and Swastika* he wrote a remarkably incisive study of the fundamental theory involved in Nuremberg's principle of accountability of the military for national crimes. The perpetration by some German military men of war crimes and atrocities as defined by the Hague and Geneva Conventions was admitted, and their punishment was accepted as just. The crux was the charge of aggression. Taylor used two examples to illustrate the complications involved in this question. The German General Seeckt was condemned for asserting the Army's independence of the politicians because his policy weakened the Weimar Republic. General Douglas MacArthur's removal from command for opposing civilian policy makers was widely lauded. If one approved of the judgments on these commanders, Taylor questioned, how can one find any basis for condemning the German generals of the Third Reich? "Did they not likewise owe full obedience to Adolf Hitler, who had been appointed Chancellor by Hindenburg, confirmed in office by popular election, and acclaimed in Hindenburg's political testament? Is it the duty of generals to obey to the letter the orders of a democratic government, but to confound, undermine and destroy an authoritarian regime?" [120]

Taylor maintains that the apparent dilemma was not a superficial puzzle but was rooted deep in basic assumptions of political and military life, because one element of republicanism in western civilization was the control of the military by civilian authority. Even acceptance of this principle, however, did not contain a

119. Ibid.
120. Teleford Taylor, *Sword and Swastika: Generals and Nazis in the Third Reich* (New York: Simon and Schuster, 1952), p. 369.

final solution to the difficulty because the real problem arises if one universalizes this tenet and affirms the doctrine of the complete obedience of the military to any political regime. "Are they mere janitors of the military machine, with no responsibility for the use to which it is put? Are they, in short, political eunuchs, deprived of the capacity of moral judgment on their own behalf?" [121] If the answer is yes, the soldier may become bloody tyranny's dread instrument of terror. If the answer is yes, the German generals were innocent and Nuremberg was unjust.

General Taylor's final answer was the addition of one word to the thesis: Military men owe allegiance and absolute obedience to any *legitimate* government. The Third Reich, according to Taylor, was not legitimate, for, although it came to power by means that technically might be democratic and constitutional, once in power its activities amounted to a revolution because it systematically violated the laws and constitution of the Weimar Republic. Consequently the German generals should have refused to support the dictatorship.

This was Nuremberg's judgment on the military and the military's judgment on Nuremberg. Although the court eliminated the world's problem of what to do with the German war leaders, it raised many perplexing questions for which men could only grope for answers. If it seemed impossible to arrive at solutions which were completely satisfying, men were still driven on in their investigations because of the ever increasing role of the military in the world of the Cold War. Although the Tribunal's verdicts on the armed forces leaders might seem to be in the sphere restricted to the professional soldier's judgment, people everywhere thought that on a much deeper level the question of the Tribunal and the generals was also their question. War in the modern world belonged to everyman. More and more men asked the right to have a say in their own destruction. This was why men looked long and hard at the different facets of the relationship between the soldier and the world as highlighted by the trials. Man must answer the question: As the power of the soldier grows should his responsibility increase? Or, is the role of the military man still essentially to do and die as ordered, and never to reason why?

121. Ibid., p. 370.

10

Behavioral Scientists
View the Major War-Crime Trials

During the committee hearing on House Joint Resolution 93 for "The Punishment of War Criminals," Congresswoman Emily Taft Douglas of Illinois expressed her interest in the psychological aspects of the Nazi atrocities: "I would like to say something contradicting a statement that was made here today that worries me very much. One of the members of the committee said that we all know about war crimes. We don't know about war crimes. We don't know at all. We know specifically of atrocities, but we do not understand the psychology of war crimes. . . . There has been a psychological sickness that has bred these crimes, which we must understand or we cannot cope with it in the future." [1]

Not only Congresswoman Douglas but many thoughtful Americans were interested in the psychological and sociological factors involved in the war crimes and the punishment related to them. The intensity and threatening nature of the human dynamics revealed by Nazi atrocities and aggression impelled intelligent men to wonder not so much about what had been done but why it was done. To this question the behavioral sciences sought an answer.

Nuremberg and the war crimes were of interest to the different behavioral sciences because the Tribunal provided a unique opportunity to study sociological and psychological variables characteristic of the modern world. Among the most obvious and important of these were the relation of personality and power, man's role in the hierarchical structure of modern bureaucracy,

1. *Punishment of War Criminals, Hearings before the Committee on Foreign Affairs, House of Representatives*, 79 Cong., 1 Sess., on H. J. Res. 93 (Washington: Government Printing Office, 1945), pp. 89–90.

the dynamics of the totalitarian state, the process of political
decision making, crowd psychology, the effects of propaganda
on cultural and ethical norms, and the validity of psychoanalyt-
ical theories of national character.[2]

Each of the three branches of the behavioral sciences that we
are primarily considering—psychology, psychiatry, and sociology—had special reasons for its fascination with the Nuremberg
court. Because aggression, tension, and international disorder
were special concerns of modern psychology, Nuremberg was for
this science a "test tube" in which psychic elements present in
the prototype of aggressive action could be studied, totalitarian
leaders' appeals analyzed, followers' responses examined, and
psychological theories tested.[3]

Psychologists also scrutinized the Nuremberg proceedings because they realized, as did the general public, that the ultimate
success of the assize depended upon men's reactions to the
judicial process.[4] They knew that in order to win mankind's
endorsement, Nuremberg had to satisfy the psychic needs of
conquering Allies, liberated nations, and defeated Germans.

To many psychiatrists war is a prime sickness of man's spirit
and reflects a basic disorder in political and economic realms and
in man's psyche.[5] Most psychiatrists have confined their studies
to the mental health of individuals, but some experts have attempted psychoanalytic interpretations of groups and states.[6] If

2. John Dawson, review of *Nuremberg Trial and Aggressive War* by
Sheldon Glueck, *American Sociological Review* 12 (February, 1947): 125
(hereafter cited as Dawson, review of Glueck's *Nuremberg Trial*).

3. "The conscious reasons for war are to gain territory, geographic disputes, to achieve political or religious independence, to gain access to raw
materials needed in industry and to gain prestige of some sort. However,
the more important ones are unconscious. It is an international mental
problem." Nolan D. C. Lewis, "Impressions of the Psychological Factors in
Nazi Ideology," *Digest of Neurology and Psychiatry* 15 (January, 1947): 70
(hereafter cited as Lewis, "Psychological Factors").

4. Sheldon Glueck, "Justice for War Criminals," *American Mercury* 60
(March, 1945): 275 (hereafter cited as Glueck, "Justice for War Criminals"); Corbett, *Law and Society*, pp. 230–31.

5. G. B. Chisholm, "The Reestablishment of Peacetime Society,"
Psychiatry 5 (February, 1946): 7; Thomas C. Rennie and Luther E. Woodward, *Mental Health in Modern Society* (Cambridge, Mass.: Harvard University Press, 1948), p. 386.

6. Theodore Abel, "Is a Psychiatric Interpretation of the German Enigma
Necessary?" *American Sociological Review* 10 (August, 1945): 457–64

the latter generalizations are not as strictly scientific as personal clinical studies, these theories at times supply rare insights into basic disorders in national and international relations.[7] The war trials uniquely lent themselves to psychiatric studies of guilt and remorse, of the superego of both western civilization and Nazi Germany, of symbolism and myth, and of identification and projection.[8]

Nuremberg also held particular interest for sociologists. Although the court posed questions which could be investigated on the individual level, the Tribunal intentionally as well as unconsciously often dealt with group dynamics and social relationships. It even treated the elusive and perhaps unscientific—perhaps suprascientific—concept of national character. Sociology in particular maintained that the solution to unjust warfare must involve social controls. No matter how many inanimate factors influenced any decision for aggression, the ultimate election was made by one group of humans interacting with another group.[9]

(hereafter cited as Abel, "Psychiatric Interpretation"); Henry V. Dick, "Personality Traits and National Socialist Ideology," *Human Relations* 3 (June, 1950): 141; Elton E. McNeil, "Psychology and War: A Review of Leonard Berkowitz, *Aggression: A Social Psychological Analysis,*" *Journal of Conflict Resolution* 7 (December, 1963): 777 (hereafter cited as McNeil, "Psychology and War").

7. Maurice Duverget, *An Introduction to the Social Sciences*, trans. Malcolm Anderson (New York: Praeger, 1964), p. 188. An interesting comparison is provided by Peter McKellar, a Scottish psychologist: "The Nuremberg trial paralleled in some ways what happens during psycho-analytic treatment. Ego-defenses of the denial, repression and isolation types are broken down, and the accused were forced to face both external reality and their own emotions. . . . If the trial is considered in terms of one of the important things which happened during psycho-analytic treatment (ridding the personality of unrealistic ego-defenses), it is interesting to note that the 'treatment' was most markedly unsuccessful in the case of the very bad obsessional." Peter McKellar, " 'Responsibility' for the Nazi Policy of Extermination," *Journal of Social Psychology* 34 (November, 1951): 160 (hereafter cited as McKellar, " 'Responsibility' for Nazi Policy").

8. Leo Alexander, "War Crimes, Their Social-Psychological Aspects," *American Journal of Psychiatry* 105 (September, 1948): 170–71.

9. Percy Winner, "The Atom at Nürnberg," *Commonweal* 43 (March 22, 1946): 569 (hereafter cited as Winner, "Atom at Nürnberg"); Wechsler, "Issues of Nuremberg," p. 9. "With the added impact of the atomic bomb the challenge to sociology becomes overwhelming. 'Cultural lag' ceases to be a trite classroom phrase. With explosive force a question is pressed upon us. Can sociology catch up to physics before man blows himself from this

The indictment of "Crimes against humanity" essentially stated a
social accusation in legal terms.[10]

All these considerations impelled experts in psychology, psychiatry, and sociology to interpret Nuremberg in terms of their
disciplines. Many amateurs adopted at least some general terms
and theories of these sciences because the trials, by their very
nature, were so concerned with the attitudes, reactions, and
motives of men and nations.

We will divide our study of the behavioral interpretation of
Nuremberg into two parts. First, we will consider opinions on
particular aspects of the actual trials proceedings, and second,
we will note comprehensive interpretations of the psychological
and sociological motivation which determined the adoption of
the trial method for punishing war criminals. Our first part
investigates specifically the Nuremberg defendants' mentality;
then, the "Mind" of the German people is studied.

Two experts who were assigned to observe the Nuremberg
prisoners published studies of their findings. Captain Gustave
Mark Gilbert, prison psychologist at Nuremberg, presented in his
Nuremberg Diary a record of the words and reactions of the
accused, not a rigidly structured psychological study of the
defendants.[11] The result was a series of psychological cameos or
psychiatric phrase diagnoses.[12] For example, we are informed
that Rudolf Hess's reactions were "typical of the hysterical per-

planet as a biological reject, too bright in some respects and in others not
bright enough?" Clifford Kirkpatrick, "Sociological Principles and Occupied
Germany," *American Sociological Review* 11 (February, 1946): 67 (hereafter cited as Kirkpatrick, "Sociological Principles").

10. Herbert W. Briggs, "New Dimensions in International Law," *American Political Science Review* 46 (September, 1952): 688–89; *Trial of the
Major War Criminals before the International Military Tribunal, Nuremberg:
14 November 1945–1 October 1946* (Nuremberg: International Military
Tribunal, 1947), 5:407.

11. Editor's introduction to Gustave Mark Gilbert, "Hermann Goering,
Amiable Psychopath," *Journal of Abnormal and Social Psychology* 43 (April,
1948): 211 (hereafter cited as Gilbert, "Hermann Goering, Amiable Psychopath").

12. Review of *Nuremberg Diary* by G. M. Gilbert, *New Yorker*, 23 (June
14, 1947): 98. See also Louis L. Snyder, Review of *Nuremberg Diary* by
G. M. Gilbert, *American Historical Review* 53 (October, 1947): 167 (hereafter cited as Snyder, Review of Gilbert, *Nuremberg Diary*).

sonality" and showed "delusions of reference and persecution." Streicher's "lewd perverted mind" showed an "obsessive-compulsive neurosis or an organic psychosis." Hermann Goering proved to the author's satisfaction that he was a moral coward, "for, he died as he had lived, a psychopath trying to make a mockery of all human values and to distract from his guilt by a dramatic gesture." [13] In spite of this last censure, Gilbert still held Goering to be an "amiable psychopath" with many outstanding qualities of leadership.

Douglas Kelley, author of 22 *Cells at Nuremberg* and a psychiatrist nationally known as an authority on Rorschach testing, reported the results of his investigation in psychological vignettes of each of the defendants.[14] Besides providing this information, Kelley's psychoanalyses of the accused exploded many American wartime myths concerning the Nazi leaders. In particular, Kelley destroyed the rumors that Baldur von Schirach was a homosexual. He found rather that Schirach was good material gone wrong. The doctor contends that Rudolph Hess's amnesia was not a hoax, but that the defendant's claim that it was a pretense was untrue. Herman Goering, in spite of all war propaganda, was not a fat fool, not impotent, and not a homosexual. "He was a shrewd, courageous, conscience-less, natural leader who took advantage of Hitler's qualities as a leader to ride to power." [15]

Doctor Kelley's general conclusion, at variance with American wartime legend as well as Gilbert's sketches, was much more disturbing than any of these factual items. The psychiatrist and others contended that the modern tragedies of aggression and atrocities documented at Nuremberg were created by individuals generally of superior mental ability who were, with few excep-

13. Gilbert, *Nuremberg Diary;* Hess mentioned pp. 11, 172, Streicher mentioned pp. 9, 73–74, and Ribbentrop mentioned p. 235.

14. The nature and value of these tests is presented in Douglas M. Kelley, "Preliminary Studies of the Rorschach Records of the Nazi War Criminals," *Rorschach Research Exchange* 10 (June, 1946): 45–48 (hereafter cited as Kelley, "Preliminary Studies").

15. Douglas McGladen Kelley, 22 *Cells at Nuremberg, A Psychiatrist Examines the Nazi Criminals* (New York: Greenberg, 1947), p. 125 (hereafter cited as Kelley, 22 *Cells at Nuremberg*).

tions, comparatively normal in the psychiatric sense.[16] At most some defendants might be considered eccentric or fanatic, but certainly they were not insane. The popular "Mad Man" theory of the enemy leaders and of the war's causation found little verification in his psychiatric studies.

The second enigma posed by the Nuremberg evidence was the twisted mind of the Nazi nation. This puzzle was: How could individuals, and indeed a whole nation, long considered an integral part of western civilization, actively or passively participate in the monstrous crimes of the Third Reich?[17]

Most explanations of the Nazi criminal mentality explored the idea of the German's acceptance of the theories of racism and social Darwinism. Experts contended that the Nazi policies, especially their barbaric outrages against the Jews, resulted from an uncritically assumed dogma held in blind faith. The German people accepted the Nazi racial doctrine that the preservation and prosperity of the Master Race was the end of a biological evolution. Therefore, when inferior races interfered with the achievement of the goals of their masters, the superior people were at liberty to use all necessary means to eliminate these hindrances.[18] The fundamental assumption of a triumphant and crude social Darwinism established for the Nazis a law of existence, one with which man could not tamper. The best survived the struggle for existence; the unfit vanished. This master race concept had tremendous psychological import because it gave Germans "a satisfying excuse and rationalization for aggression" and "flattered and convinced them that his [Hitler's] plan for the

16. Kelley, "Preliminary Studies," p. 47. "German atrocities should not be attributed to 'pathological sadism,'" Lewis, "Psychological Factors," p. 67; McKellar, " 'Responsibility' for Nazi Policy," p. 153. A contrary view was expressed by Eugene Davidson: "The Nazi period was a time when the criminal psychopaths took over, and no one knows better than the German people what it cost them." Trial, p. 586.

17. Noland D. C. Lewis asserts that the Nazis and the Germans whom they indoctrinated are atypical of western civilizations in their attitudes, thinking, and feeling. He maintains that Germany under Hitler underwent a cultural regression to pre-Christian times in its acceptance of slavery and in its disregard for the lives and property of other peoples. "They constitute a non-European island in the center of Europe." "Psycholgical Factors," pp. 67–68.

18. Max Radin, Day of Reckoning (New York: Knopf, 1943), pp. 115–20 (hereafter cited as Radin, Day of Reckoning).

society of the future was inevitable and stable because it was founded on natural law." [19]

The behavioral scientists accounted for Nazi criminal activities and mentality in particular events partly through the idea of the "sociological validity" of law. According to this theory, even if a Nazi law was illegitimate or unjust in its original enactment, it might be invoked by individuals as justification of an action done in good faith according to the statute.[20] Authors doubted that the German defendants had access to any criterion of law or morals which could transcend and test the norms created by their state.[21] One cause for the obscurity of ethical standards was that modern propaganda and other means of thought control, unlike censorship in past ages, did not merely exclude unwanted ideas but also made available only government endorsed concepts.

Behavioral sciences offered other analyses of the rationalizations performed by the German mind in the Nazi era. Authors using psychiatric theories maintained that national leaders could create a paranoia that would delude their people into believing that the most wanton aggression by them was a preventive or defensive war.[22] Anthropological theory, according to some advocates of absolute cultural relativism, taught that some societies, at certain stages, find right and profitable the exaltation of the State and the complete sacrifice of human and individual rights to the collectivity. This perhaps was the societal status of modern Germany, and consequently Nuremberg could not judge that state by the Allies' particular ethical and cultural norms.[23]

All behavioral scientists did not agree with this theory. Other experts in cultural relativism contended that "to say that certain

19. Morris E. Opler, "The Bio-Social Basis of Thought in the Third Reich," *American Sociological Review* 10 (December, 1945): 782.

20. Radin, *Day of Reckoning*, p. 118; Otto Kirchheimer, *Political Justice, The Use of Legal Procedure for Political Ends* (Princeton, N.J.: Princeton University Press, 1961), p. 328 (hereafter cited as Kirchheimer, *Political Justice*).

21. Guenter Lewy, "Superior Orders, Nuclear Warfare, and the Dictates of Conscience: Dilemma of Military Obedience in the Atomic Age," *American Political Science Review* 55 (March, 1961): 19 (hereafter cited as Lewy, "Superior Orders").

22. Vagts, *Defense and Diplomacy*, pp. 265, 319.

23. Robert L. Birmingham, "The War Crimes Trial, A Second Look," *University of Pittsburgh Law Review* 24 (October 1962): 139, 153 (hereafter cited as Birmingham, "The War Crimes Trial").

aspects of Nazism were morally wrong—is not parochial arrogance. It is—or can be—an assertion based both upon cross-cultural evidence as to the universalities in human needs, potentialities, and fulfillments and upon natural science knowledge with which the basic assumptions of any philosophy must be congruent." [24]

Some authors applied the relativistic theory and questioned whether the particular individual could know what the prescribed standard was, not whether the criteria of western civilization violated by the Nazis were valid universal norms. What western man hailed in theory as an absolute and immutable norm seemed in practice to change as new weapons appeared and new methods for their employment were developed. How could any man be sure exactly what humanity's conscience dictated for the present or for the future? The standard could change within two decades so that what was an atrocity in World War I, such as a submarine sinking a ship without warning, would be declared unsanctionable by the Nuremberg court because it was so universally accepted and practiced. [25]

These explanations or defenses of the German wartime mentality and actions led to theories which attempted to explain on a personal level how German officials could murder thousands of defenseless prisoners without any maddening sense of guilt or even any realization of the evils they were committing.

Basically science offered two theories: psychiatry stressed the growing depersonalization of war; sociology focused on the dilemma of man's impotence and lack of awareness in the web of modern bureaucracy.

Scholars first called attention to the increased mechanization of war which opened the door to new inhumanities, because no longer were men face to face with the effects of their savagery. The one who murdered at a distance by signing his name to an order had a feeling of moral security because the sight of the wounded and the dead was far removed from him psychologically as well as spatially. His peace of mind was reinforced when

24. A. L. Kroeber and Clyde Kluckhohn, *Culture: A Critical Review of Concepts and Definitions* (New York: Random House, 1953), p. 352. See also Margaret Mead, *And Keep Your Powder Dry: An Anthropologist Looks at America* (New York: William Morrow, 1943), pp. 162, 176, 183, 241, 244–46 (hereafter cited as Mead, *Keep Your Powder Dry*).
25. Lewy, "Superior Orders," p. 21.

he had some justifying mythology—always at hand in a warring nation—to settle any qualms of conscience.[26]

The second and more common theme offered to interpret the atrocities documented at Nuremberg was the social complexity of modern organizational life.[27] According to some scholars, notably Professor Kirchheimer, the scope of individual initiative and responsibility was drastically curtailed by the strict hierarchical structure of modern government.[28] In this view the ordinary public servant had a limited realization of the import of his routine implementation of policy. The only major objection urged against the complete acceptance of this theory regarding the Nuremberg defendants was that some individuals in the Nazi government did realize the significance of their actions and did resign their offices.

In view of these exceptions to total submissiveness to the Nazi program, Kirchheimer urged that a distinction be made between the top echelons of the government where decisions were made and the ordinary clerk or administrator. Only in the case of the latter could one claim that most of an official's tasks were routine and semiautomatic and that he had little control over the type and conditions of his work. Men on the higher political levels, he maintained, could recognize revolutionary changes in policy and perceive when these new programs violated basic standards of human decency. However, when this realization dawned these officials often deluded themselves by imagining that by staying at their posts they would bar even greater evils. To all following such a course a moment of truth occurred in which the official comprehended his own inability to hinder the dynamics of the situation.[29]

26. Paul Ferdinand Schilder, *Psychoanalysis, Man, and Society* (New York: Norton, 1951), p. 353 (hereafter cited as Schilder, *Psychoanalysis*). See also Wladimer Eliasberg and William Karliner, "The Psychiatric and Bureaucratic Aspects of War," *Journal of Social Psychology* 30 (November, 1939): 197–98 (hereafter cited as Eliasberg and Karliner, "Psychiatric and Bureaucratic Aspects").

27. Lewis, "Psychological Factors," p. 71.

28. "They [authors of many nations] have denied that the rejection of binding orders could ever be squared with the social reality of hierarchical command relations." Kirchheimer, *Political Justice*, pp. 329–30.

29. These rationalizations and the effects of social pressures were portrayed in the movie and book by Abby Mann, *Judgment at Nuremberg* (New York: New American Library, 1961).

Two paths lay open to the dissenting individual after he realized his predicament—active resistance or silent withdrawal. Kirchheimer and others conceded that active resistance could not be demanded by a successor regime because this would require the heroic as an ordinary policy for ordinary men. Withdrawal was a requirable alternative. The only exception to this rule would be persons who could objectively prove that such renunciation would necessarily entail a threat to their lives.[30] Experience showed, however, that even the most ruthless totalitarian state allowed public servants to relinquish their offices without vindictive action because the regime viewed such people as too weak either to resist or to serve and therefore fit only for obscurity.[31]

It was not only the "German Mind" of the Nazi period which held interest for behavioral scientists. The defeated foe's attitude in the year 1946 and, as far as it could be ascertained, the pattern of its future psychological development were elements of intrigue. German reaction to the Tribunal was crucial for world security because a prime goal of the trials was to convince the

30. Kirchheimer, *Political Justice*, p. 331. This author's principle of the Nazi elite's individual accountability was seconded by Wladimer Eliasberg, a well-known New York psychiatrist and author, in "War Trials," *Journal of Criminal Law and Criminology* 36 (May–June, 1945): 86 (hereafter cited as Eliasberg, "War Trials"). See also Davidson, *Trial,* p. 593.

31. As a final footnote to the involved question of individual responsibility, we cite one of the most eloquent affirmations of leaders' accountability for aggression and a rejection of any collective culpability of an entire nation. This "witness for the prosecution" is Hermann Goering who made a classically Machiavellian declaration to Gustave M. Gilbert: "Why, of course, the PEOPLE don't want war," Goering shrugged. "Why should some poor slob on a farm want to risk his life in a war when the best he can get out of it is to come back to his farm in one piece. Naturally, the common people don't want war; neither in Russia, nor in England, nor in America, nor, for that matter, in Germany. That is understood, but after all, it is the LEADERS of the country who determine the policy and it is always a simple matter to drag the people along, whether it is a democracy or a fascist dictatorship, or a parliament or a communist dictatorship. . . . Voice or no voice, the people can always be brought to the bidding of the leaders. That is easy, all you have to do is tell them they are being attacked and denounce the pacifists for lack of patriotism and exposing the country to danger. It works the same in any country." Gilbert, "Hermann Goering, Amiable Psychopath," p. 227. Nolan Lewis quotes Hitler's affirmation: ". . . the mood of the people was always a mere discharge of what funnelled into public opinion from above." "Psychological Factors," p. 66.

Germans of their past guilt in order to effect a *metanoia* in the Teutonic soul which would further Germany's future peaceful development.

Speculation on the trials' psychological effects upon the Germans was not limited to the experts. As we have observed in previous chapters, some magazine and newspaper writers who condemned the trials asserted that the judicial process would embitter the defeated, delay the re-establishment of those relations necessary for world reconstruction, and postpone Germany's re-admittance into the family of nations. Other authors optimistically predicted that the trials would tremendously strengthen the German sense of guilt and motivate the defeated to create a government which could regain for them the respect of the world.

Religious journals displayed a special interest in the Tribunal's impact on German attitudes. Reinhold Niebuhr in *Christianity and Crisis* pictured the defeated foe as tormented by a sense of guilt and filled with bitter hatred for their former leaders who had morally betrayed them. He believed that the trials' further dramatization of their culpability would plunge the German psyche toward despair and asocial reactions.[32]

Arnold Nash, however, recorded in the *Christian Century* that one of the most striking impressions that he obtained from visiting the Nuremberg court was the impenetrability of the defendants' psychological defense mechanisms. Professor Nash noted that Field Marshal Keitel and Admiral Raeder "both sit there like injured innocents. Both claim to be good Christian souls who have tried to do their duty." [33] Nash could not understand how the Germans could not have seen the conflicting demands of their loyalty to the Führer and to Germany, to Hitler and to God. He was informed by a psychiatrist that "even that distinction . . . took its meaning from a universe of discourse morally and intellectually beyond Keitel and his fellow prisoners." [34]

Not only popular and religious writers, but also experts in the

---

32. Niebuhr, "Report on Germany," pp. 6–7.
33. Arnold Nash, "The Nuremberg Trials," *Christian Century* 63 (September 25, 1946): 1149.
34. Ibid.

behavioral sciences dealt with this topic of the trials' influence on the conquered. By drawing an analogy between the post-World War II and post-Civil War periods, C. Arnold Anderson generalized that after every war people want only to be done with hatred and carnage and have sympathy for their fallen foe.[35] The diplomats, however, meet as victor and vanquished and, for political reasons, renew wartime bitterness. A prime element in this reversion would be the trial and punishment of the conquered leaders. The effect of this harsh policy would be that the defeated would identify with their leaders, fix their wartime hostility, and resist necessary reconstruction. The victor nation, on the other hand, would be too busy building their postwar world to be bothered about the trials, but if their interest were mobilized by publicity or the character of the offense, "their response is more likely to be a sadistic outburst or a melodramatic thrill which nourishes the tradition of violence more than it enhances the realization of the need for better instruments of social rearing and control." [36]

Postwar trials also expressed the victor's prejudice which demanded his fallen foe's reformation into the conqueror's image. The victor's attempts to impose imitation would widen the gap between the two social units by rousing the defeated's passion for preservation of his self-identity.[37] For these reasons some sociologists held that the effect of the postwar trials on the German mind would be baneful.

Perhaps the attempts which the behavioral sciences made to supply overall explanations of the Tribunal were of even greater value than these observations on the psychological and sociological factors.

The most common psychological interpretation of the Nuremberg trials depicted Allied hatred and frustration finding catharsis in revenge upon the enemy leaders. This theory maintained that Allied feelings of hostility could not find their complete satisfaction while the hated object still held power, but once military victory was achieved the conquerors felt it was neces-

35. Anderson, "Utility of Proposed Trial," pp. 1084–85, 1087. A historian might challenge the sociologist's unquestioning acceptance of the southern myth of Black Reconstruction which is the basis for Anderson's comparison.
36. Ibid., p. 1088.
37. Ibid., pp. 1086–87.

sary for the enemy to be on the receiving end of disgrace and death. Summary execution for the Nazi tyrants could not be enough because the cup of satisfaction would be at mankind's lips for a mere moment. A "ritual of revenge" had to be created for the final Götterdämmerung of the Third Reich's leaders.[38]

Critics of Nuremberg repeatedly presented the trials as a catharsis of the Allied psyche, yet one anti-Nuremberg writer acknowledged that perhaps the one positive aspect of the court's action was its therapeutic value. "Psychologically healthy expression of grief and anger may be obtained through a judicial proceeding such as the Nuremberg trials, which permit extensive public exhibition of the criminal and continued reiteration of their deeds."[39]

Other writers were not as sympathetic to supposed Allied psychic needs. We have cited the view that such trials provided for the punisher a "sadistic outburst or melodramatic thrill." We have also seen condemnation of this alleged Allied spirit of revenge in the commonly used phrases cited in previous chapters, e.g., "victors' vengeance" and "victors' justice."[40]

All those who considered Nuremberg a "ritual of revenge," however, did not automatically condemn the proceedings because many thought that the court was a necessary substitute for a wave of unbridled slaughter of German leaders by individuals who had suffered from Nazi oppression.[41] The Tribunal was an "institutional mechanism" that provided a substitute for personal vendettas and reserved the power of sanction for the public authority where a greater degree of rationality could be employed in determining guilt and gradations of culpability.[42]

Psychiatrists pointed out that the almost inevitable exaggera-

38. Glenn E. Hoover, "The Outlook for 'War Guilt' Trials," *Political Science Quarterly* 59 (March, 1944): 40 (hereafter cited as Hoover, " 'War Guilt' Trials").

39. Birmingham, "The War Crimes Trial," p. 137; Harold D. Lasswell, *World Politics and Personal Insecurity* (New York: McGraw-Hill, 1935), p. 246.

40. Anderson, "Utility of Proposed Trial," p. 1088; Erich Hula, "Punishment for War Criminals," *Social Research* 13 (March, 1945): 19; Hoover, " 'War Guilt' Trials," p. 40; Chamberlin, *Beyond Containment*, p. 73.

41. Anderson, "Utility of Proposed Trial," p. 1083; Taylor, "Nuremberg Trials," p. 247.

42. Wechsler, "Issues of Nuremberg," p. 13. See also Wright, "War Criminals," p. 260.

tion in inflicting retribution would frequently produce a feeling of guilt in the sanctioner. The punisher realizes at least subconsciously that his action is motivated not only by the desire to prevent the culprit from doing similar crimes again, to exact retribution for the atrocities, and to vent anger for what has been committed. It is also prompted by the sanctioner's desire to manifest his rage at what the criminal has made him do, to alleviate some of the guilt for the killing and hatred involved, and to rid himself of the realization that he is capable of the same aggressive tendencies as the one punished. This fits the second general psychological interpretation of Nuremberg which portrayed the Tribunal as an expression of an Allied guilt complex.[43]

The power of war to create a sense of culpability, even in a nation convinced that its intervention is justified, has been evidenced in other nations, but its most constant manifestation has been in the American psyche. Professor Dexter Perkins has asserted that Americans' ready receptivity to revisionist historians' theories of war causation displays America's recurrent post-war guilt complex, a sense of contamination from being connected in any way with the violence of war.

One element vital to the creation of a sense of guilt was the Americans' belief that war was ultimately a moral rather than a political question.[44] There arises, consequently, a psychological need and an imperative ethical demand for Americans to assure themselves that they have fought on the right side and that the enemy was an unjust aggressor.[45] This sense of righteousness could best be achieved by judicial proceedings.

Critics of Nuremberg, conscious of alleged crimes of the prosecuting countries as well as those of the defendants, at times spoke of a universal guilt. This attitude was particularly evident in religious publications such as the *Christian Century* which forcefully stated: "The court was itself a guilty court and the pros-

43. Louis Morton, "From Fort Sumter to Poland: The Question of War Guilt," *World Politics* 14 (January, 1962): 389 (hereafter cited as Morton, "Question of War Guilt"); Winner, "Atom at Nürnberg," p. 567.
44. Morton, "Question of War Guilt," p. 389.
45. Ibid., p. 388. See also Morris Janowitz, "German Reaction to Nazi Atrocities," *American Journal of Sociology* 52 (September, 1946): 46 (hereafter cited as Janowitz, "German Reaction").

ecution was a guilty prosecution. This terrible fact has to be admitted. The trial at Nuremberg was an angel born in a brothel. . . . The plain truth is that if justice of any kind is to be done anywhere in the world today it will have to be done by the guilty. There is no one else to do it!" The *Century*'s only qualification on this universal condemnation was that "the nations represented on the court are not TOTALLY DEPRAVED, even though, in varying degrees, they are all guilty." [46]

The most fully developed exposition of Nuremberg as a "struggle of guilts" and of the trials as an American symbolic hand washing was presented by Percy Winner who combined concepts from cultural Christianity, modern psychology, and psychiatry to explore the Tribunal in depth.

At Nuremberg, this author contended, America wished to exorcise the devil of anxiety, a monster born of three subconscious drives or obsessions. This triad consisted of a direct sense of guilt for the vastness of the physical destruction the United States had wrought in the war, a torment of soul caused by its succumbing to the modern heresy of the collectivization of the spirit, and, finally, the disquietude of spirit created by the United States having adopted, willingly or unwillingly, the role of lord of the world. In assuming the mantel of universal authority, America subconsciously realized that it had cloaked itself in the garb to which its fallen enemy had aspired.

These American anxieties, the *Commonweal* article continued, forced the nation to create a judicial ritual of purification. "The Nürnberg trial," Percy Winner maintained, "was predominantly an American undertaking because we more than the other peoples sought to achieve by it some part of what we most needed —a symbolic purging of guilt." [47] The Tribunal was an *auto da fé*, not a trial of law, and this was in Winner's opinion the reason the proceedings consumed so much time; this was why the trial was unsuccessful. "The trial failed precisely because it was not a judgment of crime but an attempted public portrayal of guilt." [48]

46. "Majestic Justice," *Christian Century* 63 (October 16, 1946): 1239–40. See also Moira Walsh, "Judgment at Nuremberg," *America* 106 (January 20, 1962): 544.

47. Winner, "Atom at Nürnberg," pp. 566–67.

48. Ibid. It is interesting to note the exact wording found in President Truman's State of the Union Message of January 21, 1946, in relation to

Men's minds are able to embrace not only paradox but contra-
diction. As a result we are not surprised when an interpretation
of Nuremberg, which apparently denied the concept of an Allied
guilt complex, was offered as a complementary, not an excluding,
theory. Experts did affirm that Nuremberg was at the same time
an acknowledgement of culpability and a ritual acting out of the
conqueror's sense of innocence and moral superiority.

The prosecution gave substance to this allegation by envision-
ing itself as morally battling for the Lord at Armageddon. Statements by American presidents, judges, and lawyers involved
with Nuremberg patently expressed the United States' traditional attitude of self-righteousness and a so-called "Boy-Scout
morality." [49] Indeed, writers pointed out that this American sense
of moral superiority and indignation was the United States'
particular contribution to the ethos of the Tribunal.[50] Critics of
Nuremberg vehemently condemned this trait; trial advocates

Winner's phrasing in the above quotation. Truman said: "We have high
hopes that this public portrayal of the guilt of these evildoers will bring
wholesale and permanent revulsion on the part of the masses of our former
enemies against war, militarism, aggression, and nations of racial superiority." Truman, *Public Papers, January 1 to December 31, 1946*, p. 46.

49. William H. Blanchard, "National Myth, National Character, and
National Policy, A Psychological Study of the U-2 Incident," *Journal of
Conflict Resolution* 6 (June, 1962): 144. See also Clifford Kirkpatrick,
"Sociological Principles and Occupied Germany," *American Sociological
Review* 11 (February, 1946): 69 (hereafter cited as Kirkpatrick, "Sociological Principles"); Mead, *Keep Your Powder Dry*, pp. 11, 157, 162. This
theme of American moralism and righteousness was, of course, a major
criticism of the diplomatic realists George F. Kennan and Hans Morgenthau. See the chapter on Foreign Affairs.

50. Hauser, "Backstage Battle at Nuremberg," p. 18. See also Orville C.
Snyder, "It's Not Law—The War Guilt Trials," *Kentucky Law Journal* 38
(November, 1949): 100.

One of the most eloquent condemnations of American moralism and its
spirit of self-righteousness was delivered by Hermann Goering to Captain
Gilbert. The psychologist observed the Reichsmarshal's growing irritation
with the prosecution's absorption with moral issues. " 'What do you mean,
morality—word-of-honor.' Goering snorted. 'Sure you can talk about word-
of-honor when you promise to deliver goods in business.—But when it is
the question of the interest of a nation? Phooey! Then morality stops. . . .
It is a statesman's DUTY to take advantage of such a situation for the
good of the country! . . . You Americans are making a big mistake with
your talk of democracy and morality. . . .' " Gilbert, "Hermann Goering,
Amiable Psychopath," pp. 227–28.

lauded its idealism. "Those who want to punish the Axis leaders," one political scientist wrote, "also want the world to believe they are right in pressing their charges; and to give a feeling of righteousness nothing is so effective as vindication by a judicial tribunal, even if improvised for the occasion. The Apaches might be content with the scalp of the defeated enemy chief, but those who demand the punishment of the defeated Axis leaders want that punishment to mean something more than that they were inept and unlucky in war. It must be demonstrated that their punishment was deserved, and the decision of the God of Battles must be confirmed by the Goddess of Justice." [51]

Another writer explained his psychological objections to Nuremberg in this way. "It invites and nourishes an orgiastic indulgence in the vicious narcotic of self-righteousness. . . . For the plain citizen of every country, it serves to reduce the vast and infinitely complex tragedy of the Second World War to the simple abstraction of a movie melodrama, so that with the final titillating scene on the gallows or before the firing-squad, he can relax in an untroubled glow, confirmed in his abiding faith that 'crime never pays,' that his own country is the fount and citadel of all the virtues, and that everything would go perfectly well if it were not for 'trouble-making foreigners.' " [52]

An extreme accusation of America's desire for acknowledgement of its moral superiority was the assertion that at Nuremberg the United States suffered from the psychotic fixation of a "Jehovah Complex." This term was first applied to the victors judging at Nuremberg to designate the mental attitude of one who believed he possessed universal authority, that vengeance was his prerogative, and that Old Testament fear rather than New Testament love should be the mode of his operation. [53]

Authors adopting this concept asserted that the United States played God at Nuremberg. This country made laws for all mankind and determined by its "divine will" a new international

51. Hoover, " 'War Guilt' Trials," pp. 40–41.
52. Waldo Browne, "The Nuremberg Trial," *New Republic* 113 (December 24, 1946): 872.
53. Paul W. Tatage, "The Nuremberg Trials 'Victor's Justice'?" *American Bar Association Journal* 36 (March, 1950): 247 (hereafter cited as Tatage, "Nuremberg Trials 'Victor's Justice'?").

morality because the judges "took upon themselves the task of speaking on behalf of abstract reason 'above all good and evil' of existing law." [54]

Most behavioral scientists did not even vaguely imply that the Allies claimed divinity, but a number considered the prosecution to be obsessed with the role of avenging angel of the Lord. Some saw this theory implied in the frequent Allied declarations that they were enforcing the "conscience of mankind."

Other major concepts and theories applied to Nuremberg by the behavioral sciences were projection and identification. In studying these explanations, we will employ a minimal definition or description of these mental operations. Identification here is taken as the psychological process by which one seeks his self-identity by assumption under another reality. Projection, on the other hand, is the process by which that which is intolerable to or beyond the control of the self is attributed to some object or person outside the self. In this activity the self refuses to identify with an obnoxious item even though it be an actual deed of the individual or a dream or fantasy from within its own subconscious.

The tendency of humans to identify with external objects was a basic consideration of those authors who feared that Nuremberg would create martyrs to the cause of Nazism or of German chauvinism. Columnist Dorothy Thompson popularly presented this notion, but sociologists set forth more scientific and detailed exposition of the possibility that war-crime trials would result in the German peoples' identification with their former leaders. [55] It was explained that "to punish these leaders on an extensive scale —particularly when we keep in mind the newspaper obbligato in the victor nations about war guilt—may impel their erstwhile followers to say: 'Our leaders could not really have been such villains, else how could we have followed them so loyally?'" [56] Critics concluded that "the subtleties of this identification of follower with leader require emphasis, for this is a pivotal point

54. Winner, "Atom at Nürnberg," p. 569. See also Hoover, "'War Guilt' Trials," p. 48; Corbett, Law and Society, p. 232.
55. Dorothy Thompson, "Germany Must Be Salvaged," American Mercury 56 (June, 1943): 658. See also "The Nuremberg Blunder," Chicago Daily Tribune, October 16, 1946, p. 22.
56. Anderson, "Utility of Proposed Trial," p. 1097.

in deciding upon the utility of these trials under the auspices of winning nations." [57]

Professor Clifford Kirkpatrick, sociologist of the University of Minnesota, also considered probable German identification with former Nazi leaders as an impediment to the trials' success. He began his argument by affirming all men's basic biological and psychological similarities and then explained the obvious diversity among men by his generalization: "HUMAN BEINGS ALL OVER THE WORLD TEND TO HAVE A DUAL PATTERN OF ATTITUDES AND BEHAVIOR; ONE FOR THE IN-GROUP; ANOTHER FOR THE OUT-GROUP." [58]

This principle was used to explain not only the ramifications of identification but also the psychological possibility of monstrous brutality as documentarily evidenced at Nuremberg. "All social living with its controls, competition and frustration rouses hate as well as love," Kirkpatrick wrote. "It is natural and simple therefore to displace disturbing hate to out-groups and their members. If no out-group is conveniently at hand, one can be created (there are always the Jews). Cruelty to out-group members does not count. An S.S. guard who has tortured and butchered helpless prisoners might well return after a hard day's work to fondle his children and tenderly embrace his wife. Psychologically he might be similar to a Chicago stockyard worker who sticks pigs and hangs them on hooks. Pigs and dehumanized out-group members do not rate the moral consideration due in-group members." [59]

This sociological principle had further and more special reference to Nuremberg and to psychological identification. Kirkpatrick asserted that probably the most fertile field for the operation

57. Ibid. "Neither punishment nor education will break the solidarity between the group and its leader." Abel, "Psychiatric Interpretation," p. 464.
58. Kirkpatrick, "Sociological Principles," p. 68. The capitals are in the original.
59. Ibid., p. 69; McKellar, " 'Responsibility' for Nazi Policy," p. 162. A proof of this strange ability of men to hold a double set of values was the fact that twenty years after Nuremberg the defense lawyers in war crimes cases would argue that the guards at Auschwitz were very ordinary people. "The defense also asserts that the defendants—who look like any Germans one might rub shoulders with here daily—have led blameless, middle-class lives since the Third Reich's collapse." *Greensboro Daily News*, August 16, 1965.

of in-group bias was in connection with the concepts of criminality, aggression, and punishment.[60] The question therefore was raised: Did the Nuremberg verdicts express anything more than unconscious American prejudices against a group conceived of as "foreign" or different?

A corollary of this dual pattern of attitudes and behavior was the affirmation that *different* in-groups had widely diverging conceptions of reality. This was illustrated by showing that the enemy's concept of those realities under judgment at Nuremberg differed vastly from the Allied version because the Germans started from a different frame of reference. The conclusion was that man's power to identify and to project seriously called into question the objectivity of the war-crime trials.[61]

This last principle, the power of sociological factors to determine the world view of specific groups, was also a key consideration of other psychiatrists who asserted that the problem of the Teutonic psyche resulted from an inability of the ego to mediate between the individual and the external world. This psychosis revealed itself, it was said, in the fundamental psychological distortion of the Germans' universe and their incapacity for

60. "From a sociological point of view, however, there seems to be danger in identifying leadership in aggressive war with criminality. It is not easy to be sure that men are tried as aggressors rather than leaders of an out-group." Kirkpatrick, "Sociological Principles," p. 69. See also Ferdinand A. Hermes, "Collective Guilt," *Notre Dame Lawyer* 23 (May, 1948): 499, and Paul W. Tatage, who argued: "It does not take a lawyer to appreciate that the judge, like any other human being, is subject to the predilections acquired in the country of his domicile no matter how 'immaculately ethical' he may be. It might be appropriate to speculate on what the finding would have been of a panel of either German or Japanese judges of a victorious Germany or Japan, 'composed of men of unimpeachable integrity and of the highest moral fabric,' if they had to pass on the war crimes of the Americans, the French, the British and the Russians." "Nuremberg Trials, 'Victor's Justice'?" p. 247.

61. The most authoritative and destructive criticism of all the proposed theories expressing fear of popular German identification with their former Nazi leaders because of the trials is that of Hermann Goering. He affirmed Nuremberg's psychological effectiveness. "Brooding in his cell Goering admitted that his attempts to build a heroic legend had been a failure. 'You don't have to worry about the Hitler legend any more,' he told me. 'When the German people learn what has been revealed at the trial it won't be necessary to condemn him. He has condemned himself.'" Gilbert, "Hermann Goering, Amiable Psychopath," p. 228.

rational reaction to reality. "The most important deficiencies of the members of the German social-cultural system," it was alleged, "lie in that part of the personality the function of which is to deal rationally with reality in a responsible and relevant manner—that is, in the ego. . . . Brinckner, especially, pointed out clearly that one of the outstanding features of German culture is a resentment of reality and a denial of it, which he compared to the attitude of the paranoid person in reference to reality. A propensity for fanatical, and even delusional, thinking in Germans is indeed, striking to those who come in contact with them. It exists not only among the defendants in the recent trials but also in the population at large." [62]

Because Nuremberg dealt with crime and defeat, one would expect that men might react not only by identifying with their national leaders and values, but also by rejecting the bitter truths and the guilt which the court's evidence proved beyond a shadow of a doubt. The Germans accomplished the rejection by the mental process of projecting these disturbing concepts to other people or impersonal forces.

The United States Department of Psychological Warfare sought to develop among the Germans a sense of collective responsibility for the results of national socialism and in particular for concentration camp atrocities. The efforts of the psychological warriors was to little avail because, although the Germans would admit that they knew of the existence of the concentration camps, they claimed that they did not know the manner or the extent of their operation. Positively, the German people rejected American allegations by assuming the role of injured innocents and by claiming that they were the prime victims of Nazi tyranny who should not be identified with the Nazi leaders. [63]

When writers applied these methods of projection to Nurem-

62. Leo Alexander, "Sociopsychologic Structure of the SS," *Archives of Neurology and Psychiatry* 59 (May, 1948): 627. See also McKellar, " 'Responsibility' for Nazi Policy," p. 157.

63. Morton, "Question of War Guilt," p. 390. Janowitz observed that postwar interviews showed the effectiveness of German defense mechanisms. "Probing and discussion never produced any feeling of guilt. When a sense of shame was noted it was a purely personal reaction without any feeling of coresponsibility." "German Reaction," p. 145.

berg, they developed the two concepts of the "scapegoat" and the "devil." [64] These two ideas were closely intertwined and frequently were used interchangeably because both were rooted in projection techniques and both terms were facile oversimplifications of complex psychological mechanisms.

Although Goering attempted to keep the ranks of his fellow-defendants solid in defense of past policy and Hitler's leadership, the others accused at Nuremberg tried to place all guilt upon the Führer. Outside the judicial chamber Germans claimed that Nuremberg's evidence proved that if it was not all Hitler's doing then the blame certainly should be placed on the scapegoat of the Third Reich's leaders or organizations. "Almost universally the individual German projects responsibility upon the Nazi Party or the SS." [65]

The scapegoat theory was used to explain the defense mechanisms not only of the defeated but also of the conquerors. Critics of Nuremberg and of American wartime and postwar administrations claimed that war-crime trials were a search for a victim to bear the onus of Allied leaders' share in the causation of the war and in the victors' wartime atrocities. They asserted that one reason the court should be considered a ritual rather than a trial was that the proceedings were established to delude the average citizen into assuming that the conquerors were in no way responsible for hostilities or the manner of their prosecution. "The surviving tentacles of the Nazi incubus were not to be destroyed until they had taken upon themselves our guilt as well as theirs." [66]

64. The term "scapegoat" is derived from the biblical practice of separating out a goat, and praying that God would remove the sins of people and place the burden of their guilt upon the selected animal. "He shall bring forward the live goat, and laying both his hands on the head of the live goat, Aaron shall confess over it all the iniquities of the Israelites and all their transgressions and all their sins, and laying them on the head of the goat, send it off to the desert by a man standing in readiness. Thus the goat shall carry all their iniquities away with it into a desolate region; . . ." Lev. 16:22–23.

65. Janowitz, "German Reaction," p. 141.

66. Winner, "Atom at Nürnberg," p. 567. Popular presentations of this theory often illustrated a political bias. See Tatage, "Nuremberg Trials, 'Victor's Justice'?" p. 248, and *Chicago Daily Tribune*, October 2, 1946, October 16, 1946.

Closely allied with the concept of the scapegoat was that of the devil. This defense mechanism rejected personal accountability and projected guilt to an object which was conceived of as the essence of evil. The individual employing this mental device gained satisfaction from the idea that, if the object was all bad, then certainly he must be good.[67]

The accusation that Nuremberg was the Allied acceptance of the devil theory appears in most opinion media. *Time* magazine on a number of occasions drew attention to the dangers involved in the refusal to learn the pervasiveness of evil and guilt in the modern world. Nuremberg, *Time* maintained, was based on the "old, dubious view that Hitler's New Order had been the work of only a few Nazi gangsters."[68] Harry Elmer Barnes, the revisionist historian, claimed that Nuremberg sought to create a world vision of absolute good and bad where the Allies must be Angels because the enemy was the emobodiment of satanic malevolence.

Not only popular writers but also sociologists were interested in this projective technique of the devil theory to avoid acknowledgement of personal guilt. "A serious objection to planning war-guilt trials is," one authority believed, "that such planning fosters the belief that world peace can be assured by the elimination of a few bad men. The assumption that the woes of this world are caused by devils, whether spiritual or terrestrial, is a popular error that continually thwarts realistic analysis and intellectual action. It would be tragic if we ever believed that the creation of a special tribunal to judge the Axis leaders *ex post facto* would materially contribute to the preservation of peace."[69]

Consequently, we can perceive that the Tribunal created a strange psychological paradox. A prime motive for the trials was to force the enemy to be conscious of his culpability, but the Allied prosecution, by its emphasis on personal responsibility of Nazi leaders, furthered this "devil" defense mechanism for the

67. McNeil, "Psychology and War," p. 777; Hoover, " 'War Guilt' Trials," p. 47.
68. "Awful Blackout," *Time* 46 (November 5, 1945): 30.
69. Hoover, " 'War Guilt' Trials," p. 47.

German people. Nuremberg's principle of individual accountability in this way may be seen as insulating the enemy people
from acceptance of their share of the burden of guilt.

Collectivization was another sociological phenomenon of modern life which was used to interpret the Nuremberg trials. For
some authors the tendency to treat men in the mass and regard
individuals as if they were merely cells within a giant organism
rose as a haunting specter from the trials. They perceived collectivization in the depersonalization of modern war, in the court's
turning men into symbols of professions or occupations, and in
the Tribunal's tendency to affirm guilt by association. These
aspects indicated to some that at Nuremberg even a man's sins
were not his own. They asserted that the last redoubts against
collectivization should be the womb and the tomb.[70] At these
moments man should be one, alone, separate with his God. For
them, Nuremberg invaded this sphere and sought mass guilt and
mass punishment.[71]

A final aspect of the behavioral scientists' interest in Nuremberg arose from the concerns of criminology. The question that
this discipline pondered was the effectiveness of Nuremberg as
a deterrent. We have repeatedly discussed opinions on the Tribunal's capacity to prevent war and international crimes in other
chapters, and, therefore, we will present here the viewpoints of
criminologists in a condensed form by enumerating one author's
statement of principles supposedly demonstrating the ineffec-

70. Eliasberg, "War Trials," p. 85; Wladimer Eliasberg, "Criminal
Prophylaxis and Protection in Emergency Times," *Journal of Criminal Law
and Criminology* 35 (September–October, 1944): 144. This theory is also
found in Leon Bramson, *The Political Context of Sociology* (Princeton, N.J.:
Princeton University Press, 1961), p. 129, and in the speech of Clare
Booth Luce, *Cong. Rec.*, 79 Cong., 1 Sess., 91:A-5575.
71. Winner, "Atom at Nürnberg," p. 569. A classic political statement of
the spirit of Eliasberg and Winner is to be found in Edmund Burke's
speech in Commons in 1775: "The thing seems a great deal too big for any
idea of jurisprudence; it should seem to my way of conceiving such matters
that there is a wide difference in reason and policy between the mode of
proceeding on the irregular conduct of scattered individuals or even of
bands who disturb order within the state and the dissensions on great questions. It looks to me narrow and pedantic to apply the ordinary ideas of
criminal justice to the great public contest. I do not know the method of
drawing up indictment against a whole nation." As cited in Eliasberg and
Karliner, "Psychiatric and Bureaucratic Aspects," p. 200.

tiveness and inadvisability of the Nuremberg trials as a deterrent. Only minor explanations will be added when deemed necessary for clarification. After each principle, examples of writers or publications which share the particular argument will be listed. We have cited all of the latter in other chapters.

The ten sociological principles Professor Donald R. Taft enumerated were:

1. "Punishment fails when the potential criminal feels that the punishers are themselves also criminals." (*Fortune, Saturday Evening Post*, Chamberlain, Wyzanski, Utley, Davidson, Barnes, Tansill, Tatage)
2. "Punishment is apt to be inflicted by those who are not the peers of the punished . . . here victors judge the vanquished." (Reel, Utley, Lunau, Tansill, Snyder, Tatage)
3. Punishment is ineffective when the pain inflicted is less impelling than the social approval created by the criminal act.[72] (Schick, Alexander, April)
4. "Punishment is ineffective if many committing similar acts escape punishment." The point here was that many Nazis would not be tried. The potential criminal realizes this and by nature is a notorious gambler. Aggression's stakes are high, and therefore the lesson of World War II for the potential criminal leaders is not the completeness of Hitler's defeat but the closeness of his victory. (Graber, O'Brien)
5. "Punishment is ineffective when acts similar to the crimes punished, or acts which cause crime, go unpunished." Reference here is to such acts as racial doctrines, discrimination against aliens, anti-semitism practiced by others besides the Nazis. (Opler, Radin, Chamberlain, Rheinstein)
6. "To be effective punishment should be accepted by former enemies and potential supporters of the punishment as just." (Utley, Davidson, McIntyre)

72. One indication of the psychological ineffectiveness of Nuremberg's physical punishment might be seen in the attitude of Goering. "Another aspect of this personality insofar as we may extract it from the mixture of fact and fancy that Goering was willing to reveal about his early development, was an apparent love of excitement and insensitivity to danger. He boasted, "Hell, I haven't been afraid of death since I was twelve or fourteen years old!" Gilbert, "Hermann Goering, Amiable Psychopath," pp. 212–13.

7. "Closely related to the last fact is the evidence that punishment is ineffective when the punished are supported by a gang." Today, the nation constitutes sociologically a "gang." It was questionable, though, how much postwar Germans supported former leaders. Although investigations proved that the defeated people were politically indifferent, these surveys did not show positively that the people were anti-Nazi. (Anderson, Doman, Janowitz)

8. "Perhaps as important as any consideration is the knowledge that punishment by itself never changes attitudes from antisocial to social. It is not punishment itself but the total situation—the gestalt—that determines future behavior." (Birmingham, Utley, Kunz)

9. "Punishment is ineffective when it expresses the hatred of the punisher. At the close of a horrible war such hatred is in some degree inevitable." (*Fortune*, Chamberlain, Barnes, Gault)

10. "Finally punishment of war criminals is ineffective because it is in practice moralistic rather than scientific. A moralistic policy is one which is satisfied with determining guilty parties without going behind them to ask why they were guilty." [73] (Birmingham, Barnes, Davidson, Lunau, Rheinstein, Dickinson)

The one sociological argument against Nuremberg's deterrent value not presented by Professor Taft was that of the *avant-garde* behavioral scientist who maintained that all vindictive punishments were evil and unavailing. Such authors usually denied or drastically restricted the traditional doctrine of man's free will, emphasized environmental factors in crime's causation, and looked on violations as asocial acts. The import of the last was that the perpetrator of crime was not evil but sick, and consequently all sanctions should be medicinal rather than punitive.[74]

Scholars in the behavioral sciences did not universally deny Nuremberg's deterrent value. Pro-Tribunal experts stressed that

73. Donald R. Taft, "Punishment of War Criminals," *American Sociological Review* 11 (August, 1946): 441–43.
74. Birmingham, "The War Crimes Trial," p. 137.

many of the opponents' criticisms were based on theory without foundation in fact or on misrepresentation of expectations. Advocates pointed out that the court not only tried to establish the threat of physical punishment as a bar to future aggression, but it also wished by its sanctions to change the psychological climate surrounding such wars. By outlawing aggression the Tribunal hoped to create a worldwide revulsion against such ventures and to change the attitudes of governments and of people, especially the potential international criminal's own citizens.[75]

The Tribunal's defenders claimed, moreover, that their opponents distorted the hope of Nuremberg to aid the peace when they considered its whole influence to be exclusively effective at the moment of decision on invasion. "The threat of punishment is not limited in the mode of its operation to the weight that it carries as a factor in decision at the climactic moment of choice. It also operates, and perhaps more significantly, at anterior stages in the patterns of conduct, the dark shadow of organized disapproval eliminating from the ambit of consideration alternatives that might otherwise present themselves in the final competition of choice."[76]

Another argument for the deterrent value of Nuremberg was that although the court's verdicts would not totally inhibit man's propensities to international crime, the Tribunal's sanctions were necessary, practical measures needed to aid world order. As one criminologist stated: "It is high time that the awesome power of disciplined punishment for violations of law be made evident throughout the world."[77]

These are judgments on Nuremberg stated in terms and concepts of the behavioral sciences. Evaluations from this frame of reference were usually not a facile approbation or condemnation, but an investigation of various aspects of the Tribunal. These writings searched for insight and revealed a zeal to learn, from the court's proceedings, new knowledge concerning the dynamics of human behavior.

Nuremberg offered the behavioral sciences an intriguing phenomenon of great importance in a complex modern world. Ameri-

75. McNeil, "Psychology and War," p. 778.
76. Wechsler, "Issues of Nuremberg," p. 16.
77. Glueck, "Justice for War Criminals," p. 279.

cans, with Congresswoman Emily Douglas, when confronted with war crimes and Nuremberg, wondered not only about what had happened in Nazi Germany but also why it had happened. They sought answers to this question in the ideas and theories of the sciences of human behavior.

11

In Its End Is Its Beginning

The last gavel sounded in the Nuremberg court October 1, 1946, but the trials live on. Immediately after the proceedings the Tribunal's principles and procedures were employed with modifications by the major Tokyo trials and the twelve group trials of "second line" leaders of Nazism conducted under Control Council Law No. 10. Denazification boards created later did not directly apply Nuremberg's principles, but the methods and precedents of the major assize aided the military commission in conducting this program.

More theoretical but more significant than the influence on these trials was Nuremberg's impact on the enactments by nations and organizations. The federal constitution of the Bonn Government and the United Nations declarations exemplified these enactments. Article 25 of the constitution decreed that the general rules of international law took precedence over German federal law; Article 26 stated that any act done to prepare for aggression was unconstitutional and therefore punishable.[1]

The United Nations has officially given its general approbation to the London Charter and the Nuremberg judgment as well as establishing a commission which codified the Tribunal's principles.[2] This assembly in the spirit of Nuremberg drew up a number of draft codes outlawing offenses against world peace and adopted a genocide convention condemning atrocities and the annihilation of minorities.[3]

1. Harris, *Tyranny on Trial*, p. 561.
2. "Report of the International Law Commission Covering Its Second Session, June 5–July 29, 1950," *American Journal of International Law*, Supplement of Documents 44 (October, 1950): 125–34.
3. United Nations Resolution 96 of December 9, 1948, as cited in Morris Greenspan, *The Modern Law of Land Warfare* (Berkeley: University of California Press, 1959), p. 199.

These constitutions, treaties, and covenants attest to Nuremberg's influence on the contemporary world. Of even greater eventual significance, however, will be the acceptance or rejection by men and nations of the Tribunal's principles, because only mankind's general endorsement will make Nuremberg's doctrine the desired shield against aggression and violations of human rights.[4]

Because men's reactions to the Tribunal and its principles are so crucial, we have attempted to discover America's exact judgments on Nuremberg and the reasons for these evaluations. In our study we have noted that statesmen and politicians presented perhaps the most complicated pattern of attitudes on Nuremberg. President Franklin Roosevelt, although favoring a number of plans at different times, finally decided upon international trials. President Truman gave the proceedings his full endorsement and support. Other presidents or presidential aspirants generally approved of these executives' policies, although Norman Thomas was a voice of dissent.

The cabinet was sharply divided. Henry Morgenthau, Jr. violently objected to a trial policy as an unwarranted leniency which would result in the Nazis escaping punishment for their crimes. Henry L. Stimson, on the other hand, was one of the prime proponents of formal international trials because he believed that such legal actions were the only way to achieve justice, legally outlaw aggression, and prove to all the wickedness of the Third Reich.

Legislative reaction was characterized by early support for vague declarations favoring trial and punishment of Axis war criminals. When in May 1945 a concurrent resolution was adopted declaring the "sense of Congress" urging postwar sanctions, most members considered their task accomplished. Legislative applause greeted the court's verdicts.

In Congress a triumvirate arose in opposition to the war-crime trials. Representative George A. Dondero stressed Nuremberg's threat to the military; Senator William Langer asserted that Communist influences dominated the trials; and Senator John E. Rankin declared that the Nuremberg trials were an orgy of

4. "Trial by Victory," *Time* 48 (August 5, 1946): 31.

Jewish vengeance. The most famous congressional condemnation of the International Military Tribunal was voiced far from Washington by Senator Robert A. Taft who denounced the court for applying retroactive law in its conviction of the Nazis.

The general attitude of Americans toward Nuremberg followed a definite pattern. In public opinion polls, newspaper editorials and columns, and popular periodicals we have found a fair amount of homogeneity: in all these, votes of approval of the Tribunal greatly outweighed the dissenting ballots.

We have suggested two sources for this favorable judgment— wartime hostility and just anger against the Nazis' barbaric aggression and atrocities and an intense postwar internationalism which induced Americans to favor any measure involving common action and a common law for the nations.

Popular endorsement of the Tribunal, however, was not a temporal phenomenon, for Nuremberg embodied traditional assumptions of United States foreign policy. It expressed Americans' legalism through their effort to solve world problems by new decrees and codes, their moralism through subjection of nations to scrutiny by ethical norms, their desire for peace through attempts to establish barriers to future aggression, and their idealism through submitting the fate of the Nazis to reason and law rather than to the arbitrary dictates of power. Popular faith in Nuremberg, which at times espoused a "devil theory" of history and which hoped that the Tribunal would be a "once-and-for-all" antidote to the world's ills, revealed the American propensity for oversimplifying complex questions in foreign affairs.

Popular disapproval of Nuremberg issued from a minority who questioned these values of the typical American. Dissenting votes did not come from any particular geographical area, but there was at times an identification with the conservative, Republican viewpoint. Certainly some papers and magazines such as the *Chicago Daily Tribune* and *Fortune* were motivated in their condemnation of the war-crimes policy partially because of antiadministration partisanship.

Other criticism seemed to be inspired by an American nationalism which demanded that international law coincide with the Anglo-Saxon tradition. These writers claimed the Tribunal was vitiated by its application of retroactive law which was explicitly forbidden by the United States Constitution. This nationalistic frame of mind was often joined to an advocacy of "realism" in foreign affairs which viewed the world in terms of power and therefore judged that the trials proved only that losers in war will be punished and that future victors will visit vengeance upon the vanquished by a judicial ritual.

Articles and books written for specialized professional audiences tended to reveal a clear relationship between the authors' ultimate judgments on Nuremberg and their basic assumptions in their particular fields.

The views of the major religious communities concurred with their secular counterpart's approval of the trials, but each of the three major religious divisions was particularly interested in a specific aspect of Nuremberg. The Protestant press, influenced by a long tradition of support for peace movements, if not pacifism, was mainly concerned with the legality of the Tribunal and with the court's outlawing aggression. Jewish attention centered on the verdicts and considered them inadequate punishment for Nazi outrages upon their coreligionists. The acquittals of Schacht, von Papen, and Fritzsche were especially disconcerting, as was the Tribunal's limiting its own jurisdiction to only those atrocities which were directly connected with aggressive war.

Catholic news media bifurcated. The more conservative element condemned the Tribunal because it claimed that at Nuremberg the real criminal was not in the dock but on the bench. This opinion was part of the general pattern of conservative Catholic intransigent opposition to Russia and Communism. More liberal Catholics hailed Nuremberg as the renaissance of the natural-law doctrine and the reassertion of moral principles in international life.

American lawyers tended to duplicate the pattern of approval found in popular media, but an added factor operative here was that most writers had personally participated in the war-crime trials. This had two effects. These lawyers generally lauded the tribunals, as would be expected of people examining their own handiwork, and they stressed the practical aspects of the Tribunal's problems and accomplishments.

To obtain a more theoretical evaluation of Nuremberg, we

must turn to jurists who specialize in international law. Concepts and theories only vaguely alluded to by trial lawyers and American legal journal writers were clearly delineated.

International lawyers condemning the Tribunal often reached their conclusions because they subscribed to the doctrine of legal positivism. This judicial theory maintains that the sovereign state was the only subject of international law and that a nation has no obligations except those created by explicit agreements or clear compliance with a general custom. Legal positivism, therefore, looked askance on Nuremberg's indictment for crimes against peace and humanity derived from an alleged international common law, on the court's principle of individual responsibility, and on the judges' affirmation of a progressive, dynamic law of the nations which could not be emasculated by uncompromising demands for precedence.

Adherents of the natural-law philosophy generally endorsed Nuremberg because the court supposedly vindicated their theory. This theory declared that law was derived from the ontological nature of things, that rights and duties were discovered by reason rather than made by the sovereign's will, and that consequently there existed immutable, inalienable human rights and a fundamental law above all human legislation.

Nuremberg embodied tenets of the natural-law philosophy, for the court affirmed individual accountability, claimed to be speaking for a rule of reason which judged the actions of all men and nations, and decided that, whatever the lack of statutory enactments, the laws of God and nature were enough to condemn the Nazis.

The natural-law advocates' commendation of Nuremberg was seconded by the legal pragmatist for reasons almost directly opposite to those motivating the naturalist philosophers. Followers of legal pragmatism hailed Nuremberg as an attempt to escape from rigid legalism and debilitating absolutism and to supply a legal code essential to mankind's survival. For these followers the Tribunal correctly had looked on law as an instrument for social engineering capable of creating order and security in international relations and rightly had decided that service to man's needs was the norm and justification for legal enactments.

Experts in foreign affairs shattered the usual ratio of three to one approval of Nuremberg and, indeed, they exactly reversed this pattern. The number of disapproving votes attested to the popularity in the "Great Debate" of the doctrine of realism. The doctrine shared many principles of legal positivism but also asserted that State and Power were the ultimate realities in world affairs and that national self-interest was the dynamic element in international relations.

The *bête noire* of such realists as George Kennan and Hans Morgenthau was the idealist's moralism and legalism which they saw in all their mawkish futility at Nuremberg. They could commend acknowledgement by amnesty that the Second World War was essentially a struggle for a balance of power; they could justify executive executions to achieve national aims; but the legal trappings, the confusion of morality and politics by the International Military Tribunal, were denounced. Nuremberg was a starry-eyed American program unheedful of the consequences which would at best create a power vacuum in central Europe, at worst ally the New Germany with Russia.

The idealist in foreign affairs, as we have observed, affirmed that ideas have consequences: there was power through purpose. These intangibles gave the actions of men and nations force and value, and therefore right and wrong were of the utmost importance in international relations. Consequently the second World War for the idealist was not merely a power conflict but an ideological struggle in which one set of values was vindicated. The Nuremberg court rightly affirmed aggression's evil nature and proved that initiators of an unjust war should pay for their crimes. The court reestablished for the idealist the norms and values to which all decent men adhered and from which the Nazis had so egregiously fallen.

This idealism in international relations was found among experts in foreign affairs and also in the military establishment. Such leaders as Henry L. Stimson, secretary of war, and his assistants John McCloy and Murray C. Bernays were in the forefront of those urging a return to a world in which law and morality coincided.

These military executives and many civilians saw Nuremberg's beneficial effect upon armed forces leaders in its development of a sense of responsibility among soldiers. They hoped that stern sentences for Nazi generals and admirals would inhibit the military mind's propensity for violent, clear-cut solutions to the intricate problems facing a nation.

Military officers whose activities bound them to the battlefield rather than to a Washington desk were filled with great trepidations by the Tribunal's verdicts. To some of these the court was a form of civilian revenge and catharsis for the evils of war which popular opinion somehow identified with the military. Others stressed that soldiers were being punished merely for obeying orders and thought that Nuremberg was endangering the military profession by making it a precarious vocation.

If the military's attitude was one of worry about survival as a profession, experts in the behavioral sciences had more scientific judgment on Nuremberg. Most of these sociologists, psychologists, and psychiatrists were less interested in evaluating the Tribunal than in learning, from the proceedings, facts concerning the many facets of human behavior in the totalitarian state and in the crucible of wartime violence.

These judgments by Americans on Nuremberg are of interest in themselves, but they are also significant because they reveal some aspects of the modern "American Mind."

The United States in 1945–46 faced novel and unique difficulties resulting from its new role as leader of the world and decider of the fate of the nations. How was it to blot out the Nazi past and Hitler's attempt at universal hegemony? How was the United States to usher in the brave new world? Nuremberg was a "successor trial" seeking political justice. The Tribunal sealed the past and initiated a new order by dramatizing the difference between the evils of the old and the virtues of the new world leader.

Nuremberg, moreover, was part of the solution to the postwar question of how to reconstruct Germany to achieve the American goal of turning the defeated peoples into a free, democratic, and antimilitaristic nation. The war-crime trials aimed at freeing Germans from Nazi mythology by showing the conquered, through stern justice, that international crime did not pay and that their best interests lay along a path of political development other than totalitarianism.

But, as we have pointed out, Nuremberg both dealt with these

questions of the postwar period and raised fundamental considerations concerning the ultimate nature of the law, the state, and
the relations between states in their manifold ramifications. The
Tribunal crystallized developments in international law of which
men had been only dimly aware.

Finally, our study has shown that judgment on Nuremberg
revealed much about Americans in general and about specific
groups in particular. We have considered their attitudes, opinions, values, assumptions, and mythology. We have tried not to
render judgment upon these characteristic traits but to point
them out, investigate some of their ramifications, and note that
they must be taken into consideration if American intellectual
and diplomatic history of this period is to be understood.

In the last analysis Nuremberg presents a paradox. The most
important thing about the Tribunal was that it happened, but its
significance is derived not from what happened but from people's attitudes toward the happenings.

Nuremberg is a fact of history; international law will never be
the same. Legal precedents have been established, new judicial
principles have been declared, and new procedures for international criminal courts have been developed. The Tribunal has
affirmed personal responsibility; the court has asserted judicial
protection for human rights.

But Nuremberg's principles will affect the world decisively
only insofar as men either accept the legality and utility of the
proceedings in the Bavarian courtroom or decide that the Tribunal illustrated pitfalls to be avoided in contemporary mankind's imperative struggle against unjust war and violations of
human rights. This judgment on the trials must be made explicitly or implicitly by the nations of the world. But the United
States must pass judgment because the power of world leadership which has been thrust upon it demands that the nation
make the decision. Now it is America's turn to be foremost in
providing the penetrating mind, the ready hand, and the right
heart needed in the quest for peace and justice. In 1946 Nuremberg was a typical American solution to the pressing problems of
aggression and atrocities. Future history will judge the court and
the people whose attitudes Nuremberg embodied.

Will there ever be an end to discussion of the Nuremberg

trials? Although only limited new or startling facts or opinions may appear in the future, each new intellectual mood or development may return to judge the Tribunal. As long as the monstrous outrages of Dachau, Buchenwald, and Belsen are vivid in men's minds, as long as the long bloody years of the Second World War are remembered personally and ruefully, men will return to stand in judgment upon the Tribunal which sought to establish the verdict of human justice upon those accused of causing the death, misery, and sorrow of those bitter years.

But even when the last person who experienced the war is dead, men will return to the Nuremberg court because it was a test of men's basic concepts of law, politics, and morality. Nuremberg is significant not so much because of what happened once and for all in 1946 in a Bavarian city, but because of what it has become for many men—sign and symbol of greater realities.

Bibliography

A. PUBLIC OR OFFICIAL DOCUMENTS

Congressional Record, 77–86 Congresses, 1942–1959.

JACKSON, ROBERT H. *The Case Against the Nazi War Criminals.* New York: Knopf, 1946.

JACKSON, ROBERT H. *The Nurnberg Case as Presented by Robert H. Jackson, Chief of Counsel for the United States Together with Other Documents.* New York: Knopf, 1947.

NAVAL WAR COLLEGE. *International Law Documents, 1946–1947.* Washington: Government Printing Office, 1948.

Punishment of War Criminals: Hearings before the Committee on Foreign Affairs, House of Representatives, Seventy-Ninth Congress, First Session on H. J. Res. 93. Washington: Government Printing Office, 1945.

ROOSEVELT, FRANKLIN D. *The Public Papers and Addresses of Franklin D. Roosevelt.* Compiled with special material and explanatory notes by Samuel I. Rosenman, 13 volumes. New York: Harper, 1950.

TAYLOR, TELFORD. *Final Report to the Secretary of the Army on the Nürnberg War Crimes Trials Under Control Council Law No. 10.* Washington: Government Printing Office, 1949.

Trial of the Major War Criminals Before the International Military Tribunal, Nuernberg, Germany: 14 November 1945—1 October 1946, 42 volumes. Nuernberg: International Military Tribunal, 1947–49.

Trials of War Criminals Before the Nuernberg Military Tribunals Under Control Council Law No. 10, 15 volumes. Nuernberg: International Military Tribunal, 1949.

TRUMAN, HARRY S. *Public Papers of the Presidents of the United States, Harry S. Truman: Containing the Public Messages, Speeches, and Statements of the President, January 1 to December 31, 1946.* Washington: Government Printing Office, 1962.

United States Chief of Counsel. *Nazi Conspiracy and Aggression* 8 volumes and 2 supplements. Washington: Government Printing Office, 1946–48.

United States Chief of Counsel. *Nazi Conspiracy and Aggression: Opinion and Judgment.* Washington: Government Printing Office, 1947.
United States Department of State. *Papers Relating to the Foreign Relations of the United States: The Paris Peace Conference 1919,* 13 volumes. Washington: Government Printing Office, 1943.

B. LETTERS

John M. Anspacher to the author, May 29, 1965.
James F. Byrnes to the author, May 14, 1965.
George A. Dondero to the author, May 11, 1965.
Murry I. Gurfein to the author, April 22, 1965.
Whitney R. Harris to the author, May 9, 1963, and May 18, 1965.
Mrs. Herbert H. Lehman to the author, September 24, 1965.
Alpheus T. Mason to the author, October 11, 1965.
Allan Nevins to the author, August 25, 1965.
Samuel I. Rosenman to the author, May 21, 1965.
W. Edward Sell to the author, February 1, 1965.
Telford Taylor to the author, May 14, 1965.
Pamela Turnure, on behalf of Mrs. John F. Kennedy, to the author, September 27, 1965.
Henry A. Wallace to the author, September 20, 1965.
LeRoy Whitman to the author, April 29, 1965.

C. NEWSPAPERS

1. SECULAR

Atlantic Constitution, 1945–46.
Baltimore Sun, 1945–48, 1967.
Boston Herald, 1946.
Charlotte Observer, 1945–46.
Chicago Daily Tribune, 1945–48, 1966.
Dallas Morning News, 1945–46.
Detroit Free Press, 1945–46.
Detroit News, 1945–46.
Gaelic-American, 1946.
Greensboro Daily News, August 16, 1965.
Los Angeles Times, 1945–48, 1966–67.
Miami Herald, 1946.
Milwaukee Journal, 1945–46.
Minneapolis Tribune, 1966–68.
New York Daily Mirror, 1945–46.
New York Daily News, 1945–46.

New York Journal American, 1945–46.
New York Staats-Zeitung und Herald, 1946.
New York Times, 1945–68.
Newark Evening News, 1945–46.
Oregonian, 1945–46.
PM, 1945–46.
Philadelphia Inquirer, 1946.
Rocky Mountain News, 1946.
San Francisco Chronicle, 1945–46.
St. Louis Post-Dispatch, 1945–67.
Times-Picayune, 1946.
Wall Street Journal, 1945–46.
Washington Evening Star, 1946.
Washington Post, 1945–46, 1967.
Washington Telegram, 1946.
Washington Times-Herald, 1945–46.
Worker, 1945–46.
World Telegram, 1945–46.

2. RELIGIOUS

a. Jewish
B'nai B'rith Messenger, 1946.
Intermountain Jewish News, 1946.
Jewish Advocate, 1945–46.
Jewish Examiner, 1946.
Jewish Exponent, 1946.
Jewish Times, 1945–46.
National Jewish Post, 1945–46.
Youngstown Jewish Times, 1946.

b. Protestant
Christian Advocate, 1946.
Christian Science Monitor, 1945–46.
Presbyterian Outlook, 1946.
Watchman-Examiner, 1946.

c. Catholic
Boston Pilot, 1945–46.
Brooklyn Tablet, 1945–46.
Catholic News, 1945–46.
Catholic Transcript, 1946.
Michigan Catholic, 1946.
Pittsburgh Catholic, 1946.
San Francisco Monitor, 1946.
Universe Bulletin, 1946.

d. News Agencies
Information Service of the Federal Council of Churches of Christ in America, 1945–46.
Jewish Telegraphic Agency, 1946.
National Catholic Welfare Council Information Service, 1945–46.

D. PERIODICALS

ABEL, THEODORE. "Is a Psychiatric Interpretation of the German Enigma Necessary?" *American Sociological Review* 10 (August, 1945): 457–64.
"After Nuremberg: Tito." *America* 76 (October 12, 1946): 3.
ALDERMAN, SIDNEY. "Background and High Lights of the Nuremberg Trial." *I.C.C. Practitioners' Journal* 14 (November, 1946): 99–113.
ALEXANDER, LEO. "Sociopsychologic Structure of the SS." *Archives of Neurology and Psychiatry* 59 (May, 1948): 622–34.
———. "War Crimes: Their Social-Psychological Aspects." *American Journal of Psychiatry* 105 (September, 1948): 170–77.
ALLAN, FLORENCE E. "Nuremberg Trial Implements World Law." *Women Lawyers Journal* 34 (Winter, 1948): 6–8, 26–28.
ANDERSON, C. ARNOLD. "The Utility of the Proposed Trial and Punishment of Enemy Leaders." *The American Political Science Review* 37 (December, 1943): 1081–100.
APRIL, NATHAN. "An Inquiry Into the Judicial Basis for the Nuremberg War Crime Trial." *Minnesota Law Review* 30 (April, 1946): 313–31.
"Awful Blackout." *Time* 46 (November 5, 1945): 30.
"Back to Business." *Newsweek* 69 (June 5, 1967): 30.
BARTH, KARL. "Karl Barth on Germany." *Christianity and Crisis* 2 (December 10, 1945): 3–4.
BEHLE, CALVIN A. "The War Crimes Trials." *Nevada State Bar Journal* 12 (April, 1948): 55–67.
BENNETT, JOHN C. "Some Impressions from Geneva." *Christianity and Crisis* 6 (October 14, 1946): 3–5.
BERNAYS, MURRAY C. "Legal Basis of the Nuremberg Trials." *Survey Graphic* 35 (January, 1946): 4–9; 35 (November, 1946): 390–91.
———. "Letters to Fortune; The Nurnberg Novelty." *Fortune* 33 (February, 1946): 10–11.
BIDDLE, FRANCIS B. "Nuremberg: The Fall of the Supermen." *American Heritage* 13 (August, 1962): 65–76.
———. "The Nurnberg Trial." *Virginia Law Review* 33 (November, 1947): 679–96.
———. "Report from Francis Biddle to President Truman." *Department of State Bulletin* 15 (November 24, 1946): 956–57.

BINGHAM, JOSEPH WALTER. "The Continental Shelf and the Marginal Belt." *American Journal of International Law* 40 (January, 1946): 173–78.

BIRMINGHAM, ROBERT L. "The War Crimes Trial, A Second Look." *University of Pittsburgh Law Review* 24 (October, 1962): 132–54.

BISHOP, WILLIAM W., JR. "Robert H. Jackson—Obituary." *American Journal of International Law* 49 (January, 1955): 44–50.

BLANKENEY, BEN BRUCE. "International Military Tribunal, Argument for Motions to Dismiss." *American Bar Association Journal* 32 (August, 1946): 475–77, 523.

BLANCHARD, WILLIAM H. "National Myth, National Character, and National Policy, A Psychological Study of the U-2 Incident." *Journal of Conflict Resolution* 6 (June, 1962): 143–48.

BORCHARD, EDWIN. "International Law and International Organization." *American Journal of International Law* 41 (January, 1947): 106–8.

BRAND, JAMES T. "Crimes Against Humanity and the Nurnberg Trials." *Oregon Law Review* 28 (February, 1949): 93–119.

BRIGGS, HERBERT W. "New Dimensions in International Law." *American Political Science Review* 46 (September, 1952): 677–98.

BROWN, JOHN MASON. "Nuremberg—Century of Progress." *Saturday Review of Literature* 29 (August 24, 1946): 20–24.

BROWN, PHILIP MARSHALL. "World Law." *American Journal of International Law* 40 (January, 1946): 159–61.

BROWNE, WALDO. "The Nuremberg Trial." *New Republic* 113 (December 24, 1946): 871–72.

BURNHAM, JAMES. "Hanoi's Special Weapons System." *National Review* 18 (August 9, 1966): 764.

BURRELL, DAVID DE FORREST. "The New International Law." *Presbyterian* 116 (October 17, 1946): 10–11.

CARTER, EDWARD F. "The Nuremberg Trial, A Turning Point in the Enforcement of International Law." *Nebraska Law Review* 28 (March, 1949): 370–86.

CALVERT, SAMUEL MC CRAE. "What Hope for Germany?" *Christian Century* 63 (October 23, 1946): 1274–76.

"The Chalice of Nuremberg." *Time* 46 (December 10, 1945): 25–28.

CHAMBERLIN, WILLIAM HENRY. "Don't Call It Justice." *Forum* 104 (December, 1945): 329–31.

"Charter of the International Military Tribunal." *American Bar Association Journal* 31 (September, 1945): 454–57.

CHISHOLM, G. B. "The Reestablishment of Peacetime Society." *Psychiatry* 5 (February, 1946): 1–35.

CLARK, DELBERT. "Bubble, Bubble, Toil and Trouble." *Saturday Review of Literature* 35 (December 6, 1952): 29, 38.

"Communications: Our Law was Broken." *Commonweal* 45 (November 29, 1946): 164–66.

CORBETT, PERCY E. "National Interest, International Organization and

American Foreign Policy." *World Politics* 5 (October, 1952): 46–56.

COURIER, GABRIEL. "Hanging." *Christian Herald* 69 (October, 1946): 10.

"Court Action." *Air Force Times* 27 (July 5, 1967): 12.

COWLES, WILLARD B. "Trial of War Criminals by Military Tribunals." *American Bar Association Journal* 30 (June, 1944): 330–33, 362.

————. "Universality of Jurisdiction Over War Crimes." *California Law Review* 33 (June, 1945): 177–210.

CRAIG, GORDON A. "The Army and National Socialism, 1933–1945; The Responsibility of the Generals." *World Politics* 3 (November, 1949): 426–38.

DALY, EDWARD J. "War Crime Trials." *Connecticut Bar Journal* 23 (March, 1949): 2–10.

DAWSON, JOHN. Review of the *Nuremberg Trial and Aggressive War*, by Sheldon Glueck. *American Sociological Review* 12 (February, 1947): 124–25.

DEAN, VERA M. "More Important than the Bomb!" *Rotarian* 29 (October, 1946): 8–10.

————. "United States Policy in Europe." *Foreign Policy Report* 21 (January 15, 1946): 282–95.

"Declaration of German Atrocities." *Department of State Bulletin* 9 (November 6, 1943): 311.

"Deplorable and Repulsive." *Time* 88 (July 29, 1966): 13.

DEWEY, THOMAS E., "International Justice Requires the World Court." *American Bar Association Journal* 31 (June, 1945): 295–96, 323.

DICKINSON, EDWIN D. "International Law, An Inventory." *California Bar Review* 23 (December, 1945): 177–218.

DICKS, HENRY V. "Personality Traits and National Socialist Ideology." *Human Relations* 3 (June, 1950): 111–54.

"Dissent Ahead." *Commonweal* 86 (May 16, 1967): 252.

DOMAN, NICHOLAS R. "The Nuremberg Trials Revisited." *American Bar Association Journal* 47 (March, 1961): 260–64.

————. "The Political Consequences of the Nuremberg Trial." *Annals of the American Academy* No. 246 (July, 1946): 81–90.

DULLES, JOHN FOSTER. "International Law and Individuals, A Comment on Enforcing Peace." *American Bar Association Journal* 35 (November, 1949): 912–13.

EHRENBERG, ILYA. "History's Morality, The Nuremberg Trial." *Embassy of the Union of Soviet Socialist Republic Information Bulletin* 5 (December 8, 1945): 1–3, 7.

"Eisenhower's Report on ETO Tour." *Army and Navy Bulletin* 2 (October 26, 1946): 2.

ELBE, JOACHIM VON. "The Evolution of the Concept of the Just War in International Law." *American Journal of International Law* 33 (October, 1934): 665–88.

ELIASBERG, WLADIMER G. "Criminal Prophylaxis and Protection in Emergency Times." *Journal of Criminal Law and Criminology* 35 (September–October, 1944): 143–51.

———. "War Trials." *Journal of Criminal Law and Criminology* 36 (May–June, 1945): 85–86.

———, and KARLINER, WILLIAM. "The Psychiatric and Bureaucratic Aspects of War." *Journal of Social Psychology* 30 (November, 1939): 189–205.

EMMET, CHRISTOPHER. "Verdict on Nuremberg." *Commonweal* 45 (November 22, 1946): 138–41.

"End of an Evil Epoch." *Watchman-Examiner* 34 (November, 1946): 1035–36.

EULAU, HEINZ. "The Nuremberg War-Crime Trials, Revolution in International Law." *New Republic* 113 (November 12, 1945): 625–28.

Executive Board. "The Punishment of War Criminals." *Lawyers Guild Review* 4 (November–December, 1944): 18–23.

FALK, RICHARD A. "The Realities of International Law." *World Politics* 14 (January, 1962): 353–63.

"The Fallen Eagles." *Time* 46 (December 3, 1945): 28–30.

FERENCZ, BENJAMIN B. "Nuremberg Trial Procedure and the Rights of the Accused." *Journal of Criminal Law and Criminology* 39 (July–August, 1948): 144–51.

FINCH, GEORGE A. "The Nuremberg Trial and International Law." *American Journal of International Law* 41 (January, 1947): 20–37.

———. "The Progressive Development of International Law." *American Journal of International Law* 41 (July, 1947): 611–16.

FRANKLIN, MITCHELL. "Sources of International Law Relating to Sanctions Against War Criminals." *Journal of Criminal Law and Criminology* 36 (September–October, 1945): 153–79.

"Games Men Play." *Newsweek* 69 (May 15, 1967): 44.

GAULT, P. F. "Prosecution of War Criminals." *Journal of Criminal Law and Criminology* 36 (September–October, 1945): 180–83.

GENÊT (JANET FLANNER). "Letter From Nuremberg." *New Yorker* 21 (January 5, 1946): 46–50.

———. "Letter from Nuremberg." *New Yorker* 21 (March 23, 1946), 78–84.

———. "Letter From Nuremberg." *New Yorker* 22 (March 30, 1946), 76–83.

GILBERT, GUSTAVE MARK. "Hermann Goering, Amiable Psychopath." *Journal of Abnormal and Social Psychology* 43 (April, 1948): 211–29.

GINGOLD, KURT. "Letters: Captain Levy and Army System." *Science* 157 (July 14, 1967): 140.

GLASSER, IRA. "Judgment at Fort Jackson." *Law in Transition* 4 (September, 1967): 123–56.

GLUECK, SHELDON. "Justice for War Criminals." *American Mercury* 60 (March, 1945): 274–80.
———. "The Nuernberg Trial and Aggressive War." *Harvard Law Review* 59 (February, 1946): 396–456.
GOLDEN, HARRY L. "Justice Jackson Will Unfold Nazi Tragedy." *Carolina Israelite* 2 (December, 1945): 10.
GREGORY, TAPPAN. "The Nuremberg Trials." *Connecticut Bar Journal* 21 (January, 1947): 2–20.
———. "The Nuremberg Trials." *Illinois Bar Journal* 34 (June, 1946): 469–82.
GREW, JOSEPH C. "Cooperation with the United States Chief of Counsel for the Prosecution of Axis Criminality." *Department of State Bulletin* 12 (July 1, 1945): 40.
———. "Discontinuance of Services of Herbert C. Pell." *Department of State Bulletin* 12 (January 28, 1945): 123.
GROSS, LEO. "Can Human Rights Be Enforced?" *Menorah Journal* 25 (January–March, 1947): 85–91.
———. "The Criminality of Aggressive War." *American Political Science Review* 41 (April, 1947): 205–25.
HALE, WINFIELD B. "Nuremberg War Crimes Tribunals." *Tennessee Law Review* 21 (December, 1949): 8–19.
HANDSEL, EINIFRED N. "Allied Military Rule in Germany." *Foreign Policy Reports* 21 (November 1, 1945): 222–31.
"Hanoi's Kind of Escalation." *Time* 88 (July 22, 1966): 26.
HARRIS, WHITNEY. Review of *Nuremberg Trials*, by August von Knieriem. *American Journal of International Law* 54 (April, 1960): 443–44.
HAUSER, ERNEST O. "The Backstage Battle at Nuremberg." *Saturday Evening Post* 218 (January 19, 1946): 18, 19, 137.
HERMES, FERDINAND A. "Collective Guilt." *Notre Dame Lawyer* 23 (May, 1948): 431–55.
HERTZBERG, SIDNEY. "The Month in History." *Commentary* 2 (November, 1946): 457–58.
HERZ, JOHN H. "The Fiasco of Denazification in Germany." *Political Science Quarterly* 63 (December, 1948): 569–94.
HIRSCH, FELIX E. "Lessons of Nuremberg." *Current History* 11 (October, 1946): 312–18.
HOBBS, MALCOLM. "Nürnberg's Indecent Burial." *Nation* 169 (December 3, 1949): 634–35.
HOFFMAN, NICHOLAS VON. "Conviction of Captain Levy." *New Republic* 156 (June 17, 1967): 9–11.
HOFFMAN, STANLEY. "International Systems and International Law." *World Politics* 14 (October, 1961): 205–37.
HOGAN, WILLARD N. "War Criminals." *South Atlantic Quarterly* 45 (October, 1946): 415–24.
HOOKER, WADE S., JR., *and* SAVASTEN, DAVID H. "The Geneva Conven-

tions of 1949: Application to the Vietnamese Conflict." *Virginia Journal of International Law* No. 2 (1965): 143–63.

HOOVER, GLENN E. "The Outlook for 'War Guilt' Trials." *Political Science Quarterly* 59 (March, 1944): 40–48.

HUBERT, CECIL F. "Nuremberg—Justice or Vengeance?" *Military Government Journal* 1 (March, 1948): 11–14.

HULA, ERICH. "Punishment for War Criminals." *Social Research* 13 (March, 1945): 1–23.

———. "The Revival of the Idea of Punitive War." *Thought* 82 (September, 1946): 405–34.

HULL, CORDELL. "Address by the Secretary of State Before Congress Regarding the Moscow Conference." *Department of State Bulletin* 9 (November 20, 1945): 341–45.

"If North Vietnam 'Convicts' Captured U.S. Fliers—." *U.S. News and World Report* 61 (August 1, 1966): 20–21.

"Indefensibles' Defense." *Time* 47 (March 18, 1946): 29.

"Indictment of War Criminals." *American Bar Association Journal* 31 (December, 1945): 645–46, 673.

"Instructive Episode." *Nation* 203 (August 8, 1966): 108.

International Military Tribunal. "Judgment and Sentences." *American Journal of International Law* 41 (January, 1947): 172–333.

IRELAND, GORDON. "*Ex Post Facto* From Rome to Tokyo." *Temple Law Quarterly* 21 (July, 1947): 27–59.

JACKSON, ROBERT H. "Final Report to the President from Supreme Court Justice Jackson." *Department of State Bulletin* 13 (October 27, 1946): 771–76.

———. "Nuremberg in Retrospect, Legal Answer to International Lawlessness." *American Bar Association Journal* 25 (October, 1949): 814–15, 881–82.

———. "The Nurnberg Trial, Civilization's Chief Salvage from World War II." *Vital Speeches* 13 (December 1, 1946): 114–17.

———. "The Rule of Law Among Nations." *American Bar Association Journal* 21 (June, 1945): 290.

———. "The Significance of the Nuremberg Trials to The Armed Forces." *Military Affairs* 10 (Winter, 1946): 3–15.

JACKSON, WILLIAM E. "Germany's Dance of Death." *Saturday Review of Literature* 30 (May 10, 1947): 15, 34.

———. "Putting the Nuremberg Law to Work." *Foreign Affairs* 25 (July, 1947): 550–65.

JAFFE, SIDNEY E. "Natural Law and the Nuremberg Trial." *Nebraska Law Review* 26 (November, 1946): 90–95.

JANOWITZ, MORRIS. "German Reactions to Nazi Atrocities." *American Journal of Sociology* 52 (September, 1946): 141–45.

JESSUP, PHILIP C. "The Crime of Aggression and the Future of International Law." *Political Science Quarterly* 62 (March, 1947): 1–10.

JOHANN, ROBERT O. "I Want My Rights." *America* 112 (May 20, 1965): 805.

"Judgment Day at Nuremberg, World Law Takes a Long Stride Forward." *Senior Scholastic* 49 (November 12, 1945): 5–6.

JULIN, GOSTA. "Evidence at Stockholm: The Judges are Everywhere." *Nation* 206 (June 5, 1967): 712.

"Just War," *Commonweal* 37 (December 22, 1967): 372.

KARSTEN, THOMAS L., and MATHIAS, JAMES H. "The Judgment at Nuremberg." *New Republic* 115 (October 21, 1946): 512.

KAUFMAN, MARY K. "The Individual's Duty Under the Law of Nurnberg: The Effect of Knowledge on Justiciability." *Guild Practitioner* 27 (Winter, 1968): 16.

KECSKEMETI, PAUL, and LEITES, NATHAN. "Some Psychological Hypotheses on Nazi Germany." *Journal of Social Psychology* 28 (August, 1948): 141–66.

KELLEY, DOUGLAS M. "Preliminary Studies of the Rorschach Records of the Nazi War Criminals." *Rorschach Research Exchange* 10 (June, 1946): 45–48.

KELSEN, HANS. "Sanctions in International Law under the Charter of the United Nations." *Iowa Law Review* 31 (May, 1946): 499–543.

KIRCHWEG, FREDA. "Politics and Justice." *Nation* 163 (October 12, 1946): 396–97.

KIRKPATRICK, CLIFFORD. "Sociological Principles and Occupied Germany." *American Sociological Review* 11 (February, 1946): 67–78.

KOLANDER, MORRIS. "War Crime Trials in Germany." *Pennsylvania Bar Association Quarterly* 18 (April, 1947): 274–80.

KONVITZ, MILTON R. *"Ex Post Facto* at Nuremberg." *Commentary* 1 (July, 1946): 91–92.

———. "Will Nuremberg Serve Justice?" *Commentary* 1 (January 9, 1946): 9–15.

KUNZ, JOSEF L. *"Bellum Justum et Bellum Legale."* *American Journal of International Law* 45 (July, 1951): 528–34.

———. "The Problem of the Progressive Development of International Law." *Iowa Law Review* 31 (May, 1946): 544–60.

———. "The Swing of the Pendulum: From Overestimation to Underestimation of International Law." *American Journal of International Law* 44 (January, 1950): 135–40.

LA FARGE, JOHN J. "Judgment." *America* 76 (October 12, 1946): 29.

LANGER, ELINOR. "The Court-Martial of Captain Levy: Medical Ethics v. Military Law." *Science* 156 (June 9, 1967): 1346–50.

LAUER, LAWRENCE. "The International War Criminal Trials and the Common Law of War." *St. John's Law Review* 20 (November, 1945): 18–24.

LEONHARDT, HANS. "The Nuremberg Trial, A Legal Analysis." *Review of Politics* 11 (October, 1949): 449–60.

LEVENTHAL, HAROLD; HARRIS, SAM; WOOLSEY, JOHN M., JR.; and FARR,

WARREN F. "The Nuremberg Verdict." *Harvard Law Review* 60 (July, 1947): 857–907.

LEVIN, BERNARD, "Bertrand Russell: Prosecutor, Judge and Jury." *New York Times Magazine,* February 19, 1967: 24, 55, 57, 60, 62, 67, 68.

LEVY, ALBERT G. D. "Criminal Responsibility of Individuals and International Law." *University of Chicago Law Review* 12 (June, 1945): 313–32.

LEWIS, NOLAN. "Impressions of the Psychological Factors in Nazi Ideology." *Digest of Neurology and Psychiatry* 15 (January, 1947): 64–71.

LEWY, GUENTER. "Superior Orders, Nuclear Warfare, and the Dictates of Conscience, the Dilemma of Military Obedience in the Atomic Age." *American Political Science Review* 55 (March, 1961): 3–23.

LIPPMANN, WALTER. "The Meaning of the Nuremberg Trial." *Ladies' Home Journal* 63 (June, 1946): 32, 188–90.

"MAJESTIC JUSTICE." *Christian Century* 63 (October 16, 1946): 1238–40.

MARSHALL, JAMES. Review of the *Nuremberg Trial and Aggressive War,* by Sheldon Glueck. *Saturday Review of Literature* 29 (September 21, 1946): 9–10.

MCCONNELL, G. R. "The Trial of War Criminals at Nuremberg." *Wyoming Law Journal* 1 (December, 1946): 1–12.

MCDOUGAL, MYRES S. "The Role of Law in World Politics." *Mississippi Law Journal* 20 (May, 1949): 253–83.

MCINTYRE, DINA GHAUDY. "The Nuremberg Trials." *University of Pittsburgh Law Review* 24 (October, 1962): 73–116.

MCKELLAR, PETER. "Responsibility for the Nazi Policy of Extermination." *Journal of Social Psychology* 34 (November, 1951): 153–63.

MCKINNON, HAROLD R. "Natural Law and Positive Law." *Notre Dame Lawyer* 23 (January, 1948): 125–39.

MCNEIL, ELTON B. "Psychology and War." *Journal of Conflict Resolution* 7 (December, 1963): 777–80.

MELTZER, BERNARD D. "A Note on Some Aspects of the Nuremberg Debate." *University of Chicago Law Review* 14 (April, 1947): 455–69.

"Men at War." *Time* 89 (June 2, 1967): 15.

MENDELSSOHN, PETER DE. "America's Case at Nuernberg." *Nation* 161 (December 15, 1945): 652–54.

MIGNONE, FREDERICK. "After Nuremberg, Tokyo." *Texas Law Review* 25 (May, 1947): 475–90.

MOLEY, RAYMOND. "Making History at Nuremberg." *Newsweek* 28 (September 30, 1946): 96.

MORGENTHAU, HANS J.; HULA, ERIC; and MILLAR, MOORHOUSE F. X. "Views on Nuremberg: A Symposium." *America* 76 (December 7, 1946): 266–68.

MORLEY, FELIX. "The Case for Taft." *Life* 24 (February 9, 1948): 51–66.

MORRIS, JAMES. "Major War Crimes Trial in Nuremberg." *North Dakota Bar Briefs* 25 (April, 1949): 97–101.

MORTON, LOUIS. "From Fort Sumter to Poland, The Question of War Guilt." *World Politics* 14 (January, 1962): 386–92.

NASH, ARNOLD. "The Nuremberg Trials." *Christian Century* 63 (September 25, 1946): 1148–50.

"Navy Department Participation in the Prosecution of War Crimes." *Journal of Criminal Law and Criminology* 36 (May–June, 1945): 39–40.

"Nazi Leaders Hang for War Crimes." *Lutheran Outlook* 15 (October, 1946): 294–95.

"Nazi Leaders Sing Their Swan Song." *Life* 21 (September 16, 1946): 40–41.

NEUMANN, FRANZ. "The War Crimes Trials." *World Politics* 2 (October, 1949): 135–47.

"News and Notes." *Lutheran Youth* 11 (November, 1946): 4.

NIEBUHR, REINHOLD. "A Protest Against A Dilemma's Two Horns." *World Politics* 2 (January, 1950): 338–44.

———. "A Report on Germany." *Christianity and Crisis* 2 (October 14, 1946): 6–13.

———. "Victor's Justice." *Common Sense* 15 (January, 1946): 6–9.

NIEMEYER, GERHART. "Relevant and Irrelevant Doctrines Concerning International Relations." *World Politics* 5 (January, 1952): 282–92.

"Nuremberg and History." *Opinion* 16 (September, 1946): 8.

"Nuremberg Blot." *Newsweek* 28 (October 14, 1946): 59.

"The Nuremberg Judgment." *Living Church* 113 (October 13, 1946): 18.

"Nuremberg Jurist Returns." *America* 79 (June 5, 1948): 213.

"Nuremberg Revisited." *Newsweek* 69 (May 29, 1967): 23.

"The Nuremberg Trials." *Ave Maria* 67 (March 31, 1948): 323.

"The Nuremberg Trials." *Christian Century* 63 (September 25, 1946): 1148–50.

"The Nuremberg Trials." *Interracial Review* 19 (July, 1946): 99–100.

"The Nuremberg Trials." *Opinion* 16 (December, 1945): 5–6.

"The Nuremberg Tribunal Verdicts Due Next Week." *Army and Navy Bulletin* 2 (September 21, 1945): 10.

"The Nuremberg Verdicts." *Churchman* 160 (November, 1946): 4.

"Nürnberg: Are We Sowing to Reap the Same Whirlwind Again?" *Life* 21 (October 14, 1946): 36.

"The Nürnberg Confusion." *Fortune* 34 (December, 1946): 120–21.

"The Nürnberg Debate." *Time* 48 (October 14, 1946): 29.

"The Nürnberg Novelty." *Fortune* 32 (December, 1945): 140–41.

"Nürnberg & Viet Nam." *Time* 89 (May 26, 1967): 20.

NUSSBAUM, ARTHUR. "Just War—A Legal Concept?" *Michigan Law Review* 42 (December, 1943): 453–79.

O'BRIEN, HOWARD V. "Lesson From Nuremberg." *Forum* 106 (November, 1946): 443.

"One for Fifteen." *Time* 46 (December 10, 1945): 28.

"On the Receiving End." *Time* 84 (October 2, 1964): 42–43.

OPLER, MORRIS E. "The Bio-Social Basis of Thought in the Third Reich." *American Sociological Review* 10 (December, 1945): 776–86.

"Our Law Was Broken." *Commonweal* 45 (October 18, 1946): 5.

PALMER, BEN. W. "The Natural Law and Pragmatism." *Notre Dame Lawyer* 23 (March, 1948): 313–41.

PARKER, JOHN J. "The Nuernberg Trial." *Journal of the American Judicature Society* 30 (December, 1946): 109–15.

PEGLER, CHARLES. "War Crimes and War Criminals." *Journal of the Bar Association of the District of Columbia* 13 (September, 1946): 385–92.

PEKELIS, ALEXANDER H. "To the Nuremberg Court." *New Republic* 155 (August 26, 1946): 232–33.

PHELEGER, HERMAN. "Nuremberg—A Fair Trial?" *Atlantic Monthly* 177 (April, 1946): 60–65.

PHILLIPS, C. P. "Air Warfare and Law." *George Washington Law Review* 21, Part I (January, 1953): 331–35; Part II (March, 1953): 395–422.

RADIN, MAX. "International Crimes." *Iowa Law Review* 32 (November, 1946): 33–50.

———. "Justice at Nuremberg." *Foreign Affairs* 24 (April, 1946): 369–84.

———. "War Crimes and Crimes of War." *Virginia Quarterly Review* 21 (Summer, 1945): 497–516.

"Recalling Nuernberg Trials." *Ave Maria* 71 (April 26, 1952): 514.

REDISH, MARTIN. "Military Law; Nuremberg Rule of Superior Orders." *Harvard International Law Journal* 9 (Winter, 1968): 169–81.

REDLEY, ADOLPHUS G. "International Law at Its Crossroads." *South Atlantic Quarterly* 45 (October, 1946): 165–75.

"Report of the International Law Commission Covering its Second Session, June 5–July 29, 1950." *American Journal of International Law*, Supplement of Documents 44 (October, 1950): 125–34.

"The Results of Nuremberg." *New Republic* 140 (October 14, 1946): 467–68.

RHEINSTEIN, MAX. Review of *The Nuremberg Trial and Aggressive War*, by Sheldon Glueck. *University of Chicago Law Review* 14 (February, 1949): 319–21.

ROONEY, MIRIAM, T. "Law Without Justice?—The Kelsen and Hall Theories Compared." *Notre Dame Lawyer* 23 (January, 1948): 140–72.

ROSENWEIN, SAM. "International War Crimes Tribunal: Stockholm Session." *Guild Practitioner* 27 (Winter, 1968): 22–29.

SACK, ALEXANDER N. "War Crimes and the Defense of Act of State in

International Law." *Lawyers Guild Review* 5 (September–October, 1945): 288–300.

———. "War Crimes and the Defense of Superior Orders in International Law." *Lawyers Guild Review* 5 (January–February, 1945): 11–17.

"Sartre's Séance." *Time* 89 (May 12, 1967): 30.

SCHICK, FRANZ B. "Crimes Against Peace." *Journal of Criminal Law and Criminology* 38 (January–February, 1948): 445–65.

———. "The Nuremberg Trial and the International Law of the Future." *American Journal of International Law* 41 (October, 1947): 770–894.

SCHNEEBERGER, ERNEST. "The Responsibility of the Individual Under International Law." *Georgetown Law Journal* 25 (May, 1947): 481–89.

SCHUSTER, GEORGE N. "Hanging at Nuremberg; The Truth Was Not Allowed to Emerge." *Commonweal* 45 (November 15, 1946): 110–13.

SCHWARZENBERGER, GEORG. "The Judgment at Nuremberg." *Tulane Law Review* 21 (March, 1947): 329–61.

"The Senator Takes A Chance." *Catholic World* 169 (November, 1946): 97–99.

"Settling the Issue of War Guilt, Conclusive Verdict Against Nazis." *United States News* 21 (October 11, 1946): 24–25.

SHEER, ROBERT. "Lord Russel." *Ramparts* 5 (May, 1967): 16–23.

SLOAN, F. BLAINE. "Comparative International and Municipal Law Sanctions." *Nebraska Law Review* 27 (November, 1947): 1–29.

SMITH, DELBERT D. "The Geneva Prisoner of War Convention: An Appraisal." *New York University Law Review* 62 (November, 1967): 880–914.

SMITH, WILLIS. "The Nuremberg Trial." *American Bar Association Journal* 32 (July, 1946): 390–96.

SNYDER, LOUIS L. Review of *Nuremberg Diary*, by Gustave M. Gilbert. *American Historical Review* 53 (October, 1947): 166–67.

SOLOW, HERBERT. "A Rather Startling Result." *Fortune* 39 (April, 1945): 158–64.

"The Source." *Time* 46 (December 17, 1945): 26–27.

STEPHENS, ROBERT GRIER, JR. "Aspects of the Nuremberg Trial." *Georgia Bar Journal* 13 (May, 1946): 375–83.

STIMSON, HENRY L. "The Nuremberg Trial, Landmark in Law." *Foreign Affairs* 15 (January, 1947): 179–89.

STOREY, ROBERT G. "Nuremberg Trials." *Tennessee Law Review* 19 (December, 1946): 517–25.

"A Study of the Roman Catholic Press in America." *Information Service of the Federal Council of Churches of Christ in America* 25 (June 22, 1946): 1–6.

"A Submariner Rises to Annapolis." *Life* 65 (November 22, 1968): 60.

SWEARINGER, VICTOR C. "Nuernberg War Crime Trials." *Kentucky State Bar Journal* 12 (December, 1947): 11–20.

SYNDER, ORVILLE C. "It's Not Law—The War Guilt Trials." *Kentucky Law Journal* 38 (November, 1949): 81–104.

TAFT, DONALD R. "Punishment of War Criminals." *American Sociological Review* 11 (August, 1946): 439–44.

TAFT, ROBERT A. "Equal Justice Under Law." *Vital Speeches* 13 (November 1, 1946): 44–48.

———. "The Republican Party." *Fortune* 39 (April, 1949): 108–18.

"Taking Stock." *Time* 49 (February 24, 1947): 27.

TALERICO, ANTHONY, JR. "Operation Justice." *United States Naval Institute Proceedings* 73 (May, 1947): 509–21.

TANNENBAUM, FRANK. "The Balance of Power Versus the Coördinate State." *Political Science Quarterly* 67 (June, 1952): 173–97.

TATAGE, PAUL W. "The Nuremberg Trials 'Victor's Justice'?" *American Bar Association Journal* 36 (March, 1950): 247–48.

TAYLOR, TELFORD. "Nuremberg Trials, War Crimes and International Law." *International Conciliation* No. 450 (April, 1949): 241–371.

THOMPSON, DOROTHY. "Germany Must Be Salvaged." *American Mercury* 56 (June, 1943): 647–62.

"The Trial Begins." *Newsweek* 69 (May 2, 1967): 54.

"Trial By Victory." *Time* 48 (August 5, 1946): 31.

"Trial's End." *Time* 89 (May 19, 1967): 37.

"Tripartite Conference at Berlin." *Department of State Bulletin* 13 (August 5, 1945): 153–61.

TRUMAN, HARRY S. "Prosecution of Major Nazi War Criminals." *Department of State Bulletin* 15 (October 27, 1946): 954.

———. "Reply of President Truman to Justice Jackson." *Department of State Bulletin* 15 (October 27, 1946): 776.

TUTTLE, CHARLES H. "The Lawyer and the War." *New York State Bar Association Bulletin* 16 (February, 1944): 19–22.

VAMBERY, RUSTEM. "Criminals and War Crimes." *Nation* 160 (May 19, 1945): 567–68.

———. "Law and Legalism." *Nation* 161 (December 1, 1945): 573–75.

———. "The Law of the Tribunal." *Nation* 163 (October 12, 1946): 400–401.

"The Wages of Sin." *Christian Herald* 69 (April, 1946): 7.

WALKINSHAW, ROBERT B. "The Nuremberg and Tokyo Trials, Another Step toward International Justice." *American Bar Association Journal* 35 (April, 1949): 299–302, 362–63.

WALM, NORA. "Crime and Punishment." *Atlantic Monthly* 177 (January, 1946): 43–47.

WALSH, EDMUND A. "Comments and Corollaries." *America* 76 (November 9, 1946): 151–54.

WALSH, MOIRA. "Judgment at Nuremberg." *America* 106 (January 20, 1962): 542–44.

WARNER, ADOLPHE J. "What Case Against the German Bankers?" *Commercial and Financial Chronicle* 165 (January 2, 1947): 4, 17.

WECHSLER, HERBERT. "The Issues of the Nuremberg Trial." *Political Science Quarterly* 62 (March, 1947): 11–26.

———. "*Fortune* Letters—Nurnberg Defended." *Fortune* 35 (April, 1947): 29–32.

"We Furnish the Hangman." *Ave Maria* 64 (November 7, 1946): 580–81.

WEST, REBECCA. "Reporter at Large." *New Yorker* 22 (September 7, 1946): 34–47.

———. "The Birch Leaves Fall." *New Yorker* 22 (October 26, 1946): 93–105.

WESTERMAN, GEORGE F. "International Law Protects PW's." *Army Information Digest* 2 (February, 1967): 32–39.

"West of the Pecos." *Time* 46 (November 25, 1925): 28.

"Whose Responsibility?" *Social Justice Review* 39 (February, 1947): 339.

"Will Nuremberg Stop New Aggressors?" *Saturday Evening Post* 219 (November 2, 1946): 164.

WILNER, ALAN M. "Superior Orders as a Defense to Violations of International Criminal Law." *Maryland Law Review* 26 (Spring, 1966): 127–42.

WINNER, PERCY. "The Atom at Nürnberg." *Commonweal* 43 (March 22, 1946): 566–69.

"World Judgment on Persecutors." *America* 76 (October 26, 1946): 93–95.

"A World of Criticism." *Social Justice Review* 39 (November, 1946): 230–31.

WRIGHT, QUINCY. "The Crime of 'War Mongering.'" *American Journal of International Law* 40 (April, 1946): 398–406.

———. "Due Process and International Law." *American Journal of International Law* 40 (April, 1946): 128–36.

———. "International Law and Guilt by Association." *American Journal of International Law* 43 (October, 1949): 746–55.

———. "The Law of the Nuremberg Trial." *American Journal of International Law* 42 (January, 1947): 38–72.

———. "Legal Positivism and the Nuremberg Judgment." *American Journal of International Law* 42 (April, 1948): 405–14.

———. "The Nuremberg Trial." *The Annals of the American Academy* 246 (July, 1946): 72–80.

———. "Outlawry of War and the Law of War." *American Journal of International Law* 47 (July, 1953): 365–76.

———. "War Criminals." *American Journal of International Law* 39 (April, 1945): 257–85.

WYZANSKI, CHARLES E., JR. "Dangerous Precedent." *Atlantic Monthly* 177 (April, 1946): 66–70.

———. "Nuremberg in Retrospect." *Atlantic Monthly* 178 (December, 1946): 56–59.
ZECK, WILLIAM ALLEN. "Nuremberg: Proceedings Subsequent to Goering et al." *North Carolina Law Review* 26 (June, 1948): 350–89.

E. SPECIAL STUDIES AND GENERAL WORKS

ADLER, SELIG. *The Isolationist Impulse: Its Twentieth Century Reaction.* London: Abelard-Schuman, 1957.
ALEXANDER, CHARLES. *Justice at Nuremberg, A Pictorial Record of the Trial of Nazi War Criminals by the International Tribunal at Nuremberg, Germany, 1945–1946.* Text by Anne Keeshan. New York: Marvel Press, 1946.
ALLEN, ROBERT S., and SHANNON, WILLIAM V. *The Truman Merry-Go-Round.* New York: Vanguard Press, 1950.
ALMOND, GABRIEL A. *The American People and Foreign Policy.* New York: Praeger, 1960.
ANSPACHER, JOHN. "The German Guilt." In *This Is Germany*, edited by Arthur Settler. New York: William Sloane Associates, 1950).
BAILEY, THOMAS ANDREW. *America Faces Russia, Russian-American Relations from Early Times to Our Day.* Ithaca: Cornell University Press, 1950.
———. *A Diplomatic History of the American People.* 6th ed. New York: Appleton-Century-Crofts, 1958.
———. *The Man in the Street: The Impact of American Public Opinion on Foreign Policy.* New York: Macmillan, 1948.
BARBER, HOLLIS W. *Foreign Policies of the United States.* New York: Dryden Press, 1953.
BARCK, OSCAR THEODORE, and BLAKE, NELSON MANFRED. *Since 1900: A History of the United States in Our Times.* New York: Macmillan, 1947.
BARNES, HARRY ELMER. "Revisionism and the Historical Blackout," *Perpetual War for Perpetual Peace.* Edited by Harry Elmer Barnes (Caldwell, Idaho: Caxton Printers, 1953), pp. 1–78.
BECK, EARL R. *Verdict on Schacht: A Study in the Problem of Political "Guilt."* Tallahasse: Florida State University Press, 1955.
BEMIS, SAMUEL FLAGG. *The United States As A World Power: A Diplomatic History, 1900–1955.* New York: Henry Holt, 1955.
BERKOWITZ, LEONARD. *Aggression A Social Psychological Analysis.* New York: McGraw Hill, 1962.
BERSTEIN, VICTOR. *Final Judgment: The Story of Nuremberg.* New York: Boni and Gaer, 1947.
BEWLEY, CHARLES. *Hermann Göring and the Third Reich.* New York: Devin-Adair, 1962.

BIDDLE, FRANCIS BEVERLY. *The World's Best Hope, A Discussion of the Role of the United States in the Modern World*. Chicago: University of Chicago Press, 1949.

BIRD, CHARLES. *Social Psychology*. New York: Appleton-Century, 1940.

BISHOP, WILLIAM W. *International Law: Cases and Materials*. Boston: Little, Brown, 1962.

BLUM, JOHN M.; CATTON, BRUCE; MORGAN, EDMUND S.; SCHLESINGER, ARTHUS M., JR.; STAMPP, KENNETH M.; and WOODWARD, C. VAN. *History of the United States, The National Experience*. New York: Harcourt, Brace and World, 1963.

BONNER, THOMAS NEVILLE. *Our Recent Past; American Civilization in the Twentieth Century*. Englewood Cliffs, N.J.: Prentice-Hall, 1963.

BRAMSON, LEON. *The Political Context of Sociology*. Princeton, N.J.: Princeton University Press, 1961.

BRIGGS, HERBERT W. *The Law of the Nations*. New York: Appleton-Century-Crofts, 1952.

BYRNES, JAMES F. *Speaking Frankly*. New York: Harper, 1947.

CALVOCORESSI, PETER. *Nuremberg, The Facts, the Law and the Consequences*. New York: Macmillan, 1948.

CAMPBELL, JOHN C. *The United States in World Affairs, 1945–1947*. New York: Harper, 1947.

CANTRIL, HADLEY, ed. *Public Opinion, 1935–1946*. Princeton, N.J.: Princeton University Press, 1961.

CARMEN, HARRY J.; SYRETT, HAROLD C.; and WISH, BERNARD W. *A History of the American People*. 2 vols. 2d ed. New York: Knopf, 1961.

CHAMBERLIN, WILLIAM HENRY. *Beyond Containment*. Chicago: Henry Regnery, 1953.

———. *The German Phoenix*. New York: Duell, Sloan, and Pearce, 1963.

CHEEVER, DANIEL S., and HAVILAND, H. FIELD, JR., *Organizing for Peace: International Organization in World Affairs*. Boston: Houghton, Mifflin, 1954.

CLAY, LUCIUS D. *Decision in Germany*. Cambridge, Mass.: Harvard University Press, 1946.

COMMAGER, HENRY STEELE. *The American Mind, An Interpretation of American Thought and Character Since the 1880's*. New York: Yale University Press, 1950.

CONANT, JAMES BRYANT. *Germany and Freedom, A Personal Appraisal*. Cambridge, Mass.: Harvard University Press, 1958.

CONNELL, BRIAN. *A Watcher on the Rhine*. New York: William Morrow, 1957.

COOK, THOMAS I., and MOOS, MALCOMB. *Power Through Purpose: The Realism of Idealism as a Basis for Foreign Policy*. Baltimore: Johns Hopkins Press, 1954.

CORBETT, PERCY ELWOOD. *The Individual and World Society*. Princeton, N.J.: Princeton University Press, 1953.

————. *Law and Society in the Relations of States*. Princeton, N.J.: Princeton University Press, 1951.

————. *Law in Diplomacy*. Princeton, N.J.: Princeton University Press, 1959.

————. *Morals, Law, and Power in International Relations*. Los Angeles: John Randolf Haynes and Dora Haynes Foundation, 1956.

————. *The Study of International Law*. Garden City, N.Y.: Doubleday, 1955.

COUSINS, NORMAN. *In Place of Folly*. New York: Harper, 1961.

CRANKSHAW, EDWARD. *Gestapo, Instrument of Tyranny*. New York: Viking, 1956.

CREEL, GEORGE. *War Crimes and Punishment*. New York: Robert M. McBride, 1944.

CURRENT, RICHARD N. *Secretary Stimson, A Study in Statecraft*. New Brunswick, N.J.: Rutgers University Press, 1954.

DAVIDSON, EUGENE. *The Death and Life of Germany: An Account of the American Occupation*. New York: Knopf, 1959.

————. "The Nuremberg Trials and One World." In *Issues and Conflicts, Studies in Twentieth Century American Diplomacy*, edited by George L. Anderson. Lawrence, Kan.: University of Kansas Press, 1959.

————. *The Trial of the Germans*. New York: Macmillan, 1966.

DEAN, VERA MICHELES. *The United States and Russia*. Cambridge, Mass.: Harvard University Press, 1947.

DE CONDE, ALEXANDER. *A History of American Foreign Policy*. New York: Scribner's Sons, 1963.

DENNET, RAYMOND, and TURNER, ROBERT K., eds. *Documents On American Foreign Policy*. Princeton, N.J.: Princeton University Press, 1948.

DICKINSON, EDWIN D. *Law and Peace*. Philadelphia: University of Pennsylvania Press, 1951.

DORNBERG, JOHN. *Schizophrenic Germany*. New York: Macmillan, 1961.

DUMOND, DWIGHT LOWELL. *America in Our Time, 1896–1946*. New York: Henry Holt, c.r. 1937.

DUVERGER, MAURICE. *An Introduction to the Social Sciences*. Translated by Malcolm Anderson. New York: Praeger, 1964.

EAGLETON, CLYDE. *International Government*. New York: Roland, 1948.

EKIRCH, ARTHUR A., JR. *The Civilian and the Military*. New York: Oxford University Press, 1956.

ELLIS, L. ETHAN. *Frank B. Kellogg and American Foreign Relations, 1925–1929*. New Brunswick, N.J.: Rutgers University Press, 1961.

FENWICK, CHARLES G. *International Law*. 3rd ed. New York: Appleton-Century-Crofts, c.r. 1948.

FERRELL, ROBERT H. *Peace In Their Time, The Origins of the Kellogg-Briand Pact*. New York: Yale University Press, 1952.

FINER, HERMAN. *America's Destiny.* New York: Macmillan, 1947.

FISHER, CHARLES. *The Columnist.* New York: Howell Soskin, 1944.

FRANK, JOHN P. *Marble Palace: The Supreme Court in American Life.* New York, Knopf, 1958.

———. *Mr. Justice Black; The Man and His Opinions.* New York: Knopf, 1949.

FREIDEL, FRANK. *America In the Twentieth Century.* New York: Knopf, 1960.

FRIEDMANN, A. *An Introduction to World Politics.* Fourth edition. London: Macmillan, 1960.

FRIEDRICH, CARL JOACHIM. *The Philosophy of Law in Historical Perspective.* Chicago: University of Chicago Press, 1958.

FRITZSCHE, HANS. *The Sword in the Scales.* Translated by Diana Pyke and Heinrich Freenkel. London: Wingate, 1953.

GALLAGHER, LOUIS. *Edmund A. Walsh, S.J.* New York: Benzinger, 1962.

GALLIN, MOTHER MARY ALICE. *German Resistance to Hitler.* Washington: Catholic University of America, 1955.

GANGE, JOHN. *American Foreign Relations, Permanent Problems and Changing Policies.* New York: Roland Press, 1955.

GARCIA-MORA, MANUEL T. *International Responsibility For Hostile Acts of Private Persons against Foreign States.* Hague: Martinus Nijhoff, 1962.

GERHART, EUGENE C. *America's Advocate, Robert H. Jackson.* Indianapolis: Bobbs Merrill, 1958.

GILBERT, GUSTAVE MARK. *Nuremberg Diary.* New York: Farrar, Straus, 1947.

GLUECK, SHELDON. *The Nuremberg Trial and Aggressive War.* New York: Knopf, 1946.

———. *War Criminals, Their Prosecution and Punishment.* New York: Knopf, 1944.

GOLDMAN, ERIC F. *The Crucial Decade: America 1945–1955.* New York: Knopf, 1959.

GREENSPAN, MORRIS. *The Modern Law of Land Warfare.* Berkeley: University of California Press, 1959.

GRENFELL, RUSSELL. *Unconditional Hatred: German War Guilt and Future of Europe.* New York: Devin-Adair, 1953.

GROTIUS, HUGH. *De Jure Belli Ac Pacis Libri Tres, The Classics of International Law.* 2 vols. Translated by Francis W. Kelsey. Edited by James Brown Scott. Oxford: Clarendon Press, 1925.

HAGEN, PAUL. *Germany After Hitler.* New York: Farrar and Rinehart, 1944.

HALLE, LOUIS J. *Dream and Reality, Aspects of American Foreign Policy.* New York: Harper, 1958.

HARRIS, WHITNEY R. *Tyranny on Trial, The Evidence of Nuremberg.* Dallas: Southern Methodist Press, 1954.

HENKIN, LOUIS. *Arms Control and Inspection In American Law*. New York: Columbia University Press, 1958.

HERO, ALFRED O. *Americans in World Affairs*. Boston: World Peace Foundation, 1959.

HEYDECKER, JOE J. *and* LEEB, JOHANNES. *The Nuremberg Trial, A History of Nazi Germany as Revealed Through the Testimony at Nuremberg*. Edited by R. A. Downie. Cleveland: World Publishing, 1962.

HILL, NORMAN. *International Relations*. New York: Oxford University Press, 1950.

HOCKING, WILLIAM ERNEST. *Strength of Men and Nations: A Message to the USA vis-à-vis the USSR*. New York: Harper, 1959.

HOFSTADTER, RICHARD; MILLER, WILLIAM; *and* AARON, DANIEL. *The American Republic*. Englewood Cliffs, N.J.: Prentice-Hall, 1959.

HOOVER, HERBERT, *and* GIBSON, HUGH. *The Problems of Lasting Peace*. Garden City, N.Y.: Doubleday, Doran, 1943.

HUDDLESTON, SISLEY. *Popular Diplomacy and War*. Rindge, N.H.: Richard R. Smith, 1954.

HUDSON, MANLEY O. *International Tribunals Past and Future*. Washington: Carnegie Endowment for International Peace and Brookings Institute, 1944.

HULL, CORDELL. *The Memoirs of Cordell Hull*. 2 vols. New York: Macmillan, 1948.

HUNTINGTON, SAMUEL P. *The Soldier and the State, The Theory and Politics of Civil-Military Relations*. Cambridge, Mass.: Harvard University Press, 1959.

JACOBINI, H. B. *International Law*. Homewood, Ill.: Dorsey Press, 1962.

———. *A Study of the Philosophy of International Law as Seen in Works of Latin American Writers*. Hague: Martinus Nijhoff, 1954.

JARMAN, T. L. *The Rise and Fall of Nazi Germany*. New York: New York University, 1956.

JESSUP, PHILIP C. *Transnational Law*. New Haven: Yale University Press, 1956.

KAPLAN, MORTON A., *and* KATZENBACH, NICHOLAS DE B. *The Political Foundations of International Law*. New York: John Wiley, 1961.

KEENAN, JOSEPH BERRY, *and* BROWN, BRENDAN FRANCIS. *Crimes Against International Law*. Washington: Public Affairs Press, 1950.

KELLEY, DOUGLAS M. *22 Cells in Nuremberg*. New York: Greenberg, 1947.

KELSEN, HANS. *General Theory of Law and State*. Cambridge, Mass.: Harvard University Press, 1949.

———. *Law and Peace in International Relations*. Cambridge, Mass.: Harvard University Press, 1942.

———. *Peace Through Law*. Chapel Hill: University of North Carolina Press, 1944.

———. *Principles of International Law*. New York: Rinehart, 1959.

KENNAN, GEORGE F. *American Diplomacy, 1900–1950.* Chicago: University of Chicago Press, 1953.
——. *Realities of American Foreign Policy.* Princeton, N.J.: Princeton University Press, 1954.
KENNEDY, JOHN FITZGERALD. *Profiles in Courage.* New York: Harper (Inaugural edition) 1961.
KERWIN, JEROME G., ed. *Civil-Military Relationships in American Life.* Chicago: University of Chicago Press, 1948.
KIRCHHEIMER, OTTO. *Political Justice: The Use of Legal Procedure For Political Ends.* Princeton, N.J.: Princeton University Press, 1961.
KIRK, RUSSELL, and MCCLELLAN, JAMES. *The Political Principles of Robert A. Taft.* New York: Fleet Press Corporation; 1967.
KLINGBERG, FRANK W., ed. *A History of the United States from 1865 to the Present.* Meredian Documents of American History. Edited by George D. Sheer. Cleveland: World Publishing, 1962.
KNAPPEN, MARSHALL. *And Call It Peace.* Chicago: University of Chicago Press, 1947.
KNIERIEM, AUGUST VON. *The Nuremberg Trials.* Translated by Elizabeth D. Schmitt. Chicago: Regnery, 1959.
KRIESBERG, MARIN. "Dark Areas of Ignorance." In *Public Opinion and Foreign Policy,* edited by Lester Markel. New York: Harper, 1949.
KROEBER, A. L., and KLUCKHOHN, CLYDE. *Culture: A Critical Review of Concepts and Definitions.* New York: Random House, 1953.
LARSON, ARTHUR. *When Nations Disagree: A Handbook on Peace Through Law.* Baton Rouge: Louisiana State University Press, 1961.
LASSWELL, HAROLD D. *World Politics and Personal Insecurity.* New York: Whittlesey House, McGraw-Hill, 1935.
LEAHY, WILLIAM D. *I Was There: The Personal Story of the Chief of Staff to Presidents Roosevelt and Truman Based on His Notes and Diaries.* New York: McGraw-Hill, 1950.
LEOPOLD, RICHARD W. *The Growth of American Foreign Policy: A History.* New York: Knopf, 1962.
LERNER, MAX. *Actions and Passions, Notes on the Multiple Revolutions of Time.* New York: Simon and Schuster, 1949.
LINK, ARTHUR S. *American Epoch.* 2d ed. New York: Knopf, 1963.
LIPPMANN, WALTER. *United States War Aims.* Boston: Little, Brown, 1944.
LUBELL, SAMUEL. *Revolt of the Moderates.* New York: Harper, 1956.
LUNAU, HEINZ. *The Germans on Trial.* New York: Storm, 1948.
MACARTHUR, DOUGLAS. *Revitalizing a Nation.* Correlated and captioned by J. M. Pratt. Chicago: Heritage Foundation, 1952.
MCCLURE, WALLACE. *World Legal Order.* Chapel Hill: University of North Carolina Press, 1960.
MANGONE, GERARD J. *The Idea and Practice of World Government.* New York: Columbia University Press, 1951.
MANN, ABBY. *Judgment at Nuremberg.* New York: New American Library, 1961.

MASON, ALPHEUS THOMAS. *Harlan Fiske Stone, Pillar of the Law.* New York: Viking, 1956.

MEAD, MARGARET. *And Keep Your Powder Dry, An Anthropologist Looks At America.* New York: William Morrow, 1943.

MEYER, HENRY CORD. *Five Images of Germany: Half a Century of American Views on German History.* New York: Macmillan, 1960.

MIDDLETON, DREW. *The Struggle for Germany.* Indianapolis, Ind.: Bobbs Merrill, 1949.

MILLER, ROBERT M. *American Protestantism and Social Issues, 1919–1939.* Chapel Hill: University of North Carolina Press, 1958.

MILLIS, WALTER. *Arms and the State, Civil-Military Elements in National Policy.* New York: 20th Century Fund, 1958.

MORGENTHAU, HANS, *In Defense of National Interest:* A Critical Examination. New York: Knopf, 1951.

———. *Politics Among the Nations: The Struggle for Power and Peace.* 3rd ed. New York: Knopf, 1961.

———. *Scientific Man vs. Power Politics.* Chicago: University of Chicago Press, 1946.

MORGENTHAU, HENRY, JR. *Germany Is Our Problem.* New York: Harper, 1945.

MORISON, ELTING E. *Turmoil and Tradition: A Study of the Life and Time of Henry L. Stimson.* Boston: Houghton-Mifflin, 1960.

MORISON, SAMUEL ELIOT, *and* COMMAGER, HENRY STEELE. *The Growth of the American Republic.* 2 vols. New York: Oxford University Press, 1962.

MORRAY, JOSEPH P. *From Yalta to Disarmament, Cold War Debate.* New York: MR Press, 1961.

MOWRER, EDGAR ANSEL. *The Nightmare of American Foreign Policy.* New York: Knopf, 1948.

MYRES, S. MCDOUGAL, *and* ASSOCIATES. *Studies in World Public Order.* New Haven: Yale University Press, 1960.

NACHT, S.; DIATHINE, R.; *and* RACAMIER, P. C. "Psychoanalysis and Sociology." In *Psychoanalysis of Today,* edited by S. Nacht. (London: Grune and Stration, 1959), pp. 203–228.

NEUMANN, INGE S. *European War Crimes Trials, A Bibliography.* New York: Carnegie Endowment for International Peace, 1951.

NEUMANN, WILLIAM L. *Making the Peace, 1941–1945.* Washington: Foundation for Foreign Affairs, 1950.

NEVINS, ALLAN. *Herbert H. Lehman and His Era.* New York: Scribners, 1963.

NORTHROP, F. S. C. *Philosophical Anthropology and Practical Politics.* New York: Macmillan, 1954.

NUSSBAUM, ARTHUR. *A Concise History of the Law of Nations.* New York: Macmillan, 1954.

PALMER, NORMAN D., *and* PERKINS, HOWARD C. *International Relations, The World Community in Transition.* Boston: Houghton-Mifflin, 1953.

PASTON, DAVID GEORGE. *Superior Orders as Affecting Responsibility for War Crimes*. New York: H. G. Publishing Co., 1946.
PERKINS, DEXTER. *The American Approach to Foreign Policy*. Rev. ed. Cambridge, Mass.: Harvard University Press, 1962.
———. *America's Quest for Peace*. Bloomington: Indiana University Press, 1962.
———. *The Evolution of American Foreign Policy*. New York: Oxford University Press, 1948.
POOL, ITHIEL DE SOLA. *Symbols of Internationalism*. Stanford: Stanford University Press, 1951.
POUND, ROSCOE. *Interpretations of Legal History*. New York: Macmillan, 1923.
RADIN, MAX. *The Day of Reckoning*. New York: Knopf, 1943.
REEL, A. FRANK. *The Case of General Yamashita*. Chicago: University of Chicago Press, 1949.
RENNIE, THOMAS C., and WOODWARD, LUTHER E. *Mental Health in Modern Society*. New York: Commonwealth Fund, 1948.
ROGERS, LINDSAY. *The Pollsters: Public Opinion, Politics and Democratic Leadership*. New York: Knopf, 1949.
ROOSEVELT, ELLIOTT. *As He Saw It*. New York: Duell, Sloan and Pearce, 1946.
ROSENAU, JAMES N., ed. *International Politics and Foreign Policy*. Glencoe, Ill.: Free Press, 1961.
ROSENMAN, SAMUEL L. *Working with Roosevelt*. New York: Harper, 1952.
ROSSITER, CLINTON. *The Supreme Court and the Commander-in-Chief*. Ithaca, N.Y.: Cornell University Press, 1951.
ST. GEORGE, MAXIMILIAN, and DENNIS, LAWRENCE. *A Trial on Trial: The Great Sedition Trial of 1944*. New York: National Civil Rights Committee, 1946.
SAYRE, PAUL. *The Life of Roscoe Pound*. Iowa City: College of Law Committee, 1948.
SCHILDER, PAUL FERDINAND. *Psychoanalysis, Man, and Society*. New York: W. W. Norton, 1951.
SCHUBERT, GLENDON A. *Constitutional Politics: The Political Behavior of Supreme Court Justices and the Constitutional Policies That They Made*. New York: Holt, Rinehart and Winston, 1960.
SETTEL, ARTHUR, ed. *This Is Germany*. New York: William Sloane Associates, 1950.
SHIRER, WILLIAM L. *End of a Berlin Diary*. New York: Knopf, 1947.
SLICK, TOM. *Permanent Peace, A Check and Balance Plan*. Englewood Cliffs, N.J.: Prentice-Hall, 1958.
SMITH, LOUIS. *American Democracy and Military Power: A Study of Civil Control of the Military Power in the United States*. Chicago: University of Chicago Press, 1951.
SMITH, PAUL A. L. "The Impact of International Events Upon Domestic Political Behavior." Ph.D. dissertation, Princeton University, 1960.

SNELL, JOHN L. *Wartime Origins of the East-West Dilemma over Germany.* New Orleans: Hauser Press, 1959.
———, ed. *The Meaning of Yalta.* Baton Rouge: Louisiana State University Press, 1956.
STANLEY, MAXWELL C. *Waging Peace: A Businessman Looks at United States Foreign Policy.* New York: Macmillan, 1956.
STETTINIUS, EDWARD R., JR. *Roosevelt and the Russians: The Yalta Conference.* Edited by Walter Johnson. Garden City, N.Y.: Doubleday, 1944.
STIMSON, HENRY L., and BUNDY, MCGEORGE. *On Active Service in Peace and War.* New York: Harper, 1947.
STIPP, JOHN L. *Devil's Diary: The Record of Nazi Conspiracy and Aggression.* Yellow Springs, Ohio: Antioch Press, 1955.
STOESSINGER, JOHN G. *The Might of Nations, World Politics In Our Time.* New York: Random House, 1964.
STONE, JULIUS. *Aggression and World Order, A Critique of United Nations Theories on Aggression.* Berkeley: University of California Press, 1958.
———. *Legal Controls of International Conflict.* New York: Rinehart, 1959.
STROMBERG, ROLAND N. *Collective Security and American Foreign Policy, From the League of Nations to NATO.* New York: Praeger, 1963.
SVARLIEN, OSCAR. *An Introduction to the Law of Nations.* New York: McGraw Hill, 1955.
TAFT, ROBERT A. *A Foreign Policy for Americans.* Garden City, N.Y.: Doubleday, 1951.
TAYLOR, TELFORD. *Sword and Swastika, Generals and Nazis in the Third Reich.* New York: Simon and Schuster, 1952.
THAYER, CHARLES W. *The Unquiet Germans.* New York: Harper, 1957.
THOMAS, NORMAN. *Appeal to the Nations.* New York: Holt, 1947.
TRUMAN, HARRY S. *Memoirs.* 2 vols. Garden City, N.Y.: Doubleday, 1955.
TUCKER, ROBERT W. *The Just War, A Study in Contemporary American Doctrine.* Baltimore: Johns Hopkins Press, 1960.
———. *The Law of War and Neutrality at Sea.* Washington: Government Printing Office, 1957.
UTLEY, FERDA. *The High Cost of Vengeance.* Chicago: Regnery, 1949.
VAGTS, ALFRED. *Defense and Diplomacy, The Soldier and the Conduct of Foreign Relations.* New York: King's Crown Press, 1956.
VAN ALSTYNE, RICHARD W. *American Diplomacy in Action.* 2d ed. Stanford: Stanford University Press, 1947.
VEALE, F. J. P. *Advance to Barbarism, How the Reversion to Barbarism in Warfare and War-Trials Menaces Our Future.* Appleton, Wis.: C. C. Nolan, 1953.
WALLACE, HENRY A. *The Century of the Common Man.* New York: Fischer, 1942.

WALSH, EDMUND A. *Total Power, A Footnote to History.* Garden City, N.Y.: Doubleday, 1949.

WEST, REBECCA. *A Train of Powder.* New York: Viking, 1955.

WESTERFIELD, H. BRADFORD. *Foreign Policy and Party Politics: Pearl Harbor to Korea.* New Haven: Yale University Press, 1955.

WHEELER-BENNETT, JOHN W. *The Nemesis of Power, The German Army in Politics, 1918–1945.* New York: St. Martin's Press, 1954.

WHITE, WILLIAM SMITH. *The Taft Story.* New York: Harper, 1954.

WHITEMAN, MARJORIE M. *Digest of International Law.* 2 vols. Washington: Government Printing Office, 1963.

WILBUR, RAY LYMAN, and HYDE, ARTHUR MASTICK. *The Hoover Policies.* New York: Knopf, 1946.

WILCOX, FRANCIS O., and KALIJARVI, THORSTEN V. *Recent American Foreign Policy: Basic Documents 1941–1951.* New York: Appleton-Century-Crofts, 1952.

WILSON, ROBERT RENBERT. *The International Law Standard in Treaties of the United States.* Cambridge, Mass.: Harvard University Press, 1953.

WOETZEL, ROBERT K. *The Nuremberg Trials in International Law.* London: Stevens, 1960.

WRIGHT, QUINCY. *Problems of Stability and Progress in International Relations.* Berkeley: University of California Press, 1954.

———. *The Role of International Law in the Elimination of War.* Manchester: Manchester University Press, 1961.

———. *The Study of International Relations.* New York: Appleton-Century-Crofts, Inc., 1955.

———, ed. *A Foreign Policy for the United States.* Chicago: University of Chicago Press, 1947.

WYNNER, EDITH, and LLOYD, GEORGIA. *Searchlight on Peace Plans, Choose Your Road to World Government.* New York: Dutton, 1949.

ZINK, HAROLD. *The United States in Germany, 1944–1955.* Princeton, N.J.: Van Nostrand, 1957.

Index

69, 71; committee declared superfluous, 70

Chamberlin, William H., 227, 228

Chicago Daily Tribune, 97, 189, 233

Christian Century, 121, 123, 216–17

Churchill, Prime Minister Winston, 23, 26, 27, 163, 175n

Clark, Attorney General Thomas, 38–39

Cold War, and Nuremberg, 112, 164, 174, 202; and "fusionist" theory, 176

Commentary, 118, 129

Common law analogy, 124; and Kellogg-Briand Pact, 8; source of international law, 58, 64, 75, 102; legal basis for Nuremberg, 69, 99, 137; principle opposed, 133, 139

Commonweal, 126, 127, 192, 217

Communism, 121, 178; Nuremberg as conspiracy of, 83, 84, 154; Catholics disturbed by, 127, 234

Concentration camps, Allied, 121; Nazi, 198. *See also* Belsen; Buchenwald; Dachau

"Consensus of mankind," as source of international law, 58, 64, 158

Conspiracy for aggression, indictment for, 10n, 11, 19; appeals to Roosevelt, 24; Stimson urges, 35, 36; difficult to prove, 113

Crimes. *See* War crimes

Crimes against humanity, 15, 121, 158, 206, 235; and London Charter, 11; and Vietnam war, 184

Crimes against peace, 11, 184, 235

Cultural relativism, 209–10

Customary international law, source of law, 58, 64; legal basis for Nuremberg, 107, 136

Dachau, 10, 18, 239. *See also* Concentration camps, Nazi; War crimes; Jews

Davidson, Eugene, 154, 162, 227, 228

Defendants, Nuremberg, 16, 118, 160, 199, 204, 211, 225; enu-

merated, 13n; leniency toward, condemned, 98, 99; psychological aspects of, 205–6. *See also* Nazis, leaders of; War crimes; and Individual defendants

Denmark, 180, 181

Depersonalization of war, 210, 226

Deterrent, Nuremberg as, 20, 48, 106, 226, 227, 228–29

"Devil theory," 111, 153, 224, 225, 233

Dewey, Governor Thomas E., 77, 78, 79

Diplomats, held accountable, 15, 100, 104

Dodd, Senator Thomas, 131, 186

Doenitz, Admiral Karl, 13n, 17, 166, 168; reaction to punishment of, 171, 181; evidence against, 173, 180

Dondero, Representative George A., 82, 83, 178, 232

Douglas, Representative Emily Taft, 203, 230

Douglas, Associate Justice William O., 132, 134, 194

Drumhead court martial, 9, 22, 31

Eisenhower, General Dwight D., 29, 171, 172

"*Ex post facto*" law, 49, 59, 99, 124, 138, 139, 143, 157, 225; condemned by United Nations, 46; forbidden in American law, 105, 132, 143. *See also* Retroactive law

Finland, invasion of, 44, 152

Flanner, Janet, 113

Forrestal, Secretary James V., 168

Fortune, 114, 227, 228, 233

France, and Nuremberg, 17, 110, 194

Fritzsche, Hans, acquittal of, 13n, 104, 234. *See also* Acquittals

Fulbright, Senator J. William, 73, 186

Gault, Lt. Col. P. F., 131, 179, 228

General Staff, and organizational guilt, 13, 104, 168; not con-

www.ingramcontent.com/pod-product-compliance
Lightning Source LLC
Chambersburg PA
CBHW020340270326
41926CB00007B/263